KARA WALKER

OCTOBER Files

Rosalind Krauss (founding editor), Annette Michelson (founding editor, 1922–2018), George Baker, Yve-Alain Bois, Benjamin H. D. Buchloh, Huey Copeland, Leah Dickerman, Devin Fore, Hal Foster, Denis Hollier, David Joselit, Carrie Lambert-Beatty, Pamela M. Lee, Mignon Nixon, and Malcolm Turvey, editors

Richard Serra, edited by Hal Foster with Gordon Hughes
Andy Warhol, edited by Annette Michelson
Eva Hesse, edited by Mignon Nixon
Robert Rauschenberg, edited by Branden W. Joseph
James Coleman, edited by George Baker
Cindy Sherman, edited by Johanna Burton
Roy Lichtenstein, edited by Graham Bader
Gabriel Orozco, edited by Yve-Alain Bois
Gerhardt Richter, edited by Benjamin H. D. Buchloh
Richard Hamilton, edited by Hal Foster with Alex Bacon
Dan Graham, edited by Alex Kitnick
John Cage, edited by Julia Robinson
Claes Oldenburg, edited by Nadja Rottner
Louise Lawler, edited by Helen Molesworth with Taylor Walsh
Robert Morris, edited by Julia Bryan-Wilson
John Knight, edited by André Rottmann
Isa Genzken, edited by Lisa Lee
Hans Haacke, edited by Rachel Churner
Michael Asher, edited by Jennifer King
Mary Kelly, edited by Mignon Nixon
William Kentridge, edited by Rosalind Krauss
Bruce Nauman, edited by Taylor Walsh
Sherrie Levine, edited by Howard Singermann
Michael Snow, edited by Annette Michelson and Kenneth White
Carrie Mae Weems, edited by Sarah Elizabeth Lewis with Christine Garnier
Donald Judd, edited by Annie Ochmanek and Alex Kitnick
Hollis Frampton, edited by Michael Zryd
Kara Walker, edited by Vanina Géré

KARA WALKER

Edited by Vanina Géré

essays and interviews by Jerry Saltz, Hamza Walker, Thelma Golden,
Anne M. Wagner, Yasmil Raymond, Lorraine Morales Cox, Tavia Nyong'o,
Vanina Géré, and Zadie Smith

OCTOBER Files 28

The MIT Press
Cambridge, Massachusetts
London, England

This book was set in Bembo Std by New Best-set Typesetters Ltd. Printed and bound in the United States of America.

Library of Congress Cataloging-in-Publication Data is available.

ISBN: 978-0-262-54447-4

10 9 8 7 6 5 4 3 2 1

Contents

OCTOBER Files addresses individual bodies of work of the postwar period that meet two criteria: they have altered our understanding of art in significant ways, and they have prompted a critical literature that is serious, sophisticated, and sustained. Each book thus traces not only the development of an important oeuvre but also the construction of the critical discourse inspired by it. This discourse is theoretical by its very nature, which is not to say that it imposes theory abstractly or arbitrarily. Rather, it draws specific ways in which significant art is theoretical in its own right, on its own terms, and with its own implications. To this end we feature essays, many first published in *OCTOBER* magazine, that elaborate different methods of criticism in order to elucidate different aspects of the art in question. The essays are often in dialogue with one another as they do so, but they are also sensitive as the art to political context and historical change. These "files," then, are intended as primers in signal practices of art and criticism alike, and they are offered in resistance to the amnesiac and antitheoretical tendencies of our time.

The Editors of *OCTOBER*

This volume would not be possible without the support and generosity of Kara Walker and Sikkema Jenkins & Co.

I most sincerely thank Huey G. Copeland for inviting me to edit this OCTOBER Files issue, and for his support throughout this project. I also warmly thank the *OCTOBER* editors for their trust. Thanks go to Adam Lehner, managing director at *OCTOBER* magazine, as well as Gabriela Bueno Gibbs, assistant acquisitions editor at the MIT Press.

I would like to express my heartfelt gratitude to the contributors of this volume, for their strong, sophisticated intellectual engagement with Walker's work, of course, but also for their warm response to this project and their spirit of collaboration as this volume moved from proposal to completion. It has been an honor to be in dialogue with such impressive artworld professionals, scholars, and writers.

My gratitude goes to Monica Truong and Scott Briscoe at Sikkema Jenkins gallery, whose diligence and competence have been invaluable for this project and so many others regarding Walker's work.

Throughout the time span of this project, I have been blessed with the help of my colleagues at the Villa Arson School of Fine Arts (Nice, France): Céline Chazalviel, editorial coordinator; Christophe Robert, head librarian; and Jean-Louis Paquelin, teacher and computer services technician. I also thank my former colleague and dear friend Frédéric Wecker, professor of aesthetics and philosophy at the National School of Art and Design (Nancy, France), for his kind assistance in the final stage of the project. I thank Christine Camara, librarian at the National

Institute of Art History (INHA). I cannot stress enough the importance of professionals such as them in public institutions, which they uphold through their complete dedication to their work.

I also thank the wonderful women of the public daycare system, who made it work whenever possible for the children and their families, despite the circumstances of the COVID-19 pandemic and the acceleration of the relentless assault on public service that has characterized recent French politics. Without these women, and without the help of family and friends, I would not have been able to edit this volume at all. Special thanks go to my partner, Henri-Christophe Audigé.

Of course, *no mere words can adequately reflect* the gratitude that goes to Kara Walker, as one of the most influential artists of the twentieth and early twenty-first centuries, for the courage, aesthetic intelligence, political relevance, and generosity of her artwork. It is a deep honor to count among the numerous students, scholars, educators, and intellectuals who have worked overtime gathering her many citations and references for use in their dissertations, as a modest tribute to her rich, complex, powerful art.

Last but not least, my gratitude goes to the presses for granting republication of the catalog essays, scholarly articles, interviews, and other texts included in this book, and for their help in collecting the texts. I specifically thank Rebecca McNamara, Brynnae Newman, Alanna Nissen, and Kayla Nordlund.

Jerry Saltz's interview, "Kara Walker: Ill-Will and Desire," originally appeared in *Flash Art* (November–December 1996): 82–86, and here appears with the permission of *Flash Art*. Hamza Walker's essay, "Cut It Out," was first published in the January newsletter of the Renaissance Society at the University of Chicago, as an introduction to Kara Walker's solo exhibition at the Society in 1997. The newsletter was republished as an edited article titled, "Nigger Lover or Will They Be Black People in Utopia?," in *Parkett*, no. 59 (2000): 152–158. The 1997 newsletter version was later reproduced in its original form (without images) in *Witness to Her Art: Art And Writings by Adrian Piper, Mona Hatoum, Cady Noland, Jenny Holzer, Kara Walker, Daniela Rossell and Eau de Cologne*, edited by Rhea Anastas with Michael Brenson (Annandale-on-Hudson, NY: Center for Curatorial Studies, 2006), 280–282. "Cut It Out" appears in its original 1997 version in this volume as well, with the permission of the Renaissance Society at the University of Chicago.

Walker's "A Mind Is a Terrible Thing to Waste" (2006), also published in *Witness to Her Art* (pp. 273–279), is reproduced here with the permission of the author and Rhea Anastas. Despite the chronological leap that the reproduction of both texts by Hamza Walker entails, it seemed clearer for the reader to make them appear as a single chapter; the 2006 text, it must be noted, was written as a response to the reception of the Renaissance Society catalog.

Thelma Golden's interview, "Thelma Golden/Kara Walker: A Dialogue," was published in the exhibition catalog *Kara Walker: Pictures from Another Time*, edited by Annette Dixon (Ann Arbor: University of Michigan Museum of Art, 2001), 43–49. It is included here with the permission of the Regents of the University of Michigan. Anne M. Wagner's essay, "Kara Walker: The Black-White Relation," was first presented in the exhibition catalog *Kara Walker: Narratives of a Negress* (Cambridge, MA: MIT Press, in association with the Frances Young Tang Teaching Museum and Art Gallery at Skidmore College and Williams College Museum of Art, 2003), 90–102. It is reproduced courtesy of the author and of the Massachusetts Institute of Technology, the Frances Young Tang Teaching Museum and Art Gallery at Skidmore College, and the Williams College Museum of Art. Yasmil Raymond's essay, "Maladies of Power: A Kara Walker Lexicon," appeared in *Kara Walker: My Complement, My Enemy, My Oppressor, My Love* (Minneapolis, MN: Walker Art Center, 2007), 347–370. It is reproduced with the permission of the Walker Art Center. Lorraine Morales Cox's journal article, "A Performative Turn: Kara Walker's *Song of the South* (2005)," was published in *Women and Performance: A Journal of Feminist Theory* 17, no. 1 (March 2007): 59–87. It is reproduced in this volume with the permission of the author and Taylor and Francis Group. Tavia Nyong'o's essay, "Subtleties of Resistance: Sweetness and Violence in Kara Walker's *A Subtlety*," was originally published in *Giving Contours to Shadows*, n.b.k. Diskurs vol. 9, edited by Marius Babias, Elena Agudio, Bonaventure Soh Bejeng Ndikung, and Storm Janse van Rensburg (Berlin: Neuer Berliner Kunstverein, Verlag der Buchhandlung Walther König, 2015), 113–121. It appears with the permission of the editors, the Neuer Berliner Kunsteverein, and the author (with new images consistent with the article added with their permission as well as that of Walker's studio and her gallery). Vanina Géré's article, "'Stories of Mortal Terror': Kara Walker's *Six Miles from Springfield* and *Lucy of*

Pulaski (2009)," initially appeared in French as a book chapter in Vanina Géré's *Les mauvais sentiments: L'art de Kara Walker* (Dijon: Presses du réel, 2019), 282–299. The book itself is an edited version of Géré's doctoral dissertation (2012). The text presented in this volume is an edited translation of the original book chapter, reproduced with the permission of Presses du réel. Zadie Smith's essay, "Kara Walker, What Do We Want History to Do to Us?," was published for the first time in the exhibition catalog *Kara Walker: Fons Americanus* (London: Tate Publishing, 2019), 32–53. It is reproduced here by permission of the author c/o Rogers, Coleridge and White Ltd., 20 Powis Mews, London W11 1JN, with the addition of two images from the Tate Modern exhibition that were not included in Smith's essay, but which appeared in the catalog. This addition has received Smith's permission, as well as that of Walker's studio and gallery. (The copyright is held by Zadie Smith.)

Each author's choice of capitalization or noncapitalization of the adjective "Black" has been left unchanged.

The images of artworks by Kara Walker are reproduced © Kara Walker, courtesy of Sikkema Jenkins & Co., New York; Sprüth Magers, Berlin (except notified otherwise in the caption). Walker and her galleries' generosity with image permissions has been remarkable.

The specific credit lines are to be found in the image captions. I express my general gratitude here to the artists, artists' estates, and galleries, as well as to the museums and foundations that granted permission to reproduce all the images of artworks other than Walker's, notably, Byron Kim and James Cohan Gallery; Adrian Piper and the Adrian Piper Research Archive Foundation Berlin (APRAF), and the Museum of Contemporary Art of Chicago; Simone Leigh and Hauser & Wirth; Karen Reimer at the Renaissance Society at the University of Chicago; the New-York Historical Society; the Wordsworth Trust; the National Galleries Scotland; the Museo Nacional del Prado; the Landesmuseum Württemberg; and the ADGAP France.

Lorraine Morales Cox is an Associate Professor of Art History at Union College in Schenectady, New York, and Chair of the Visual Arts Department. She teaches courses on modern and contemporary visual art and culture of Europe and the Americas, many of which contribute to various interdisciplinary programs. Her pedagogical research and teaching utilize critical making, design thinking, and the development of an entrepreneurial mindset using experiential and civically engaged approaches for student-centered project-based learning. Professor Cox's scholarly research and publications focus on contemporary critical artistic practices that address social and political issues including the subjects of race, gender, consumer culture, and the environment. Professor Cox earned her BFA from Virginia Commonwealth University (1992) and her MA and PhD in Art History from the University of Illinois at Urbana Champaign (2001).

Vanina Géré is a Paris-based scholar who specializes in contemporary American art, with special interests in art and activism, feminist art history, African American studies, and painting. An alumni of ENS-LYON (2004–2008), she has obtained her PhD in American Studies at the Sorbonne Nouvelle (Paris 3, France). She is the author of *Les mauvais sentiments: L'art de Kara Walker* (2019). She has also worked extensively on the writings of Sarah Schulman. She writes art criticism, and currently teaches at Villa Arson National School of Fine Arts in Nice, France, having previously taught at the National School of Fine Arts and Design in Nancy, France. She has lectured on her fields of interest and organized academic events on Black feminism and feminist self-defense. She has contributed to academic publications, art journals, and exhibition catalogs. She is the 2021 recipient of the Beauford Delaney Scholarship for African-American Visual Arts.

Thelma Golden is director and chief curator of the Studio Museum in Harlem. As a recognized authority in contemporary art by artists of African descent and an active lecturer, Golden has organized numerous groundbreaking exhibitions, from *Black Male: Representations of Masculinity in American Art* (1994) at the Whitney Museum of American Art to *Freestyle* at the Studio Museum in Harlem (2001). She has received numerous honorary doctorates, appointments, and awards, including the 2016 Audrey Irmas Award and a 2018 J. Paul Getty Medal for curatorial excellence.

Tavia Nyong'o is Chair and Professor of Theater & Performance Studies, Professor of American Studies, and Professor of African American Studies at Yale University. He was previously acting Chair and Associate Professor of Performance Studies at New York University. His current research and teaching interests span black queer cultural and performance studies, contemporary art and aesthetic theory, speculative genres, afrofuturism, and black sound studies. Nyong'o's first book, *The Amalgamation Waltz: Race, Performance, and the Ruses of Memory* (2009) won the Errol Hill award for the best book in black theater and performance studies. His second book, *Afro-Fabulations: The Queer Drama of Black Life* (2018), won the Barnard Hewitt award for best book in theater and performance studies. Nyong'o also writes for contemporary art and culture publications such as *Artforum, Texte Zur Kunst, Cabinet, n+1,* and the *LA Review of Books,* and forums like npr.org. In 2019, he curated *Dark as the Door to a Dream* at the Stedelijk Museum in Amsterdam. In 2017, he curated *The Critical Matter of Performance* at the New Museum for Contemporary Art, with Johanna Burton and Julia Bryant-Wilson. A long-standing member of the editorial collective of *Social Text,* Nyong'o has served as both print editor and web editor of the journal for many years. He is also on the editorial boards of *TDR: The Drama Review.* He edits the Sexual Cultures book series at NYU Press with Ann Pellegrini and Joshua Chambers-Letson. Nyong'o has received fellowships from the Alexander von Humboldt Foundation,

American Society for Theatre Research, Ford Foundation, Jacob K. Javits Foundation, and British Marshall Foundation.

Yasmil Raymond was appointed rector of the Hochschule für Bildende Künste–Städelschule and Director of Portikus in April 2020. Previously, she was associate curator in the Department of Painting and Sculpture at the Museum of Modern Art, New York (2015–2019) and curator at Dia Art Foundation, New York (2009–2015). She has organized exhibitions and projects with artists Allora & Calzadilla, Thomas Hirschhorn, Koo Jeong A, Jean-Luc Moulène, Tomás Saraceno, Tino Sehgal, Kara Walker, Franz Erhard Walther, Robert Whitman, and Ian Wilson. Past group exhibitions include *Abstract Resistance* (2010), *Statements: Beuys, Flavin, Judd* (2008), and Brave New Worlds (2007, co-curated with Doryun Chong). Most recently, Ms. Raymond co-curated, with Ann Temkin, Tamar Margalit, and Erica Cooke, the retrospective *Judd* at the Museum of Modern Art, New York.

Jerry Saltz is Senior Art Critic at *New York Magazine*; he was awarded the 2018 Pulitzer Prize for Criticism. A two-time ASME National Magazine Award winner, he is the author of "How to Be an Artist: 33 Rules to Take You from Clueless Amateur to Generational Talent (or at Least Help You Live Life a Little More Creatively)" (2018), as well as numerous articles and lectures on contemporary art and interviews with contemporary artists.

Zadie Smith holds a degree in English Literature from the University of Cambridge. She is a fellow of the Royal Society of Literature and has twice been listed as one of Granta's 20 Best Young British Novelists. Her first novel, *White Teeth*, was the winner of the Whitbread First Novel Award, the Guardian First Book Award, the James Tait Black Memorial Prize for Fiction, and the Commonwealth Writers' First Book Award. Her second novel, *The Autograph Man*, won the Jewish Quarterly Wingate Literary Prize. Zadie Smith's third novel, *On Beauty*, won the Orange Prize for Fiction and the Commonwealth Writers' Best Book Award (Eurasia Section) and was short-listed for the Man Booker Prize. Her fourth novel, *NW*, was short-listed for the Royal Society of Literature Ondaatje Prize and the Women's Prize for Fiction. Her most recent novel, *Swing Time*, was short-listed for the National Book Critics Circle Award for Fiction and long-listed for the

Man Booker Prize for 2017. She published her first essay collection, *Changing My Mind*, in 2009 and her second essay collection, *Feel Free*, in 2018. Her first short story collection, *Grand Union*, was published in 2019. In 2020 she published a short essay collection, *Intimations*. In 2021 Zadie Smith and Nick Laird publish their first children's picture book, *Weirdo*, illustrated by Magenta Fox.

Anne M. Wagner is an art historian, critic, and teacher who writes on a range of topics in nineteenth-, twentieth-, and twenty-first-century art, especially sculpture. Class of 1936 Professor Emerita at the University of California, Berkeley, she is now based in London, where in 2013–2014 she was Visiting Professor at the Courtauld Institute of Art. Other positions held since her move abroad include the post of Henry Moore Foundation Research Curator at Tate Britain, 2010–2011; Visiting Distinguished Professor at the University of York, 2010–2013; and Mellon Residential Fellow in Arts Practice and Scholarship at the Richard and Mary L. Gray Center for the Arts and Inquiry at the University of Chicago, 2012. Her books include *Jean-Baptiste Carpeaux: Sculptor of the Second Empire* (1986), *Three Artists (Three Women)* (1996), and *Mother Stone: The Vitality of Modern British Sculpture* (2005). *A House Divided: On Recent American Art* appeared in 2012. With T. J. Clark, she is the curator of *Lowry and the Painting of Modern Life*, a major exhibition staged at Tate Britain in 2013, as well as the coauthored book that accompanied the show. Her articles and essays have appeared in such journals as *Art History*, *Representations*, *OCTOBER*, the *London Review of Books*, and *Artforum*.

Hamza Walker is director of LAXART, a nonprofit art space in Los Angeles, and an adjunct professor at the School of the Art Institute of Chicago. Prior to joining LAXART in 2016, he was director of education and associate curator at the Renaissance Society, a noncollecting contemporary art museum in Chicago. Recent exhibitions include Kandis Williams/Cassandra Press's *The Absolute Right to Exclude* (2021) and Post Commodity's *Some Reach While Others Clap* (2020). In 2016, Walker co-curated (with Aram Moshayedi) the Hammer Museum's Los Angeles biennial *Made in L.A.* Walker has won the Walter Hopps Award for Curatorial Achievement (2004) and the Ordway Prize (2010) for impact on the field of contemporary art.

A formidable creature is sound asleep, her head in her arms, oblivious to the minuscule characters busying themselves about her; some are about to seize packages held aloft by a crane, others climb up her surface, then slide down ropes, which may be holding the figure down or trying to move her. Is she a giantess or a monument? In this rough, yet precise pencil drawing, one will recognize Kara Walker's hybrid between Egyptian sphinx–American mammy figure, *A Subtlety, or The Marvelous Sugar Baby*, named after the artist's installation at the former Domino Sugar refining plant in Brooklyn in 2014.[1]

I might look at this image as a metaphor for my own relationship to Walker's oeuvre: a tiny worker among others, toiling away at the indifferent, albeit fully alive, monument that is her practice. Yet to indulge that fantasy so would be to further perpetuate a certain sin—using the artwork to prop up an argument, rather than deriving meaning from the work itself—that has already travestied Walker's art-historical reception. This aborted metaphor, however, is a telling symptom of the process involved in compiling this volume: the return of the repressed—those fleeting attitudes and affects—that any effort to engage art in a rigorous manner is supposed to exclude.

Since Kara Walker became known as an artist and a cultural powerhouse in the mid-1990s, the ink spilled on her work has flowed continually, matched only by the flood of artworks she produced. This is due to the high degree of public, institutional exposure Walker's art has had since her 1994 debut exhibition at the Drawing Center, with no

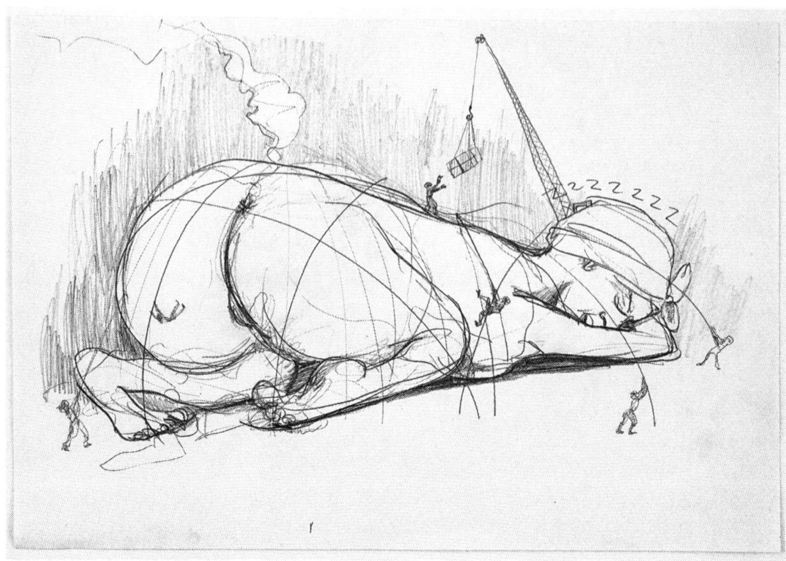

Kara Walker, detail from *Whisperer*, 2014. Gouache and graphite on paper. Set of 26: 12 × 18 inches (30.5 × 45.7 cm) each. Artwork © Kara Walker, courtesy of Sikkema Jenkins & Co., New York; Sprüth Magers, Berlin.

less than three solo shows per year between 1995 and 1998. Another reason for such an abundance of engagements is, of course, the work itself. Walker's art presents a unique combination of violent figuration and exquisite forms via the appropriation of minor art media, above all the silhouette, with the result that it pulls "the viewer into something totally demeaning and possibly very beautiful,[2]" according to Walker in the 1996 interview with art critic Jerry Saltz (reproduced in this volume). Her work borrows from an iconography linked to the fantasized and travestied history of American chattel slavery. Because of the rocket-speed institutional recognition of Walker's art—made spectacularly manifest with her reception of a MacArthur "Genius" Fellowship in 1997[3]—and the work's openly personal and often abject references to the imaginary of the antebellum South, the critical discourse around Walker quickly became laden with discussions of the controversy occasioned by the work. Such approaches did not so much interrogate Walker's art itself as they mobilized it to stress the problematic representation of minorities and of the imbalances of power within mainstream art institutions.[4]

Indeed, the very first art-historical monograph on Walker's art, Gwendolyn DuBois Shaw's *Seeing the Unspeakable: The Art of Kara Walker*, devotes no less than a full book chapter to that subject.[5] And virtually no text from the Walker literature, including my own, has engaged her art without at least a tentative account of the controversy, regardless of its approach or point of view. Thus, the exegesis has been shaped by the numerous debates on the very debates it generated, from the early stages of its formation. In a more positive light, the meta-discussions on Walker's work attest to the range of responses it has elicited, including in realms beyond the scope of the mainstream contemporary art world, starting with many writers, for instance.[6] Walker's work has illustrated numerous fascinating analyses in African American Studies on postslavery subjectivity, on trauma, on the state of racism and sexism and the peril of Black lives in United States, on the state of post-Black art.[7] However, the work has also been recruited for not so fascinating analyses on a co-opted, neoliberal version of the notion of "post-Blackness." Yet whatever light one may shed on the mass of texts her work has engendered, its sheer volume sets an obvious methodological problem. How does one look at a work that has been covered up—and maybe, to a certain extent, even obscured—by such "thick theoretical layers,"[8] to borrow a phrase from the late art historian Daniel Arasse's analysis on Cindy Sherman?[9]

The answer this volume provides, among possible others, is to favor texts that enable one to look at the work precisely and to see it—rather than those that tell us what one should, or should not, see in it. The writings collected here aim to engage the art in the long run, taking the time and pains to examine the work as artistic work, and attempting to understand the nature and process of Walker's interventions within the visual. In doing so, these texts allow us to comprehend Walker's formal research and experimental as the process of *working through* the problems and questions that her work summons. In other words, I have privileged those aspects of the Walker discourse that reckon with her "profoundly formal" sensibility,[10] bringing full attention to the "aesthetic intelligence embodied in actual works of art as objects of experience in their own right," to quote from art historian Kobena Mercer's introduction to *Travel and See* (2016), his anthology of texts on works by African American, Black British, and Afro-Caribbean artists.[11] In other words, texts centering on the practice of ekphrasis (the in–depth description of the work of art before one's eyes).

As the practice of writing about art, the ekphrasis demands a highly detailed attention to the formal qualities of the artwork; it is sometimes regarded as one of the origins of critical art discourse.[12] Yet, to follow in Mercer's footsteps in understanding ekphrasis as a political act of aesthetic justice (or an aesthetic act of political justice), taking such a tack does not mean sweeping the sociopolitical issues the work is in relation to under the rug by applying an anachronistic formalism to the analysis of Walker's art. Rather, this means trying to understand how Walker's work processes through and with form, in dialogue with the histories of cultural artifacts and visual cultures. Accordingly, the texts reproduced in this volume all share a high degree of engagement with Walker's pieces as material works of art, carefully assessing the artist's process, choice of materials, and medium, while putting those decisions in the context of the sociopolitical and cultural environment that shape but never determine them. Yet even with this vision in mind, difficult choices had to be made given the quality of the extant scholarship: preference has thus been given to texts that are not easily accessible or already in circulation, such as DuBois Shaw's landmark text.[13]

Given the artistic and cultural impact of Walker's best-known pieces, her silhouette installations, and, more recently, her public sculptures, this volume presents analyses of her most significant work. At the same time, the book aims to convey a sense of the versatility of Walker's practice from its very beginnings, with texts that highlight her writing practice, her video and performance work, and the importance of music in several of her pieces. To this end, this volume provides analyses of works by Walker that are less known, thereby stressing the range and depth of her artistic positioning, and the variety in tone and gestures of her practice.

Through some of the texts reproduced in this volume, the reader will also get a fair glimpse of one of the main tenets of Walker's art: drawing. The exclusive study of drawing *as such* in Walker's practice, however, remains a stimulating challenge for the literature on Walker in the making or yet to come. Until curator Anita Haldemann's groundbreaking exhibition of Walker's drawings, *A Black Hole Is Everything a Star Longs to Be* (and her remarkable essay catalog essay),[14] many discussions by scholars, curators, and artists on Walker's drawings have observed them *as images*, or they have not taken up Walker's drawing practice as their sole object of study but, rather, included it in more general discussions of the artist's work or in anthologies on contemporary drawing.[15] And, to be sure, it is within the contemporary that Walker's drawing has to be comprehended, as her dizzying ability to appropriate and conjure any number of Western drawing styles—Renaissance, Baroque, nineteenth-century satiric cartoons, Symbolist, Expressionist, Realist, Social modernist,[16] to the point where it might almost seem irrelevant to speak of *style* any longer (although a drawing by Walker is, paradoxically, instantly recognizable)—precisely anchors her work within the contemporary approaches to drawing in the digital information age as a practice in and of itself.

Keeping a balance between professional perspectives on Walker's work, with future artists and curators as well as scholars in mind, this volume means to provide a view of the conditions of circulation of Walker's art: hence, contributions by curators are vital to grasp those issues linked to the exhibition and contextualization of her art. Another major aspect of Walker's critical reception is her interviews, not only because they were partly instrumental to the polarization of the public reception of her work, but also because they attest to one of the most significant forces in her practice: namely, her ever-evolving artistic, political, and social self-reflexive positioning. The conversation between Walker and art critic Jerry Saltz, "Kara Walker: Ill-Will and Desire," (1996), relies on a discussion of some of her *Negress Notes* drawings (1995–1997); the artist accounts for her choice of the silhouette as a medium, but also for her eclectic visual sources. She also explains some of her most provocative statements, revealing her flair for catchphrases, but, more importantly, her mature artistic approach and a pragmatic, sophisticated view of the concepts of history, fiction, myth, and humor. Hamza Walker's "Cut It Out," from the broadside issued by the Renaissance Society at the University of Chicago on the occasion of Walker's 1997 solo show, provides an analysis of the artist's work as anachronistic. Building on the notion of excess and surplus within power relations, stressing the psychosocial and cultural issues at stake with Walker's wielding of dark humor, Hamza Walker's text highlights the way the artist's work questions and pleads for the idea of agency. His second text, "A Mind Is a Terrible Thing to Waste" (2006), written partly in response to the "Kara Walker controversy," provides a concise account of the problems the debates around her work brought to the fore, while giving the reader an invaluable insight into the process of curating the 1997 Renaissance Society exhibition, setting Walker's practice within the context of its reception and of the work carried out by art institutions to reach out to audiences. "Thelma Golden/Kara Walker: A Dialogue" provides a rare view of Walker: catching her at a point when her use of the silhouette was branching out into different directions, the dialogue unveils how Walker's use of one medium morphs into the next. The interview enables Walker to develop her thoughts on her complicated relationship to painting on a deeper level than ever previously articulated. Golden's interview also shows Walker as an artist concerned with the history, politics, and impact of the visual forms she borrows from. In "Kara Walker: 'The Black-White Relation'" (2003), art historian Anne M. Wagner starts from the criticisms leveled at Walker to conduct a thorough analysis of the way the artist transforms her source material and its function as portrait. Pointing out the simulacral nature of Walker's silhouettes as copies without originals, Wagner lays the ground for interpreting Walker's work within the field of conceptual art, as the figuration of the (interdependent) constructs of blackness and whiteness. In her essay in the shape of a lexicon, "Maladies of Power: A Kara Walker Lexicon" (2006), Yasmil Raymond, then curator at the Walker Art Center in Minneapolis, offered a penetrating insight into the artist's iconographic, literary, and textual sources. Often shifting scale in her analysis, Raymond surveys the broad range of media explored by the artist—installation, large and small drawings, film. Art historian Lorraine Morales Cox's "A Performative Turn: Kara Walker's *Song of the South (2005)*" (2007) dwells on the transition from Walker's silhouette installations with projections to shadow theater and film. Relying on precise accounts of shadow theater performances by Walker that have been recorded for documentation but not shown publicly afterward, Cox's article gives a highly original, informed perspective on Walker's performance process and on her films as video installations. With "Subtleties of Resistance: Sweetness and Violence in Kara Walker's *A Subtlety*" (2015), performance theorist Tavia Nyong'o provides the most convincing answer to the public offline and online debates raised by Walker's first take on public sculpture. Through the double critical lens of relational aesthetics and Black feminism, Nyong'o situates Walker's monumental gesture within the production chain of contemporary capitalism. My own essay, "'Stories of Mortal Terror': Kara Walker's *Six*

Miles from Springfield and *Lucy of Pulaski (2009)*" (2019), questions the relation between Walker's then unprecedented use of historical archives and the formal solutions that resulted from the artist's confrontation with actual records of terror, through an in-depth interpretation of the film diptych (*Six Miles from Springfield* and *Lucy of Pulaski*). Decentering the discourse on Walker to the Black Diaspora, writer Zadie Smith examines Walker's public art in general and her *Fons Americanus* installation at the Tate Modern (2019), in particular, as counter-propositions to colonial monuments and as a reflection on colonial history in the light of a careful and eclectic selection of Walker's work since the beginning of her career, from the personal, explicitly situated point of view of a fellow artist. Indeed, each text in this volume shares a highly personal viewpoint revealed in the choice of artworks that are discussed, conveying the author's desire to understand through specific manners of looking and ways of seeing. As such, the final ambition with this volume is to anchor the discourse on Walker within a pedagogy of the image that stems from the awareness of the contemporary necessity of image literacy, with a critical passion for art as its core.

Vanina Géré

Notes

1. This drawing was presented at *Afterword* (2014), the exhibition of Walker's preparatory work and research on the history of sugar plantations and industry that followed her installation at the former Domino factory. The full title is *A Subtlety, or the Marvelous Sugar Baby, an Homage to the unpaid and overworked Artisans who have refined our Sweet tastes from the cane fields to the Kitchens of the New World on the Occasion of the demolition of the Domino Sugar Refining Plant.*

2. Kara Walker, interviewed by Jerry Saltz, "Kara Walker: Ill-Will and Desire," *Flash Art* (November–December 1996): 82–86, 83.

3. As has been pointed out, the same year as Kerry James Marshall. One could also bring as an example of early institutional recognition the fact that as soon as 2007, the Museum of Modern Art acquired Walker's Drawing Center installation, *Gone, An Historical Romance of a Civil War as It Occurred between the Dusky Thighs of One Young Negress and Her Heart* (1994).

4. The Walker controversy has been the object of an anthology in and of itself. See Howardena Pindell, ed., *Kara Walker No/Kara Walker Yes/Kara Walker?* (New York: Midmarch Art Press, 2009).

5. See Gwendolyn DuBois Shaw, "Censorship and Reception," in *Seeing the Unspeakable: The Art of Kara Walker* (Durham, NC: Duke University Press, 2004), 103–124.

For other in-depth accounts on the controversy, also see Robert Reid-Pharr, "Black Girl Lost," in *Kara Walker: Pictures from Another Time*, ed. Annette Dixon (Ann Arbor: University of Michigan Museum of Art, 2001), 27–41; and Amy Tang, "Postmodern Repetitions: Parody, Trauma, and the Case of Kara Walker," *differences: A Journal of Feminist Cultural Studies*, 21, no. 2 (2010): 1–31. Also, for a short yet insightful analysis, see Lorraine O'Grady as "Poison Ivy," "Letter to the Editor," *Artforum International*, 37, no. 1 (October 1998). Yet, despite the range of responses to the Walker controversy, the latter has seldom been analyzed through the prism of social class.

6. Starting with the writer James Hannaham, with whom she had been in public conversation and who wrote two texts in publications related to Walker's exhibitions, *Dust Jackets for the Niggerati* (Sikkema Jenkins, New York, 2013) and *Go to Hell or Atlanta—Whichever Comes First* (Victoria Miro, London, 2015). See James Hannaham, "Pea, Ball, Bounce," *Interview* (November 1998): 114–119; James Hannaham, "Hellfire," in *Kara Walker: Go to Hell or Atlanta—Whichever Comes First* (London: Victoria Miro Gallery, 2015); James Hannaham, "Who Is Delicious?," in *Dust Jackets for the Niggerati*, by Hilton Als, James Hannaham, Christopher Stackhouse, Kevin Young, and Kara Walker (New York: Gregory R. Miller & Co., 2013), 116–123. Recently, Walker's art has also been discussed by writer Maggie Nelson, "On Kara Walker's *Event Horizon*," in *I Stand in My Specific Place with My Own Day Here: Site-Specific Art at the New School*, ed. Frances Richard (Durham, NC: Duke University Press, 2019), 162–167.

7. See Christina Sharpe's remarkable perspective on Walker's *The End of Uncle Tom and the Grand Allegorical Tableau of Eva in Heaven*: Christina Sharpe, "Kara Walker's Monstrous Intimacies," in *Monstrous Intimacies: Making Post-Slavery Subjects* (Durham, NC: Duke University Press, 2010), 154–188; Christina Sharpe, *In the Wake: On Blackness and Being* (Durham, NC: Duke University Press, 2016). Also see Nana Adusei-Poku, "The Challenge to Conceptualize the Multiplicity of Multiplicities—Post-Black Art and Its Intricacies," *Dark Matter Journal*, special issue no. 2, *Post-Racial Imaginaries* (November 2012). www.darkmatter101.org/site/2012/11/29/the-multiplicity-of-multiplicities.

8. I am borrowing this phrase from Daniel Arasse's analysis on Cindy Sherman's critical reception. Daniel Arasse, *Anachroniques* (Paris: Gallimard, 2006), 95.

9. Walker's case may not be exceptional: the critical reception of Cindy Sherman's work, for instance, offers an enlightening precedent of discourses submersing the work of the artist early on, as the OCTOBER Files volume edited by Johanna Burton made amply manifest.

10. Frances Richard, "New York: Kara Walker Brent Sikkema," *Artforum International*, 2, no. 42 (October 2003): 169. This brief, yet precious insight into Walker's work can easily be consulted in the *Artforum* online archive, https://www.artforum.com/print/reviews/200308/kara-walker-46505.

11. Kobena Mercer, *Travel and See: Black Diaspora Art Practices since the 1980s* (Durham, NC: Duke University Press, 2016), 1.

12. I mean Giorgio Vasari's in his *Lives of the Most Excellent Painters, Sculptors, and Architects* (1550, 1568).

13. DuBois Shaw's book has been reprinted twice and is available as an e-book. One may also notice the absence of a text by Darby English, whose work on Walker has been crucial precisely due to his ekphrastic approach. However, for professional reasons, Professor English declined. See Darby English, "This Is Not about the Past: Silhouettes in the Work of Kara Walker," in *Kara Walker: Narratives of a Negress*, ed. Ian

Berry, Darby English, Vivian Patterson, and Mark Reinhardt (Cambridge, MA: MIT Press, in association with the Frances Young Tang Teaching Museum and Art Gallery at Skidmore College and Williams College Museum of Art, 2003), 141–174. Also see Darby English, "A New Context for Reconstruction: Some Crises of Landscape in Kara Walker's Silhouette Installations," in *How to See a Work of Art in Total Darkness* (Cambridge, MA: MIT Press, 2007), 71–136.

14. The exhibition of Walker's drawings, which excavated many drawings from the artist's own archive as well as new drawings, took place at the Kunstmuseum Basel, Switzerland (June 5–September 19, 2021). Anita Haldemann, "Kara Walker's Drawings: 'A Dance of Skepticism and Faith,'" in *Kara Walker: A Black Hole Is Everything a Star Longs to Be*, ed. Anita Haldemann (Geneva: JRP/Editions, 2019), 561–573.

15. One notable exception is Gwendolyn DuBois Shaw's book chapter on a large drawing by Walker, *John Brown* (1996). DuBois Shaw's interest throughout the book chapter lies above all in Walker's subversion of religious and history painting iconography; however, she gives the viewer a detailed account of Walker's use of drawing as a medium. See Gwendolyn DuBois Shaw, "The Lactation of John Brown," in *Seeing the Unspeakable*, 67–102, 72.

For analyses of Walker's drawings as such within a larger perspective on contemporary drawing, see Laura Hoptman, *Drawing Now: Eight Propositions* (New York: Museum of Modern Art, 2002), 104–127.

16. I am specifically thinking of Walker's 2011 charcoal drawings in relation to large drawings by the realist African American artist Charles White (1918–1979).

Kara Walker: Ill-Will and Desire

Jerry Saltz

JERRY SALTZ: I want to hear a little about the genesis of the form, how you came to do the silhouettes.

KARA WALKER: For the most part it happened in graduate school at the Rhode Island School of Design. I was trying to find a clean and easy way to bring together a bunch of messy ideas that were troubling me. I was always looking for a way to condense broad and polarizing emotions or issues, issues of race and sex, because I grew up surrounded by them in the culture and in the arts. It's really a graphic issue, the silhouetting; it really is about an image, and growing up with my father as a painter and going to exhibitions of black art. I saw a lot of works steeped in history and in the awareness of self and pride—and enormous intangibles, issues that often get didactic.

JS: But why the silhouette, how does it function for you?

KW: It's a blank space, but it's not all a blank space, it's both there and not there. It's very polite.

JS: Polite?

KW: It comes from a sort of polite middle-class society to some extent. It's not as haughty and aristocratic as a full-fledged oil painting portrait. Everyone could get one for a few pennies;—and you had image, you had connection with physiognomy: it told you about your profile. Someone gave a speech not long ago in Washington in which

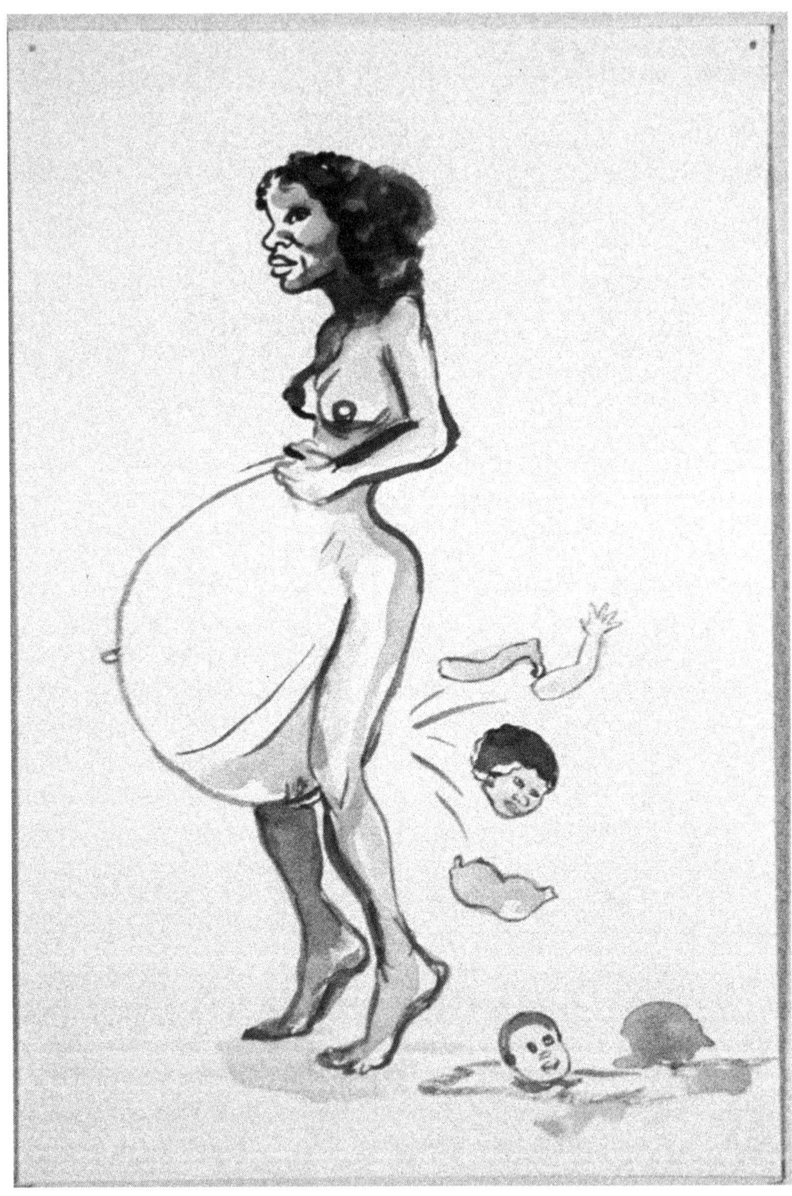

Kara Walker, *Untitled (from Negress Notes)*, 1996. Watercolor on paper. 17 works, 9 × 6 inches (22.9 × 15.2 cm) each. Artwork © Kara Walker, courtesy of Sikkema Jenkins & Co., New York; Sprüth Magers, Berlin.

they talked about profiles: the profile of a person, profile as a side-long glance, and I liked that.

JS: The side-long glance?

KW: The side-long glance: it's my answer to the male gaze. It's the little look and it's full of suspicion, potential ill-will, or desire. It's a look unreliable women give.

JS: What do you mean "unreliable"?

KW: The unreliable woman is the negress.

JS: You sign your work in an extraordinary way. The installation at Wooster Gardens last April was signed, partially: "From the Bowels to the Bosom, A Reconstruction by Miss K. Walker, a Free Negress of Noteworthy Talent," and it went on.

KW: It's a play on the slave narratives from another era. Well-meaning abolitionists would make some sort of testimonial. It was the antithesis of racism, a higher than high uplift of the oppressed peoples.

JS: So to sign yourself a "Free Negress of Noteworthy Talent" plays on historical phraseology.

KW: At one point the first draft said "of Remarkable Talent," but I had to axe that because that was too much; that was giving myself too much credit. It's a hesitant kind of word "Noteworthy Talent": somewhat anonymous, as a stereotype or as a silhouette. You find a silhouette in an antique store and you know that there's a person, a sitter, whose shadow this is.

JS: Whose shadows are these?

KW: Shadows, shadows of shadowy characters, shadows of artificial things, shadows of stereotypes, shadows of things that maybe there's only a written description of. There's this novel, *The Clansman*, which describes the deep South in a gothic Victorian style, all sorts of tantaliz-ing creatures with grotesquely large lips, whose dirty hair is tied with dirty ribbons; catlike.

JS: So in a way your silhouetting is a shorthand of a stereotype.

KW: It's silhouetting a fiction, the fiction of history; the fiction that has come out of history. We speak of history in odd terms. I sort of condensed it to the fictional—of romance fiction, or stories, books, novels, *Gone with the Wind, Uncle Tom's Cabin.* It's a genre, like the historical romance. Harriet Beecher Stowe has taken bits and pieces of real life and some of her experiences or interviews with other people, and embellished it; and in that embellishment Harriet Beecher Stowe longs to see this docile man, Uncle Tom, this simple fellow, humble, God-fearing, childlike, and she comes up with, I think, the desire to know what it is like life among the lowly. She embellishes these characters with desire.

JS: But you seem to go back to this nineteenth-century historical fiction in order to critique it.

KW: To critique it and to question why it's reoccurring. I had to make the silhouette because I think I could never really condense anything in painting form. Too many brush strokes to worry about. In the installation at Wooster Gardens there were all these little ghostly characters, these shadowy bits and pieces; bits of phraseology, the child-likeness, the tawdry vixen, the wicked; they all jumped into life—waking life—without my really controlling them. But it did make me think about the romantic implications.

JS: I'm not sure what you mean by "romantic implications."

KW: Romance. It exists in interracial romance and also in miscegenation. Each implies a different situation. Miscegenation, race mixtures, causes a lot of anxiety, anger. It depends on where you are, but it seemed very apparent in Atlanta. Hostility seemed very pronounced when I was with white boys. On the other hand there is the polite, you know, "we're-all-in-this-wonderful-world-getting-together" reaction. That's the interracial romance. Then there are the silent notes and things from the Klan. It only happened once but it had enough of an impact on me. It threw me from the present happiness all the way into what I thought was the distant past—but really it isn't so far removed. That is where this tableau comes from: as a way to recapitulate all of this and to have some impact on the viewer.

JS: How did this history play itself out in your last installation?

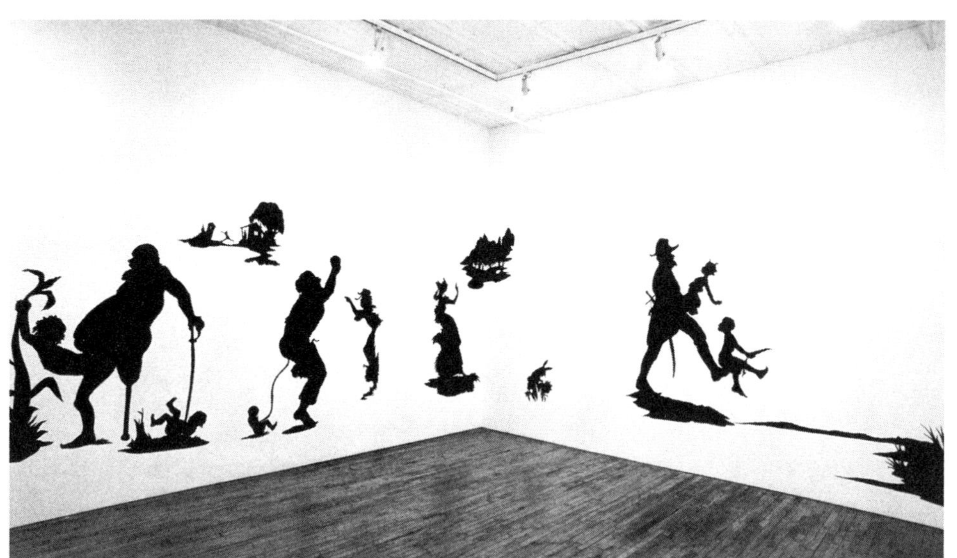

Kara Walker. Left side: detail from *The End of Uncle Tom and the Grand Allegorical Tableau of Eva in Heaven*, 1995 (wall installation), 156 × 420 inches (396.2 × 1066.8 cm); right side: detail from *The Battle of Atlanta: Being the Narrative of a Negress in the Flames of Desire—A Reconstruction*, 1995 (wall installation). Cut paper and wax adhesive on wall. 17 parts, dimensions variable. Installation view: *From the Bowels to the Bosom*, Wooster Gardens/Brent Sikkema, New York, NY, 1996. Artwork © Kara Walker, courtesy of Sikkema Jenkins & Co., New York; Sprüth Magers, Berlin.

KW: I didn't want a completely passive viewer. Art means too much to me. To be able to articulate something visually is really an important thing. I wanted to make work where the viewer wouldn't walk away; he would either giggle nervously, get pulled into history, into fiction, into something totally demeaning and possibly very beautiful. I wanted to create something that looks like you. It looks like a cartoon character, it's a shadow, it's a piece of paper, but it's out of scale. It refers to your shadow, to some extent to purity, to the mirror.

JS: There's a wild story going on in your installation.

KW: It's a wild story, but it's not. I think that the historical myths are kind of deceiving. I mentioned something about Harlequin romances. I didn't read that many of them, but I worked in a bookstore long enough to see what kind of an impact they have and who's buying them. It's love, it's desire, all of those things cloaked in a hoop skirt. The only

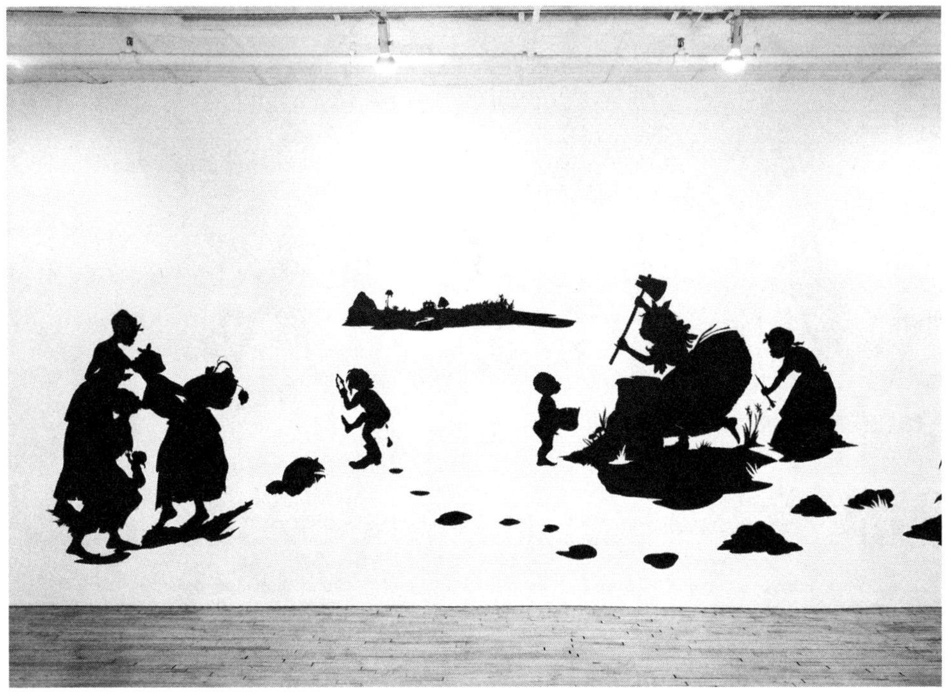

Kara Walker, detail from *The End of Uncle Tom and the Grand Allegorical Tableau of Eva in Heaven*, 1995. Wall installation, 156 × 420 inches (396.2 × 1066.8 cm). Artwork © Kara Walker, courtesy of Sikkema Jenkins & Co., New York; Sprüth Magers, Berlin.

thing that makes it a historical romance is the setting, the types of dress and the picture on the cover. On the other hand, something that really fascinates me is what happens to history. Does history die if you intentionally repeat it? If you play it out again, like those guys who go out into the fields, dressed in blue and gray, playing Civil War games, the recreational societies? To me they seem to be killing history solely in their fanatic worship of it. It turns it into absurdity.

JS: In your installation everything is right, everything is wrong. There are funny things, it's gross, everybody's a hero, nobody is a hero. It really brings high and low together, cradle and grave, funny and tragic . . .

KW: . . . and black and white. But there's got to be one little hook in there. To some extent I'm grinning while all this is happening.

JS: There's a smile? The grin of the side-long glance?

KW: A side-long glance at the viewer. I was thinking about creating a situation where the viewer would come in, be shocked of horrified, but interested, so I could see what that reaction was.

JS: In a statement about the show you used the word "Cyclorama." What did you mean?

KW: The large-scale paintings in the round that were around at the end of the last century and that were fairly popular just before cinema—grand history painting of absurd scale, almost wildly dramatic, very popular, totally obscure now.

JS: Do you think that there is a grand history painting aspect to your work, something "wildly dramatic?"

KW: I grew up in the mini-series era . . .

JS: Which ones do you remember?

KW: *Roots* was the main one. The strange thing about it, I don't remember much of the story, but I know it was very important, we all watched it. Everyone came into school—it was fourth grade—and started making fun of it. So it became just another joke.

JS: How does humor function in your work?

KW: I have a funny problem with humor I guess, because I don't consider it fun. I remember cartoons on TV that were old, pre–Mickey Mouse cartoons. These mysterious black-faced mice. I saw new prints of old Bull Durham ads with these coons scenes, genre scenes, sitting on the porch with all the animals. It's strange but this is somebody's interpretation of the good life. But this good life is full of people with a kind of peasant worship—these humorous, clowny coon images, you know these black characters. Whatever else they might be, they were also intended to be hilariously funny. The black person was the butt of all kinds of jokes from vaudeville to Hollywood on up. Where are we now? I think we've stopped being funny.

JS: This "Miss K. Walker a Free Negress," who is she, the author?

KW: "Miss K. Walker" is the author who came up North to make good.

JS: And is she "free?"

KW: She is free as opposed to expensive.

JS: Let's talk about some of your drawings. Could you read that one with the writing to me?

KW: "Afro Am or African American artists are always espousing the horrors of slavery Gen-Afro Apartheid. The continued voice of the victim seeps through all that pride. Yes! But horrors are always tolerable to repressed individuals to whom they may occur. This allows for a stronger sense of masochism in future generations, makes for great race riots, very colorful."

JS: Wow. You've talked about "my inner plantation," that's an incredible phrase. What does it mean?

KW: My inner plantation . . . I guess that's what this generation of black kids are going to inherit. And this "inner plantation" is this grand place where, to some extent, we knew our place; a place where one is whole, in that sense, and knows what to fight against, or who to obey, or how to hold on to oneself in the face of oppression. In my work I just assigned them all characters in this fictional version.

JS: And who are some of these characters, for example? Who is this figure represented in this drawing?

KW: She would be like an Aunt Dicey. She is not the big house nanny for instance. She might know some potions, she might know something about "humanness," she keeps to herself. She's sitting in front of a sign that says "Relive the past for 5¢" with one breast exposed.

JS: Why is one breast exposed?

KW: Implying suckling, implying childhood, implying history resides here. A shack in the background also refers to the black woman in this world as an anonymous root.

JS: There seems to be a lot of excrement in your work—what gives?

KW: Letting it all hang out. This terrible song that somebody came up with—kind of a rap go-go kind of song—and I guess the performer's persona was Doo-Doo Brown. It is an insult, but it comes from within the black community itself, I think. One of the great Harlem Renaissance poets once described every conceivable shade of person in Harlem and I think there was a doo-doo brown.

JS: There certainly was a whole lot of shitting going on at the installation at Wooster Gardens.

KW: It trailed across one wall. I could sort of hear this character farting. It's rather difficult to convey in black paper. It's easier if it's shitting, especially if it's sort of liquid. Really it's about finding one's voice in the wrong end; searching for one's voice and having it come out the wrong way.

JS: Could you read me the text on this one?

KW: "The side-long glance. The look unreliable women give is a profile lacking detail and full of speculation. Don't tell me you don't think evil when you see me, low cut and with a white man. Tell me it doesn't cross your mind, flitting along the wall, the specters of confusion and nasty-headedness."

JS: What's going on in this one captioned *The End of Africa*? It's just barely there. It looks like a tiny isle in the middle of blue.

KW: It's just very sad. What does Africa mean anyway, because Africa has this whole other meaning in much of the black community: T-shirts and posters glorifying this mythical Africa—this grand home island—that we don't have anything to do with.

JS: What does it mean to you then?

KW: I don't know if I really have an Africa. I embellish history in my mind, when I go back in time and try to figure out who I would have been 50 years ago, 150 years ago; I can't really jump back without getting into a sci-fi mode, or these utopian stories.

JS: Are you in your installations?

KW: I'm in it all over the place. Actually, cutting out a racist caricature draws you very close to that caricature. Art is just like this, I guess. You get very attached to the thing you do and it stops being an ironic gesture—which I like and I don't like.

Kara Walker, *Untitled (from Negress Notes)*, 1996. Watercolor on paper. 17 works, 9 × 6 inches (22.9 × 15.2 cm) each. Artwork © Kara Walker, courtesy of Sikkema Jenkins & Co., New York; Sprüth Magers, Berlin.

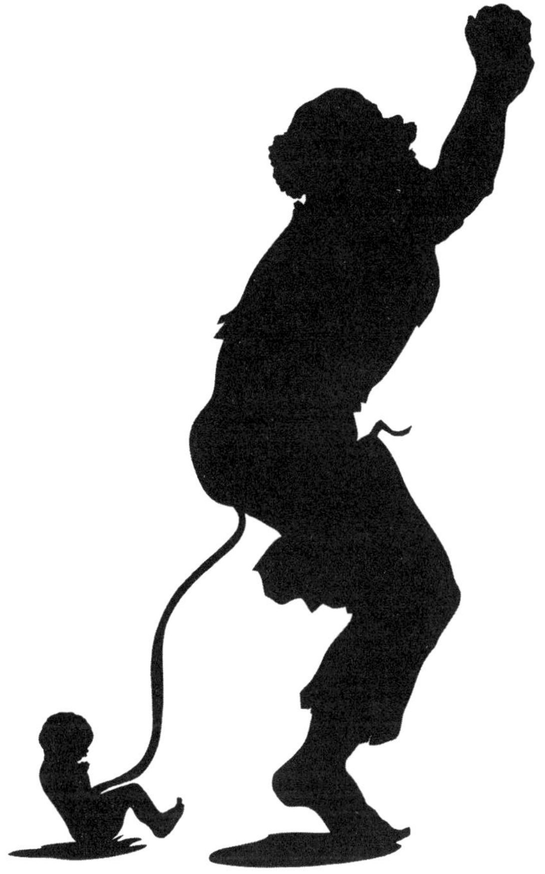

Kara Walker, detail from *The End of Uncle Tom and the Grand Allegorical Tableau of Eva in Heaven*, 1995. Artwork © Kara Walker, courtesy of Sikkema Jenkins & Co., New York; Sprüth Magers, Berlin.

JS: You don't seem to assign fixed meaning to your images . . .

KW: Yes and no. It really depends on what picture you're looking at. And if I did assign a meaning, I would be very angry at myself, and the next day I would see a different meaning.

JS: Here's another drawing, what's going on here?

KW: Black woman with the side-long glance; attractive, buxom; small blond boy at her breast, enraptured; older black man with white hair;

his thumb in white boy's ass; his tongue out. Everyone is in ecstasy—except for the black woman.

JS: And what is she doing?

KW: She's simply putting up with it.

JS: How do you connect to fiction, particularly historical fiction?

KW: Thinking of bad historical fiction, contemporary stuff; it's a very middle-class thing and it seems to go hand-in-hand with this silhouette esthetic. You can go into the mall, for instance, and get a Harlequin romance—the same way you can get your silhouette cut—they're all tied into the same sort of late twentieth-century fascination with something called "history."

JS: Didn't you write something about this? Would you read it to me?

KW: "Once you get a clear grasp on the fundamentals of history: who's writing it, what emotions are involved in reshaping it, what kinds of people are subjected to it—well, like being the guinea-pig . . . European-style enlightenment: 'Thems that are most doomed to repeat it are thems who believe in it'—taking history like a faith, a new religion of time and events and more time and more events. So in a way the follower's actions are in keeping with his or her creed. Me? Me, I say consciously and conscientiously: 'repeat actual events out of someone's history text book.' Conscientious repetition is the surest way to kill memory, and at that, history."

JS: Can I read you a quote and ask you for your reaction to it? It's a quote by John Brown. "Without the shedding of blood there can be no remission of sins."

KW: Someone yelled at me on the street: "Don't you know anything about your history?," and you know there's just too much to know. It's almost impossible to know everything about your history without getting romantic or crossing that line into fiction. I'm all for war, as long as I'm not in it and nobody gets hurt. I was still in Atlanta gathering material, as it were, for this work, sequestered in my room, when the L.A. riots broke out, and I thought, "what a great moment this is for me to be sitting here quietly, burning up, silently sitting at the typewriter, and trying to delicately write out my feelings when somebody else has just taken the initiative, and taken that anger, or whatever, and done something." It probably doesn't even matter what sparks a riot, it just happens; it releases so much.

JS: What do you think of dogmatism?

KW: I have no use for it. I can't make a clear statement anyway.

JS: What role does theory play in your work?

KW: It doesn't play much of a role. I feel that it should; I feel inadequate in my grasp of it. I feel I should be really tough and on-the-ball, instead I just try to look tough and on-the-ball. There's a place for dogmatism, but somebody's got to be better at it.

JS: Your work feels very handmade. What's your connection to craft?

KW: I always wanted to be an artist. I do the drawings by hand and cut them out completely different.

JS: So the silhouettes start as drawings?

KW: Craft, ladies work, minor art, a minor thing, ladies and maybe a couple of negroes and anyone who has some time on their hands.

JS: I want to read you another quote. I think you might recognize the author: "All black people in America want to be slaves just a little bit."

KW: That sounds like Kara Walker. That didn't go over too well with a couple of people in Atlanta. I think the rest of that quote went something like, "It gives people heaping teaspoons of dignity and pride." I guess slavery is the ultimate oppression. To be a slave runs along the lines of being a better masochist and knowing how to put up with things. It's that strength that entitles you to brace yourself for—I don't know—finding that thing that helped your grandmother or great-grandmother get through it all; made her such a strong person. Without that sense of oppression, ironically, it seems difficult to progress.

JS: Does it connect to sex at all? The masochism, the sadism?

KW: There is still a prevalent myth about the black woman and the black man: better, stronger, the big dick, the big cunt. I figured out I was a

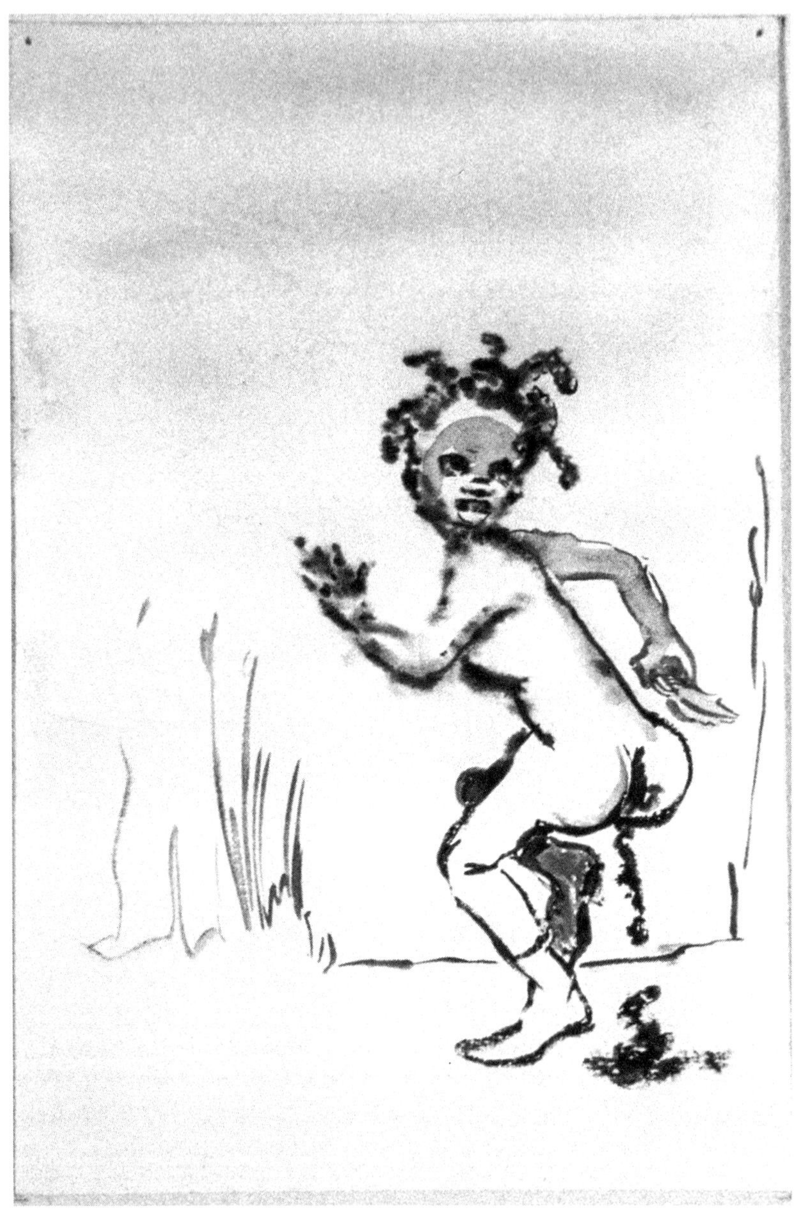

Kara Walker, *Untitled (from Negress Notes)*, 1996. Watercolor on paper. 17 works, 6 × 9 inches
(22.9 × 15.2 cm) each. Artwork © Kara Walker, courtesy of Sikkema Jenkins & Co., New York;
Sprüth Magers, Berlin.

milestone in people's sexual experience—to have made it with a black woman was one of those things to check off on your list of personal sexual accomplishments. That already has a slightly masochistic effect: to have just been the body for somebody's life story. I guess that's when I decided to offer up my side-long glances: to be a slave just a little bit. It's like what happened when that person on the street confronted me, hollered something at me, or when the Ku Klux Klan gives out flyers about disease-ridden black people; why my boyfriend shouldn't be with me. To be immediately thrust into history. So I used this mythic, fictional, kind of slave character to justify myself, or reinvent myself in some other situations.

JS: This week's issue of the *New Yorker* is called "the black issue." In the front of the magazine they asked a number of prominent black people to share their thoughts on the N-word, on the word nigger. How would you have responded?

KW: For me, it's a word that precedes violence, or at least it has in the past. You scream it and the ropes go up, or gunshots. I can understand, to some extent, why black folks would use it affectionately. But a word that seems to hurt more for me, and maybe you can tell me how this works, is nigger-lover.

JS: There's another drawing with writing on it. What does it say?

KW: It says, "The consistent use of the black body is to stand in for the: (a) Unnamed, (Vulgar), illicit sexuality, low-class, dirty humor, cannibalism, poverty, voodoo, insanity, death, envy; (b) Unnamable (Sublime), like pity, remorse, absolute oppressives and its we-shall-overcomeness, can-dance, can-do pride and all that. Looks better in black, perceived as a contrast to (a)."

JS: Now that sounds like a theory.

KW: It's somewhere between theory and paranoia. It goes on: "White, on the other hand, white peeps, as leaches, suckling, eating, licking, seeking qualities (a) or (b) or of course, as The Master, but also the Poor Cracker, and receive the benefit of multiple characteristics of this Afro-American Artists [*sic*]." It goes on. It's another note to myself.

JS: Anything going on with you and cannibalism?

KW: I'm a vegetarian. But cannibalism—eating the other—is wanting to have everything of the other person, body and soul. In the cartoons where African savages get pictured, the European explorers are often placed at the mercy of savages. There is a little bit of masochism, I think, involved with making pictures like these: so much love and hate involved in eating something; to kill something and eat it. It's very sexual, very sensual.

JS: How are things in general?

KW: Busy. I guess if I knew something about how to be an artist, I'd put out a handbook. I didn't move to New York, for instance, because I can't handle it. It's too much and I think something would be lost for me if I finally did come. I might at some point, but I'm always a little worried. When I was in Atlanta, New York was so far away, such an impossibility. Now, it's closer, and I have some access, and I could even move a little bit closer.

JS: Should people move to New York right now?

KW: I don't know what it means to be a "New York artist." I'm a Ted Kaczynski kind of artist right now. I'm just out there in the woods, making trouble. I don't really want to be a Kaczynski kind of artist, but in a way, that is a character that I find truly fascinating—on his own, completely undefinable.

Cut It Out/A Mind Is a Terrible Thing to Waste

Hamza Walker

These two essays have been written respectively in 1997 and 2006. They are reproduced here as two sections according to chronological order.

Cut It Out

Which of us has overcome his past? And the past of a Negro is blood dripping down through the leaves, gouged out eyeballs, the sex torn from the socket and severed with a knife. But this past is not special to the Negro. The horror is also the past, and the everlasting potential, or temptation, of the human race. If we do not know this, it seems to me, we know nothing about ourselves, nothing about each other; to have accepted this is also to have found a source of strength—source of all our power. But one must first accept this paradox, with joy.

—James Baldwin

It was from a personal perspective that James Baldwin arrived at the question: What does it mean to be human? As a black gay man who took pride in his skill as a polemicist, Baldwin felt obliged, if not entitled, to address the question of humanity. He immediately understood that the question was accountable to race and sexuality, making the stakes

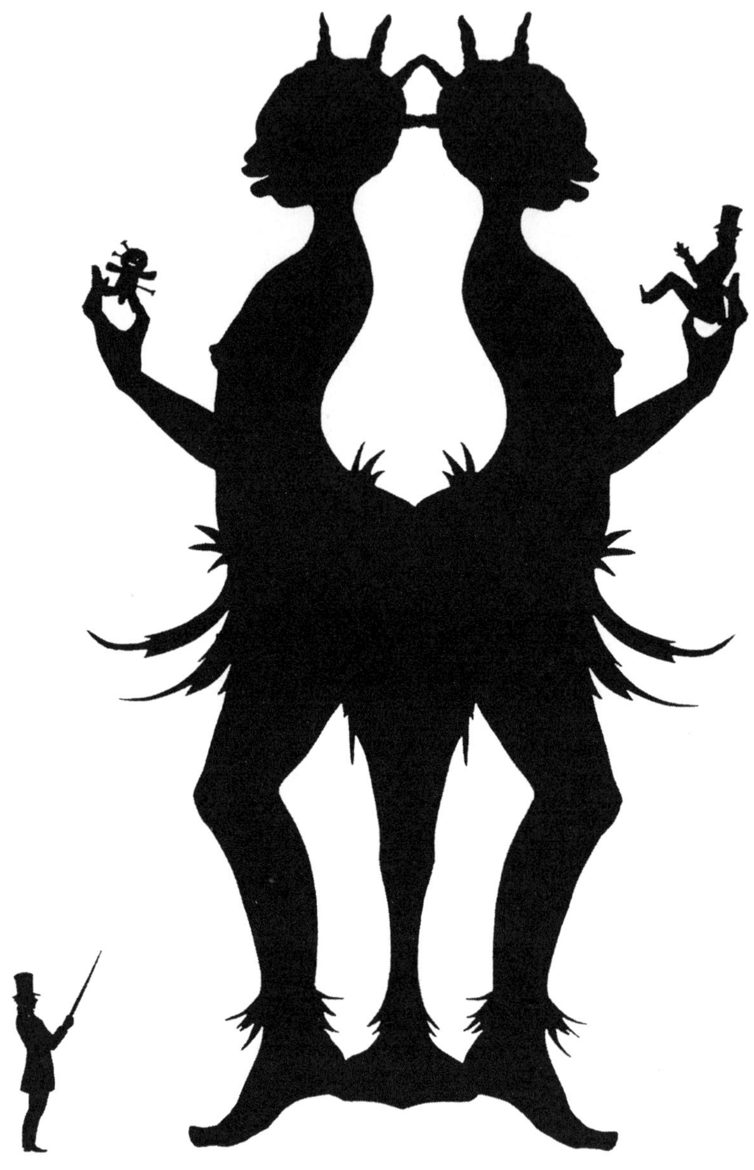

Kara Walker, *You Do*, 1994. Cut paper on canvas, 55 × 49 inches (139.7 × 124.5 cm). Artwork ©
Kara Walker, courtesy of Sikkema Jenkins & Co., New York; Sprüth Magers, Berlin.

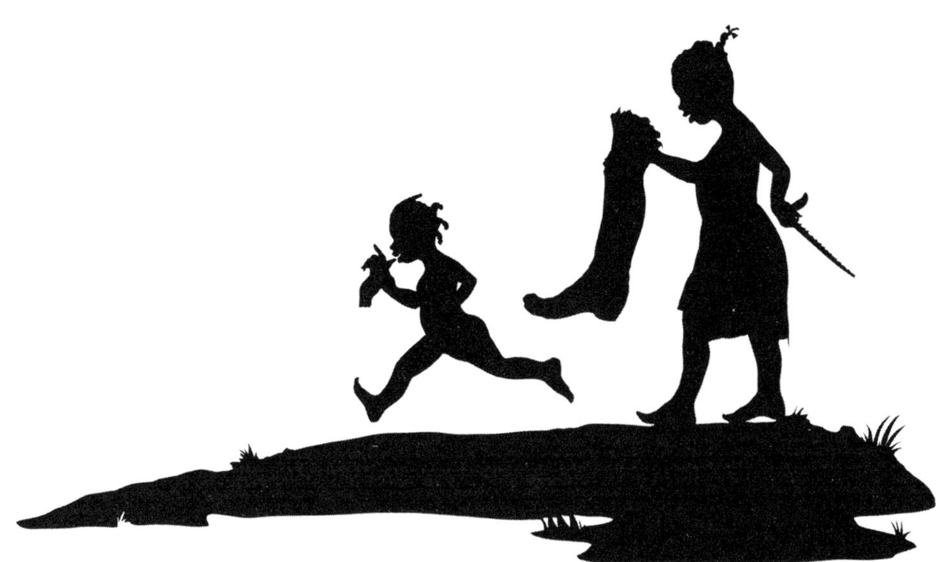

Kara Walker, detail from *The Battle of Atlanta: Being the Narrative of a Negress in the Flames of Desire—A Reconstruction*, 1995. Cut paper and wax adhesive on wall. 17 parts, dimensions variable. Artwork © Kara Walker, courtesy of Sikkema Jenkins & Co., New York; Sprüth Magers, Berlin.

at once both personal and social. The question of humanity, however, allowed Baldwin to consider the past outside of a historical context. Not only do the words "past," "potential," and "temptation" establish a trajectory that transcends history; they also paint a dark picture of human nature by calling into question the idea of moral progress. But Baldwin's comment was far more than a condemnation of this country's inability to come to terms with its historical underbelly of racial violence. Implicit in his suspicion of moral progress was a critique of the question. Baldwin knew that the use of the word "human" was rhetorical in that the question of humanity could never yield answers universal in scope. It is a question whose answer ultimately depends on who is doing the asking and what period is under examination. In short, Baldwin understood that the question would always falter before history, making it a paradox rather than an inquiry capable of resolution.

In light of this quote from Baldwin, one could without reservation characterize Kara Walker's imagination as joyful. That is a scary thought for an artist whose work often includes sexually explicit images which at their most harrowing have depicted acts of pedophilia and bestiality. Then again, some imaginations are more active than others. As black paper cutouts adhered directly to the white walls of the gallery, Walker's work is put forth in no uncertain terms. Her world is quite frankly black and white. In fact, it is shameless. The work's refusal to acknowledge shame when dealing with issues of race and desire set within the context of slavery allows Walker to challenge, indeed taunt, our individual and collective historical imaginations. From Baldwin's generation to Walker's, the issue as to how to come to terms with a painful past persists. How does one write oneself into a painful history without first inquiring into the human capacity for lust, disgust, and violence? And if one is African American, as is Walker, where does one begin this task amid the pickaninnies, sambos, mammies, mandingos, and mulatto slave mistresses depicted on sought-after flotsam and jetsam hiding in the back of antique stores, bric-a-brac that goes by the name of bygone Americana? As bizarre, beautiful, or violent as her imagery may be, Walker understands that a historical imagination is a prerequisite for genuine ownership of the past. And if the task of writing oneself into history is conducted at the level of Baldwin's paradox of what it means to be human, then this task must take into account pain, parody, pleasure, poetry, and ultimately the perverse.

Although her cutouts have been likened to the literature of Toni Morrison, Alice Walker, and Toni Cade Bambara, Walker's work actually shares more in common with dime-store historical romances that use the antebellum as a backdrop. With human chattel as part of the historical mise-en-scene, it begs to be asked to what extent a romance could follow conventions of decency before the specter of perverse power relations would come into play. For Walker, this extent certainly is not great. Her vignettes are designed to upstage the entire genre. But Walker's work exceeds parody. Using her artistic hindsight, slavery could just as easily have been dubbed "the perverse institution" by Sigmund Freud as it was "the peculiar institution" by Frederick Law Olmsted. Her vision is a skewed triad of race, history, and desire, that when it avails itself to a reading, avails itself to one of such surreal and psychological dimension that perhaps it is better to call it a diagnosis.

Shame, the psychic force of prohibition, is a good place to begin. Walker's work is shameless three times over. In her choice of imagery, she has abandoned the historical shame surrounding slavery, the social shame surrounding stereotypes, and finally a bodily shame regarding sexual and excretory functions. To put it bluntly, as the legibility of her imagery warrants, Walker's installations are a freak scene à la de Sade. Lick, suck, devour. Prod, poke, puncture. Shit, fuck, bludgeon. They are a psycho-sexual mess of Looney Tunes proportion. Needless to say, it is the two-hundred-year history of a shameful act conducted squarely within our consciousness that makes it possible for Walker not only to refuse shame but to blur the distinction between forms of shame. Even more important, Walker is aware that to speak of shame is simultaneously to speak of disgust, the overcoming of which is a prerequisite for sexual pleasure. Given the volume of shame, it is no wonder that the pleasures derived by her characters are often sadistic in nature. Even her victims victimize, as is the case with the detail from *The End of Uncle Tom and the Grand Allegorical Tableau of Eva in Heaven*, in which an amputee stabs one child and through some perverse polymorphous gluttony is attempting to ingest another whole. The psychology behind this perpetuated cruelty recalls a scene cited by Frantz Fanon, from the film *Home of the Brave* in which a Pacific War veteran turns to an African American and says, "Resign yourself to your color the way I got used to my stump; we're both victims."

Walker, however, is capable of more subtle forms of confounding, as is the case when the economy surrounding slavery is overlapped with that surrounding sex. As Walker's baby-plopping pickaninny in her 1994 installation *Gone, An Historical Romance of a Civil War as It Occurred between the Dusky Thighs of One Young Negress and Her Heart* suggests, slavery was a labor force meant to reproduce itself. If sex is theoretically defined as an economy whose poles are reproduction—read work or utility—on the one hand, and pleasure—read play or surplus—on the other, then slavery would fall into the former category. The tier of breast suckling from *The End of Uncle Tom and the Grand Allegorical Tableau of Eva in Heaven* depicts the transition of sex from reproductive utilitarian ends to an erotic surplus that stands outside the ends of slavery. In short, sexual pleasure becomes the locus of an individual bodily sovereignty, pleasure as a form of power. But pleasure should not simply be equated with power. As theorist Michel Foucault would have it, this is "power that lets itself be invaded by the pleasure it is pursuing; and opposite it, power asserting itself in the pleasure of showing off,

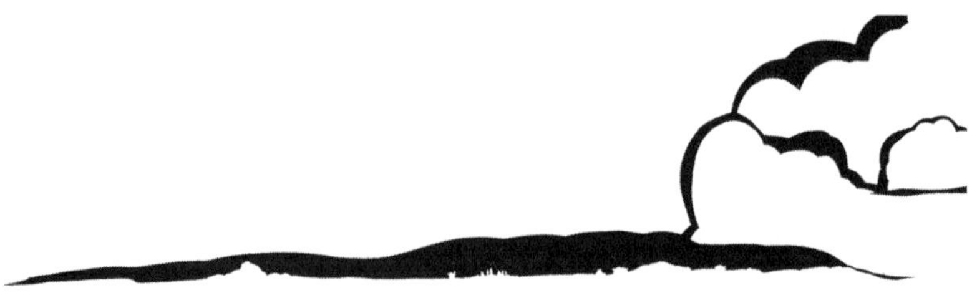

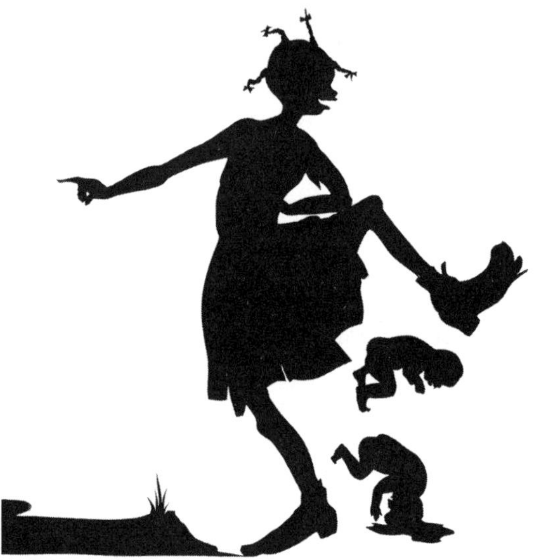

Kara Walker, detail from *Gone, An Historical Romance of a Civil War as It Occurred between the Dusky Thighs of One Young Negress and Her Heart*, 1994. Cut paper on wall. 156 × 600 inches (396.2 × 1524 cm). Artwork © Kara Walker, courtesy of Sikkema Jenkins & Co., New York; Sprüth Magers, Berlin.

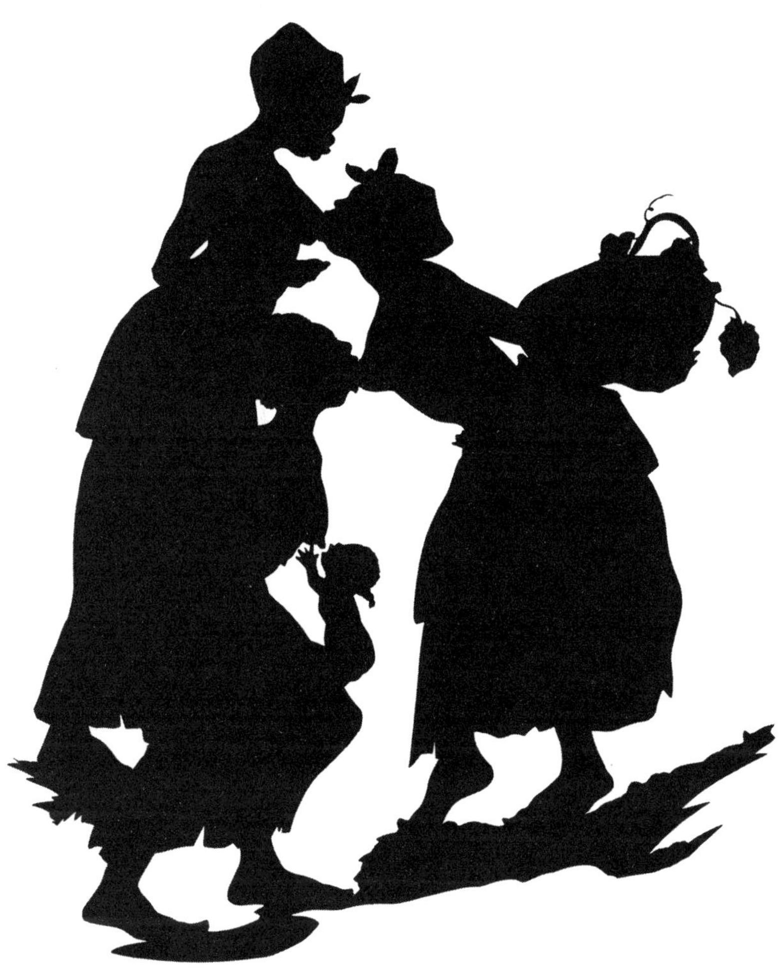

Kara Walker, detail from *The End of Uncle Tom and the Grand Allegorical Tableau of Eva in Heaven*, 1995. Cut paper. Wall installation. 150 × 420 inches (396.2 × 1066.8 cm). Artwork © Kara Walker, courtesy of Sikkema Jenkins & Co., New York; Sprüth Magers, Berlin.

scandalizing, or resisting. Capture and seduction, confrontation and mutual reinforcement; parents and children, adults and adolescents, educators and students, doctors and patients." And for Walker, this list would include the slave mistress and her conscripted lover. Liberation is not in the form of the plantation rebellion or the runaway slave in search of the underground railroad. Instead, it is the naughty tongue of a slave mistress tickling the barrel of a kneeling soldier's rifle, or the chicken drumstick, willfully abandoned in favor of his tender sexual advances. Did Walker's suggested forms of bodily sovereignty exist in spite of slavery? Or were they more so the case under the confines of slavery? Although Walker seems to leave very little to the imagination, the spaces she does leave blank are reserved for questions such as these. With historical accuracy effectively suspended, her cutouts, for all their clarity, in the end become a Rorschach test whose highly subjective readings are consciously overdetermined. In avoiding Walker's conclusions, however, it begs to be asked, where does our imagination go? Does it lapse into a moralizing tone? Or does it allow for more complex human relations to emerge, relationships which for better or worse either hurt, haunt, or simply hover over us today, whether these specters be relationships between blacks and whites or simply our relationship to the stereotypes Walker employs?

Walker does not control these specters as much as she wields them. Violently humanized through acts involving the grotesque, Walker's characters are violently racialized through her use of stereotypes. Her stereotypes, however, exceed the immediate pain associated with demeaning images of African Americans. Her images encompass the obverse, the fear that one's actions will correlate to a stereotype. Under these circumstances, the onus is to prove what one is not rather than what one is. While the stereotypes a group creates of itself fall under the category of parody, the dilemma arises when a group, because of preexisting imagery, is unable to parody itself before others. Filled with a shameless humor, the early careers of Richard Pryor, Redd Foxx, and Rudy Ray Moore, for example, involve African Americans parodying themselves to themselves through the exploitation of stereotypes. Walker likewise embraces, even exaggerates stereotypes. But Foxx's, Pryor's, and Moore's exploitation of stereotypes was at the service of humor, while Walker's work moves toward anger as her attempts to violently humanize stereotypes only leads to the creation of even more

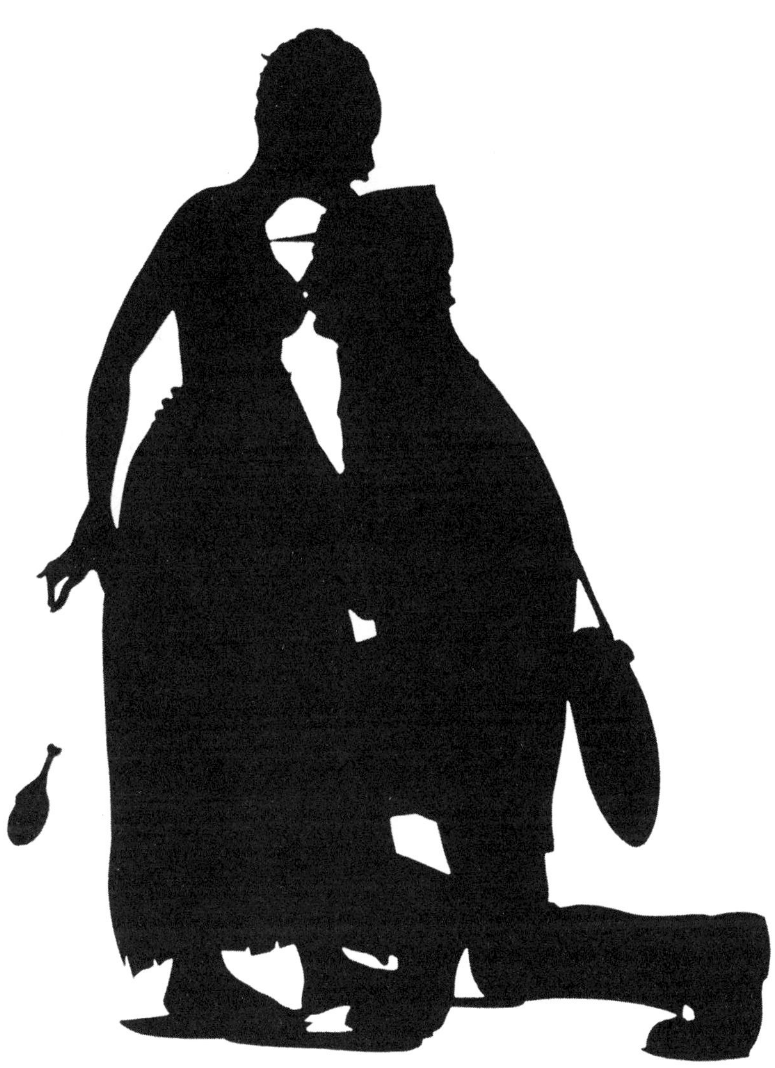

Kara Walker, *Before the Battle (Chickin' Dumplin')*, 1995. Paper on canvas. 48 × 54 inches (121.9 × 137.2 cm). Artwork © Kara Walker, courtesy of Sikkema Jenkins & Co., New York; Sprüth Magers, Berlin.

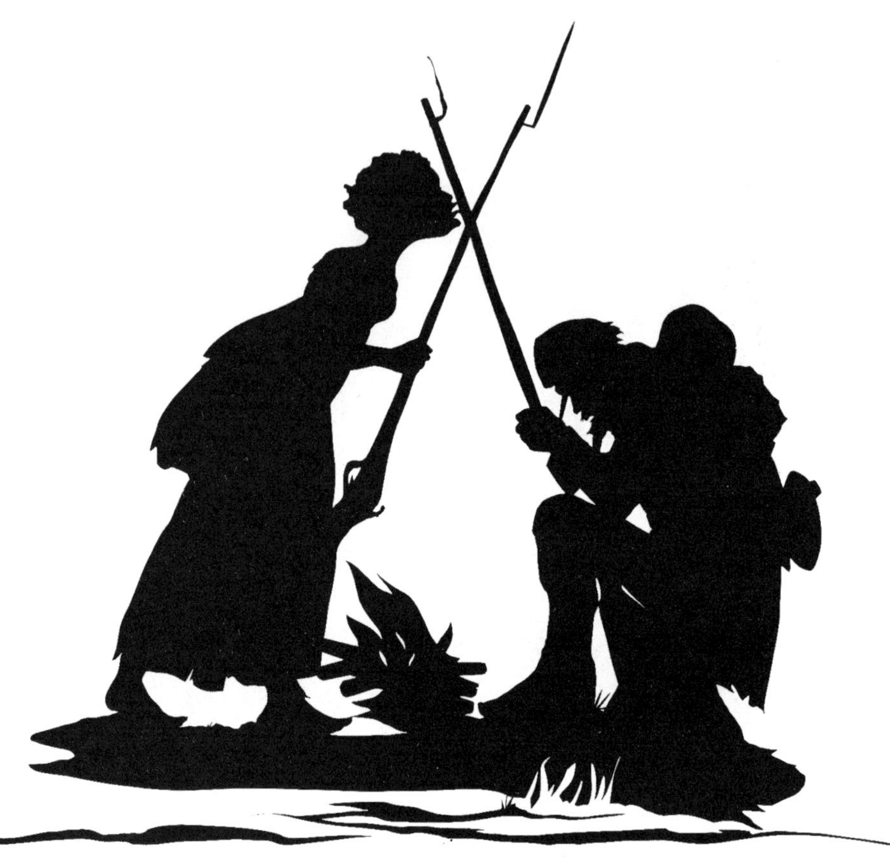

Kara Walker, detail from *The Battle of Atlanta: Being the Narrative of a Negress in the Flames of Desire—A Reconstruction*, 1995. Cut paper and wax adhesive on wall. 17 parts, dimensions variable. Artwork © Kara Walker, courtesy of Sikkema Jenkins & Co., New York; Sprüth Magers, Berlin.

questionable stereotypes. Walker's recasting of stock black antebellum characters is an exchange of one stereotype for another as the sexual sovereignty of her mammies, sambos, pickaninnies, and slave mistresses is eclipsed by the myth's surrounding black sexuality, myths which contemporary reality has only further confounded. For proof, one need only refer to the Anita Hill/Clarence Thomas hearings, the confessionals of Magic Johnson or Wilt Chamberlain, or the psychosocial, psychosexual drama of O. J. Simpson; these examples corresponding to myths of black hypersexuality and the evils of miscegenation. Again, the fear being that one's actions fulfill rather than negate stereotypes. The result is frustration over issues of audience and representation perhaps best expressed in the following bit of dialogue between Archibald and Village, two black characters from Jean Genet's play *The Blacks.*

ARCHIBALD: They tell us that we're grown-up children. In that case, what's left for us? The Theater! We'll play at being reflected in it, and we'll see ourselves—big black narcissists—slowly disappearing into its waters.

VILLAGE: I don't want to disappear.

ARCHIBALD: You're no exception! Nothing will remain of you but the foam of your rage.

Since they merge us with an image and drown us in it, let the image set their teeth on edge!

Walker's work is relentless. It ekes out much of its poetry through its excessiveness. Since her stereotype's quest for liberation through pleasure has been foiled by yet another layer of myths, Walker has had to proceed to taboos such as animality. This seems logical if not inevitable given the workings of her imagination. Legally classified as property and categorized as a species less than human, blacks fell prey to a whole series of myths as to their animal nature. Work horses, raging bulls, and sexual bucks, blacks, as the myth would have it, like animals had no choice but to obey their instincts. In the silhouette chosen for the invitation, Walker has juxtaposed animality with high culture. The dancer is oblivious to the snarling rodents which populate her dress. The maintenance of a Degas-like grace indicates that the events transpiring around her lower half are not foreign to her. Perhaps they are somehow a part of who she is, in which case, these animals are meant to signify our lower selves, our animal selves, vestiges of which are to be found in our hairy parts. The raging animals on the young girl's dress can then be read as a substitute for the untamed hair between our legs as opposed to the sculpted hair on our heads. Poised between sex and civilization, between an aggressive animal act and an elegant refinement of manners, Walker's young dancer and her pet pals represent the height and depth of humanity.

Animal Nature/Human Nature, Life/Death, Pleasure/Pain. Walker, however, unlike Bruce Nauman, is concerned with the cruel aspects of human nature set within a historical context as the anachronistic character of her medium suggests. Skiagraphy, Decoupure, Shadowgraphy, Papyrography, Scissorgraphy, and Black Shade, these are some of the names that black paper portraiture has had throughout its life from the mid-seventeenth century to the end of the nineteenth century. Although he did not invent black paper portraiture, the name and indeed the word "silhouette" were taken from Étienne de Silhouette (1709–1767), Louis XV's miserly minister of finance who apparently practiced the art. The word was brought to England and popularized by the most famous practitioner of cut black paper portraiture, Auguste Edouart (1789–1861). Edouart's career represents the height of the genre's popularity, which was between 1770 and 1850. Although it was destined to become a poor man's portraiture, silhouettes gained their dignity by having been used to capture the aristocracy and the haute bourgeoisie. Mechanized, however, within the first decade of the nineteenth century, silhouette portraiture lost most of its prestige shortly thereafter. Not only was photography a mere four decades away, but silhouette portraiture had been deemed a craft rather than an art form, securing for it a place at carnivals and in classrooms devoted to the training of "good ladies."

To say that Walker has exploited the irony inherent in the medium is an understatement. With respect to the dates that cut black paper portraiture was practiced, the form certainly reinforces the content. Slavery was practiced in the United States from 1619 until the end of the Civil War in 1865. Walker's genuine historical affinity, however, is with the slave narrative, an autobiographical genre unique to the slaves of North America. Although there are only estimated to be a hundred or so full-length book accounts by former slaves, according to scholar Marion Wilson Starling, all in all, some 6,000 slaves recorded their tales through interviews, essays, and books. The invitations Walker has designed for her exhibitions, including the one for this show, were done after a combination of typographical designs for posters announcing eighteenth and nineteenth century spectacles as well as the designs for the title pages of slave narratives. In this instance, Walker has aimed her wit directly at the audience. By extending this invitation under the assumption that you are indeed one of "our Negro Brethren," Walker, with all the playful antagonism of Fats Waller, is asking, "Is you is, or is

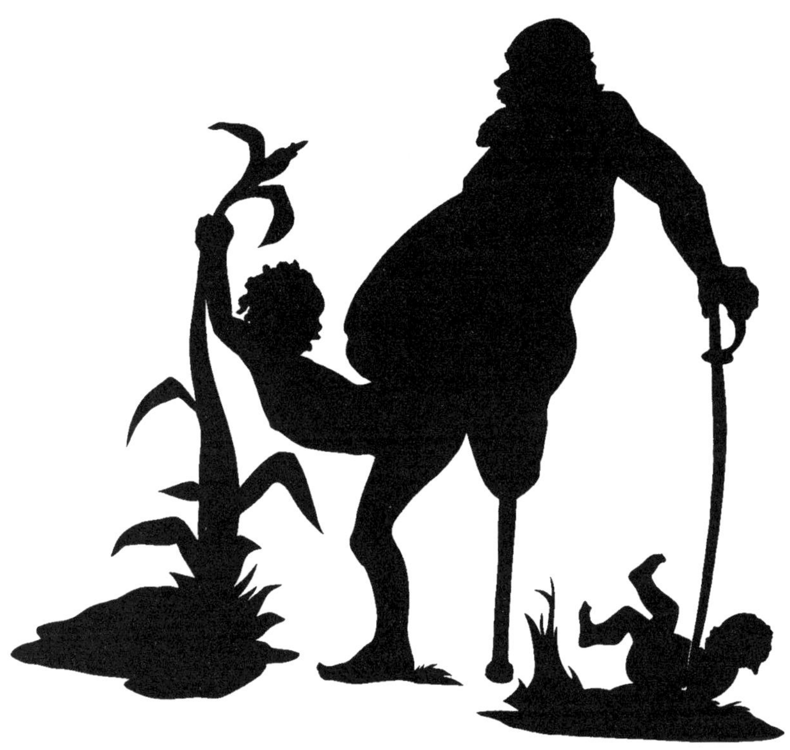

Kara Walker, detail from *The End of Uncle Tom and the Grand Allegorical Tableau of Eva in Heaven*, 1995. Wall installation. 156 × 420 inches (396.2 × 1066.8 cm). Artwork © Kara Walker, courtesy of Sikkema Jenkins & Co., New York; Sprüth Magers, Berlin.

you ain't." Perhaps less subtle is the blurring of her own name with that of W. E. B. DuBois and Madame C. J. Walker, an early entrepreneur in the black beauty industry and inventor of the hot comb. Maybe the issue is not whether some imaginations are more active than others but what some imaginations are willing to wield and therefore yield. Needless to say, in Walker's mind, a Harlequin Romance becomes a deadly weapon. As Lou Rawls put it, "A mind is a terrible thing to waste." In Walker's case, however, he would probably have cut it short to "A mind is terrible thing." The mind can be a terrible thing, a frightening thing, only because it is a powerful thing; a thing, as Walker proves, capable of breaking the shackles of history.

A Mind Is a Terrible Thing to Waste

Kara Walker is something of a Nat Turner for black folk in Museum Ed. Departments tired of aiding and abetting yet another feel-good discussion about race. The work prompts the impulse either to shout or shut up. But maybe I should speak for myself in that regard since I copped a Fifth Amendment plea when it came to developing materials for her 1997 exhibition at the Renaissance Society, including her first catalogue.

Walker's work is a challenge for museums, which have an obligation to clarify artwork whose beauty may reside in its absurdist logic. Saddled with some form of explication, press releases, brochures, and invitations tread a line of speaking to and for work whose hallmark in the case of Walker is a delightful revelry in the perverse. As a result, such materials run the risk of over-framing the work, dampening its spirit. If the work is to be effective, the museum may have to refrain from, say, using wall text in favor of letting the work speak for itself, which for Walker includes her writings, as they have become a critical extension of the work.

From the outset, Walker's Renaissance Society exhibition was to be accompanied by a catalogue. Walker was kind enough to temporarily part with one of her sketchbooks, giving it to the Society's director, Susanne Ghez, during a studio visit in the spring of 1996, at which time they confirmed the exhibition for the winter of 1997. Susanne learned about Walker's work through her friend and colleague Vasif Kortun, director of the museum of the Center for Curatorial Studies at Bard College during the time of Walker's 1995 exhibition *Look Away! Look Away! Look Away!* The sketchbook revealed facets of her practice that were overshadowed by the work, so to speak. The decision to use it as the basis for her catalogue was made without knowledge of her writings, which were not included in the sketchbook she gave to Susanne. These she would fax later. As for text, the catalogue was initially going to contain an essay with installation photos. We approached the literary scholar and theorist Hortense Spillers, who graciously declined due to her workload.

The model for Walker's catalogue was a facsimile reproduction of Ulrike Ottinger's working notebook for the film *Madam X—An Absolute Ruler*.[1] Walker, like Ottinger, keeps a diary with photographic clippings

interspersed with notes and drawings. Together, these visual and written fragments form something of a field through and out of which
the work matriculates. Even without the writings, Walker's sketchbook
contained a wealth of information solely in its visuals. Her inspiration
is drawn from a well that, if not deeper, is certainly more expansive
than the historical period suggested by the work. In her sketchbook, for
example, the odd wood engraving was accompanied by the delectable
deviance of Jean Genet represented by a photocopy of a production still
from his 1956 play *The Balcony*.[2] It is a racy image of a powder-wigged
magistrate kissing Ruby Dee's foot as she sits poised in an electric chair.
And if Walker's doodles were not enough, a classified ad she placed in
a local Providence, Rhode Island, newspaper ("SBF, 23, painter, seeks
tall, affectionate bastard, 30's, for coffee and paranoia") should dispel
any doubt as to whether she is a trickster in the performative sense.[3]

More than engage history, Walker's work inhabits history. In this
respect, the work itself is a form of role playing, a preposterous historical reenactment of which Walker is the narrator. Her characters are
animated by a voice steeped in hyperbole. The silhouettes, however, are
far more illustrative than they are psychological. Unlike her silhouettes,
Walker's writings are fodder for the analyst's couch. As a mixture of
voices and literary genres (dime-store romance, slave narratives, phone
sex script, the reflections of a self-deprecating art), they are the primor-
dial slurry of thought from which the silhouettes emerge. They are raw
and messy by turns, less historical than the silhouettes and more visceral
in both their anger and eroticism, portraying their narrator as a psy-
chopath whose imagination is decidedly unhinged from the television
mini-series *Roots*. They are over the top, and as a result expose Walker's
project as profoundly ahistorical. Rather than frame her characters as
stereotypes, Walker's writings allow them to be discussed as perhaps all
too human. Based on her writings, the work is not about "slavery and
its legacy" as a recent *Art News* review stated.[4] Instead, the antebellum
South is a trope through which desire is expressed, and specifically,
desire as a turbulent combination of pleasure and power, a relationship
that encompasses submission and domination.

There were only a couple snippets of writing in the sketchbook,
certainly not enough to consider writing an integral part of her practice.
We became aware of the writings through a text the Aldrich Contemporary Art Museum had used as a handout, referring to it as an artist

statement.[5] This led me to casually ask Walker if there were more writings, which to my surprise there were. She described them nonchalantly as "the rantings of a crazy lady who spends too much time alone in her attic."[6] Walker modestly said she did them to amuse herself in a creative writing class she had taken in college. Based on the highly charged nature of Walker's imagery and the voices she adopts in her writing, one might expect Walker to be a cross between Sapphire, Lil' Kim and Robert Colescott, which is hardly the case. She actually comes across as somewhat demure. During a reading she gave at the opening reception of her Renaissance Society exhibition, however, Walker came across as supremely confident.[7] Writing would seem a natural for Walker, whose work is plagued by its legibility. Her characters not only behave in a grossly literal fashion; they are recognized as the stock-in-trade of any antebellum or Reconstruction-era narrative. Walker's stereotypes are the stuff of stories made familiar through film, photography, writing (fiction and nonfiction), the decorative arts, painting—you name it. The work is steeped in historical narrative to the extent that there is a free and circular exchange between the visual and the literary. Her vignettes illustrate plots laid thick, and conversely scenes from stories such as *Gone with the Wind, Incidents in the Life of a Slave Girl, Birth of a Nation, Uncle Tom's Cabin, Narrative of the Life of Frederick Douglass*, and Toni Morrison's *Beloved*, to name but a few, are the lenses through which we read her vignettes. Her writings, however, remained separate from her visual work save for her flair for prosaic titles.

After seeing two previous exhibition announcements that Walker designed for her exhibitions at Wooster Gardens gallery (*From the Bowels to the Bosom*, 1996, and *The High and Soft Laughter of the Nigger Wenches at Night*, 1995), we asked her to design one side of her poster/invitation for her exhibition at the Society. The announcement followed our standard poster/invitation design, a 28 × 24-inch poster that folds down into a 6 × 9-inch mailer. This format proved successful for listing public programs as well as accommodating a seven-hundred-word introductory essay. Walker's poster was the first time we would forego the essay, which would have distracted from the intrigue kindled by her design.

As a template for her poster, Walker provided Jason Pickleman of KNL Graphic Design, the designer with whom we worked on both the poster and the book, a photocopy of an 1859 playbill for a staged reading of *Uncle Tom's Cabin*, and an 1851 runaway slave announcement.

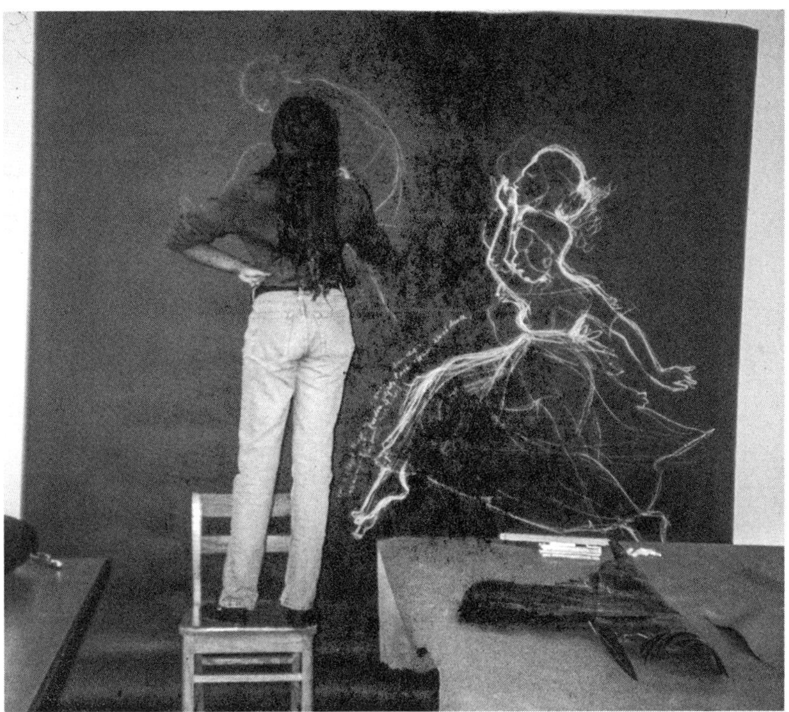

Kara Walker at work during the installation of her exhibition at the Renaissance Society. Courtesy the Renaissance Society at the University of Chicago.

Walker wanted to use the same aggressive mix of typefaces and was explicit about the visual weight of each line of text. She reserved italics exclusively for "Lascivious Subjects," for example, and wanted "The South" to be rendered in an ornate typeface such as that on the Konriko wild rice packaging, a copy of which she also sent. Walker's poster is not only an announcement for a fictitious spectacle, it is itself a spectacle. Visually, the various sizes and kinds of typefaces correspond to a huckster's hyperbole. These theatrics are solicited even when the poster is read in silence. As a result, the reader is seamlessly implicated in a parody in which Walker fictitiously recast the Society as an exclusively black membership organization. The poster, in addition to serving as an announcement, ultimately stood as a work in its own right. Walker generously agreed to allow us to print two hundred single-sided versions

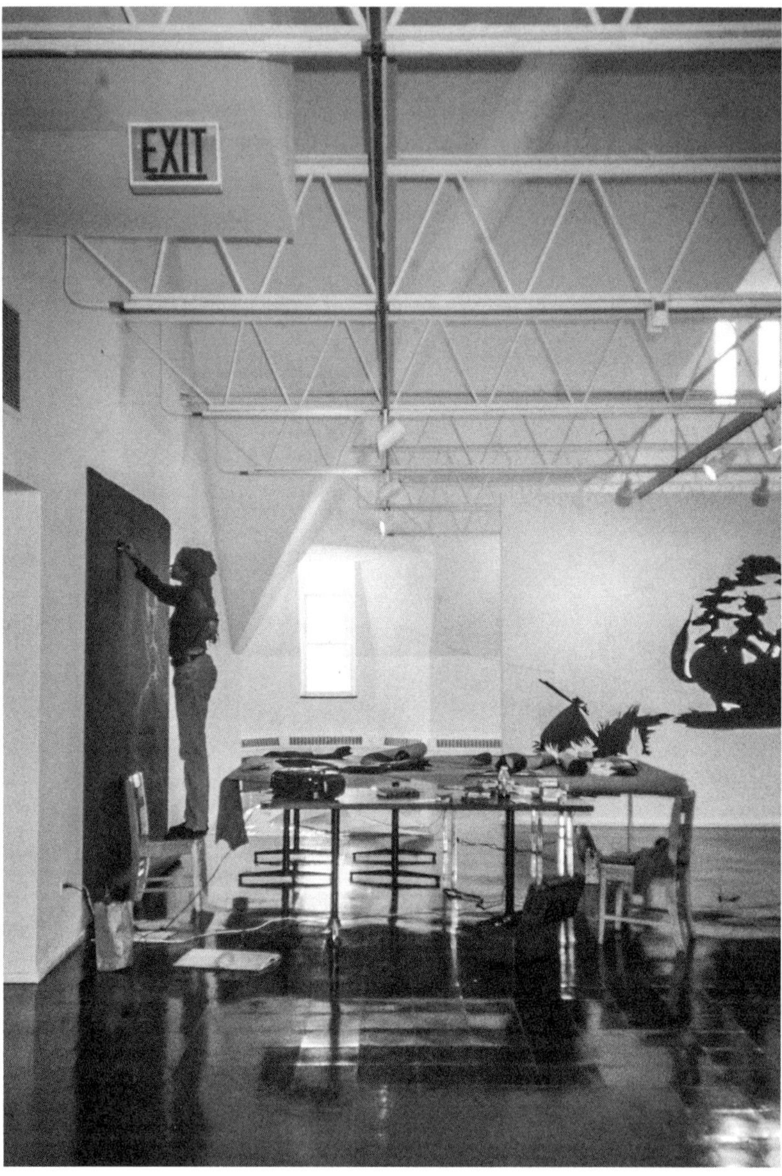

Kara Walker at work during the installation of her exhibition at the Renaissance Society. Courtesy the Renaissance Society at the University of Chicago.

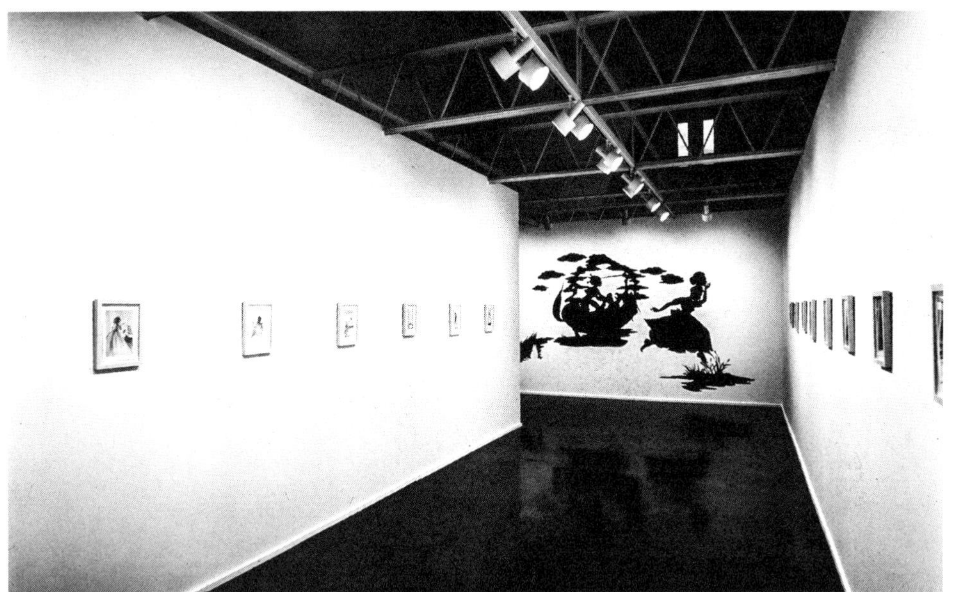

Kara Walker, the Renaissance Society at the University of Chicago, 1997 (two installation views). Courtesy the Renaissance Society at the University of Chicago.

featuring only her text. These were printed on heavier paper stock and made available for sale.

Walker doesn't pussy-foot her subject matter, to say the least. On the wall furthest from the entrance to the Society was a scroll-shaped sepia drawing, roughly 4 × 3 feet, featuring the words "Nigger Lover," which to my knowledge was the first textual element to appear in one of her installations. In the context of Walker's sexually explicit vignettes, "Nigger Lover" was to be taken literally, and absurdly so, as a lover of "niggers" in the physical sense, rather than to be taken figuratively, as a racist slur referring to whites who sympathized with the plight of blacks. It punctuated to the point of puncturing the exhibition. A caricature of history is one thing, while racist slurs susceptible to gross misinterpretation are another.

Walker's exhibition was accompanied by a newsletter/brochure containing an essay I wrote in December 1996, on the eve of the controversy surrounding her work as a result of her winning a prestigious MacArthur Fellowship in the summer of 1997. I wrote the essay not

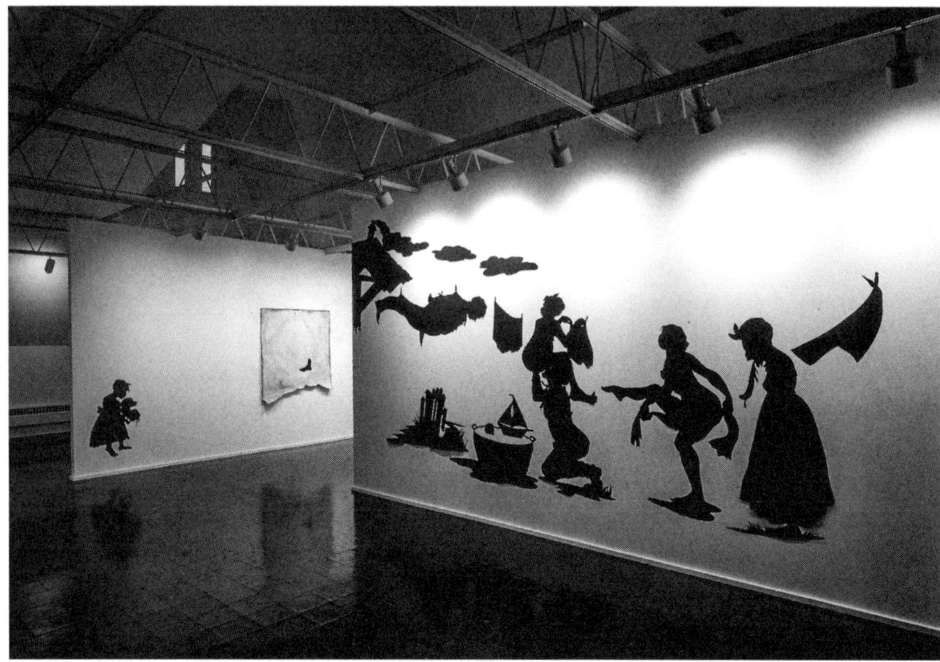

Kara Walker, the Renaissance Society at the University of Chicago, 1997 (two installation views). Courtesy the Renaissance Society at the University of Chicago.

in response to storm clouds brewing on the horizon (those, I did not foresee) but in response to Walker having substantially upped the ante by introducing the word "Nigger" into her exhibition at point-blank range. More important than making up for the lack of an introductory essay on her poster was contextualizing Walker's irreverence, which for her Society exhibition was now forthright in its tone.

History is something of a red herring in Walker's work. Despite the work's rich historical and art historical references, these do not comprise its content. The work smacks of history in order to smack history, which, needless to say, are very different things. Walker's work is also ahistorical relative to the wealth of scholarship on slavery unearthed during the artist's lifetime, which is marked not merely as post–civil rights but post-*Roots*. It was the "Nigger Lover" scroll which rescued me from a pat interpretation, pushing me away from its cloying historical baggage and more toward the likes of the late Richard Pryor, who,

THE RENAISSANCE SOCIETY

IS GIVEN THE OPPORTUNITY TO PRESENT TO YOU

OUR NEGRO BRETHREN

{ WORKS OF CERTAIN INTEREST }

CREATED

ENTIRELY BY A YOUNG

NEGRESS

OF UNUSUAL ABILITY

SILHOUETTES

CUT

FROM BLACK PAPER

BY

MADAM K.E.B. WALKER

UPON HER RETURN FROM

THE SOUTH

THIS FEMALE ARTISAN IS WONT TO ILLUSTRATE

LASCIVIOUS SUBJECTS

{ MISCEGENATION IS KEY AMONG THEM }

THEREFORE,

IT IS ILL-ADVISED FOR LADIES & CHILDREN
TO ATTEND THIS EXHIBITION

JANUARY 12 - FEBRUARY 21, '97

A RECEPTION WILL BE HELD

JANUARY THE TWELFTH FROM 4–7pm

Kara Walker, poster design for exhibition at the Renaissance Society, 1997. Courtesy of the Renaissance Society at the University of Chicago.

like Walker, could redeem the expression "Nigger Lover" by turning it on its head through the human capacity for folly. If, in the newsletter I had written, humor formed one cardinal orientation, then shame formed yet another. Just as the work is not simply about history, neither is it simply about stereotypes. More important than a question of who her characters are is the question of what they are doing as they shamelessly engage in the most shameful acts. Between humor and shame, I felt I had found something of a True North by which to write about the work in a manner neither bogged down by nor hiding behind history.

The controversy attending Walker's work came both as a result of her subject matter as well as her being named a MacArthur fellow. Along with the increased exposure came a vocal black audience angered not just by the work, but by the validation it received from critics, collectors, and curators deemed part of a white power structure. Walker's most vocal critics were the artists Betye Saar and Howardena Pindell, both of whom spearheaded letter-writing campaigns to museums and the press. As Saar stated in a 1998 interview, "How do young persons just a few years out of school get a show at a major museum? The whole arts establishment picked up their work and put it at the head of the class. This is the danger, not the artists themselves. This is like closet racism. It relieves them of the responsibility to show other artists. Here we are at the end of the millennium seeing work that is derogatory and racist."[8] The controversy, however, came well after the work had been critically received. By 1997, there was plenty of discussion contextualizing the work, as it had been the subject of several feature articles in major publications, not to mention its being shown in museums with increasing frequency (The Drawing Center, 1994; Bard College, 1995; Musée d'Art Moderne, Paris, 1995; The ICA, Boston, 1996; The Aldrich, 1996; Site Santa Fe, 1996). At that time, anyone bothered enough to inquire about the work could have obtained *Look Away! Look Away! Look Away!*, a beautiful lil' purse packer of a catalogue accompanying her 1995 Bard College exhibition which featured an excellent essay and interview with Walker by Sydney Jenkins.[9] In no way, shape, or form did controversy figure into plans for her exhibitions at the Society. Moreover, within a very short time of debuting here, the same exhibition traveled to Cincinnati and Seattle with nary a peep. This would change within two years when the controversy reached its peak as a suite of Walker's prints, *A Means to an End: A Shadow Drama in*

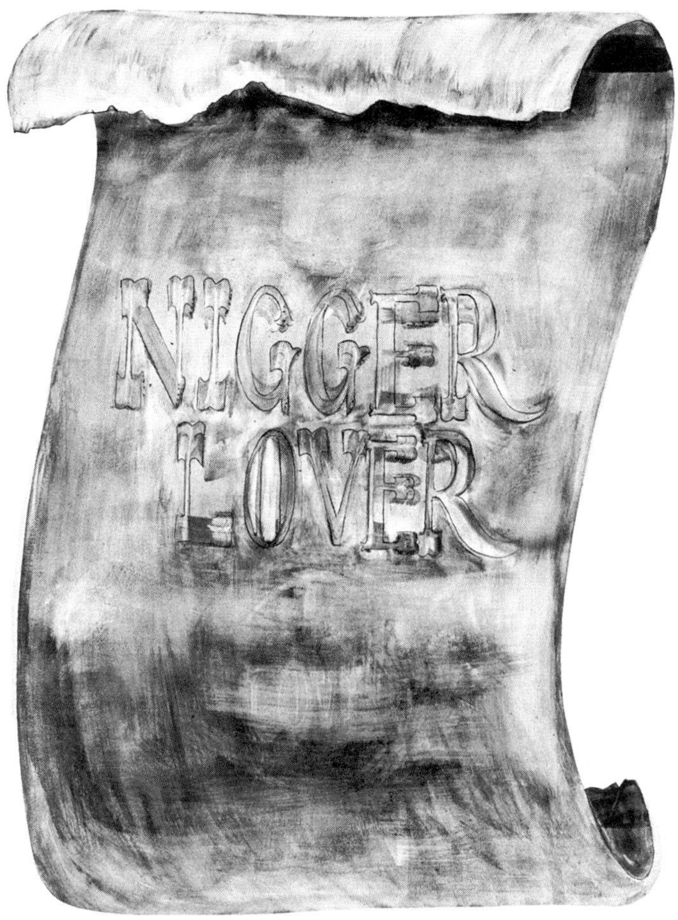

Kara Walker, *Nigger Lover*, 1997. Artwork © Kara Walker, courtesy of Sikkema Jenkins & Co., New York; Sprüth Magers, Berlin.

Five Acts, was pulled from an exhibition at the Detroit Institute of Arts at the request of an advisory group, the Friends of African and African American Art.[10]

Although it had been conceptualized during the run of her Renaissance exhibition, Walker's catalogue didn't roll off the press until over a year later, during which the controversy was full-blown. This formed the backdrop against which the catalogue was received. With no intermediary voice other than the installation views of her exhibition, what we had been calling a catalogue was actually an artist's book, which, as an extension of the work itself, only fueled the fire. Although her use of stock antebellum stereotypes would seem to initiate a discussion about slavery, that is more of a willful projection on the viewer's part, as anything that could pass for historical accuracy has been dutifully warped. That the work is cloaked in history, however, serves to provoke a reflexive response, underscoring the relationship between museums and a larger black community seeking to have its history institution-ally acknowledged and therefore validated. For an older generation of Blacks, notably those who participated in the civil rights movement, these cultural aspirations would remain of central concern. In addition, Walker's work emerged in the wake of a multicultural moment that was devolving into a kind of knee-jerk rhetoric of inclusion. These two factors would create an atmosphere fraught with expectations, if not a sense of obligation, regarding how museums would negotiate the color line.

To me, the appeal of Walker's work lay in its upbraiding of that very expectation, creating something of a disconnect between the museum and an already elusive demographic. Putting it bluntly, the controversy surrounding Walker's work is symptomatic of the segregation we all muster an overwhelming amount of earnestness to ignore, that is, repress. The result is that museums unconsciously adopt a patronizing tone in their efforts to attract (placate) a black audience in what I'll call "February Syndrome." Walker's work for better and or worse relieves the museum of being a slave to history in a manner that equates black artists with black audiences. If black history, no matter how dignified it may be rendered at the hands of a black artist, is considered solely the province of a black audience, then we haven't gotten anywhere since *Plessy v. Ferguson.* Through her work, Walker is proposing that we *not* buy in at the level of history but at the level of humanity, in which black and everybody else has equal stakes. Under those circumstances, the work would indeed alienate so as to pull us together, rather than placate only to keep us apart.

My guess is that museums, through exhibition-related ephemera, would be tempted to bridge that disconnect by discussing the work in the dignified light of a history that in this instance is a ruse. Dis-guised as a period piece, Walker's work is not about dignity but a shame over a cruelty that is seemingly instinctual, and therefore ever present.

Although Walker's Renaissance Society exhibition and its related materials were not designed in relationship to any potential controversy, I sought to make this last point explicit in the brochure essay accompanying the exhibition, an essay that was subsequently retooled for *Parkett*.[11] At the same time that it is specific to Walker, the controversy exposed circumstances that will no doubt occur again, circumstances where related materials may be called upon to speak on behalf of work that perhaps won't speak as forthrightly as Walker's. But with her recent Metropolitan Museum of Art exhibition under her belt,[12] controversy is well behind Walker, leaving those in the museum ranks who develop these materials that much more wary of the fire next time.

Notes

1. Ulrike Ottinger, *Madame X—An Absolute Ruler* (Frankfurt: Stroemfeld/Roter Stern, 1978).

2. Kara Walker, *Kara Walker* (Chicago: Renaissance Society at the University of Chicago, 1997), not paginated.

3. Walker, *Kara Walker*, 1997.

4. Ann Landi, "Kara Walker Metropolitan Museum of Art," *Art News*, 105, no. 7 (Summer 2006): 173.

5. For *No Doubt*, a 1996 group exhibition at the Aldrich Contemporary Art Museum in Ridgefield, Connecticut, Walker has entitled this text "My Little War." It was reproduced on a single page in her Renaissance Society catalog without a title. Its opening sentence is: "Lots of people create wars for fear of humiliation, I have a little war occurring now that I like to call The Civil War."

6. Conversation with the artist.

7. This reading took place on January 12, 1997, at the Renaissance Society of Chicago.

8. Gwendolyn Dubois Shaw, *Seeing the Unspeakable: The Art of Kara Walker* (Durham, NC: Duke University Press, 2004), 115.

9. Sydney Jenkins, *Look Away! Look Away! Look Away!* (Annandale-on-Hudson, NY: Center for Curatorial Studies, Bard College, 1995).

10. DuBois Shaw, *Seeing the Unspeakable*, 105.

11. Hamza Walker, "Nigger Lover, or Will There Be Any Black People in Utopia," *Parkett*, no. 59 (2000): 152–158.

12. *Kara Walker at the Met: After the Deluge*, March 21–August 6, 2006, curated by Gary Tinterow.

Thelma Golden/Kara Walker: A Dialogue

Thelma Golden

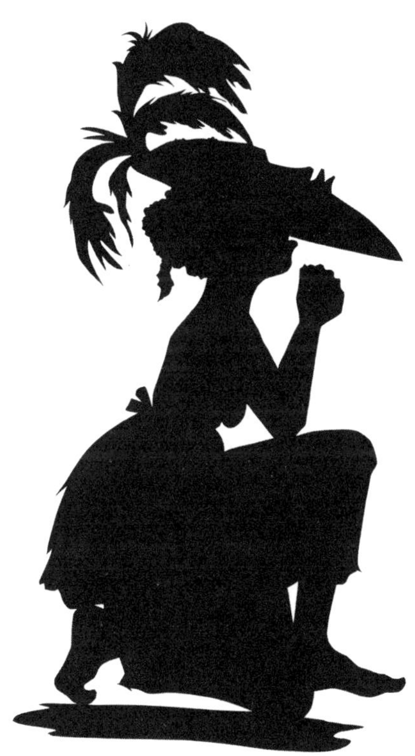

Kara Walker, *Untitled (Kneeling Woman with Mask)*, 1998. Cut paper and adhesive on wall. 55.25 × 32 inches (140.3 × 81.3 cm). Artwork © Kara Walker, courtesy of Sikkema Jenkins & Co., New York; Sprüth Magers, Berlin.

This conversation between Kara Walker and Thelma Golden took place in December 2001 and was transcribed by Damion Lawyer.

THELMA GOLDEN: First, I would like to talk about the project for the University of Michigan Museum of Art. What are you thinking of doing? How does it fit within the trajectory of what you have been doing?

KARA WALKER: The piece I have developed for Ann Arbor is a reworking of *The Emancipation Approximation*, my piece from the Carnegie International. It will have a slightly new title, *An Abbreviated Emancipation (from The Emancipation Approximation)*. It includes elements from the Carnegie installation that were on the white walls rather than the gray walls. It's sort of traditional in a way; it is very similar to my earliest work and it's a little bit of a slight step backward in a way.

TG: Well, not exactly . . .

KW: I mean it's traditional—white wall, black images. Which fits with the space at the Carnegie, which is architecturally very interesting, and very classical.

TG: You haven't seen the space in Ann Arbor, but you've been working out the re-creation of this piece conceptually?

KW: With sketches.

TG: Tell me how you think this fits in with what you've been making and showing most recently, because you've made this big leap forward with color and moving images. Your most recent exhibition at Brent Sikkema in September of 2001 centered on projection installations. Are projections where your mind is now?

KW: My mind is completely in projections and really light, basic film or video. Very low tech. I think projections are sort of the antithesis of high tech.

TG: So video and film and moving image are where the work is moving?

KW: Well, that's where I'm leaning right now; projection is sort of as far as I've gotten, and I have to make these aesthetic jumps in increments. The idea of shadow and puppet theater has been on my mind for the longest time. It seems like the obvious solution somehow for some issues that I'd like to talk about formally, like how one interacts with the work and how the work acts on you. But I can't just make the shadow theater, so I'd make the projection pieces. I haven't really done much with the film or video yet; I've got a little bit of footage, but I don't think it's exactly what I am going to wind up working on. I think it just requires a little more patience—and more time.

TG: I would love to talk about subject matter and themes. You and I are probably the least qualified people to talk about the controversial nature of your work in that I know that you don't think it's controversial because you make it, and I don't think it's controversial because, curatorially, my work has been based on the presentation of such work. It seems that in a progressive way in which the work has developed, there are ways in which you've approached your themes that are interesting and unique, confrontational and pointedly disturbing. Can you talk about the context from which you have developed the themes for your work?

KW: Gosh, it seems like a "once upon a time" kind of story . . .

TG: But it probably is.

KW: Let me have a pregnant pause for a moment . . . at some point in my developing vocabulary as a painter, I started realizing that the kind of work that I enjoyed was genre-oriented. My father is an abstract painter. I grew up with this vague sort of sense of modernism, but I love little pictures from another time, and this led me in a lot of different directions, a lot of pathways. It led me to thinking about time and history—how we perceive history, how we romanticize history, and at the same time when life and art merge and converge around those conflicts. I got to thinking about the way black people represent ourselves in our artwork and also about the ways that I was avoiding that representation in my work, trying to find some universal, which, when I took a step back, I realized was Eurocentric, white-male identified. So this led to a long series of intense questions. It's impossible to condense in a way; some of the impetus for my work comes from reexamining, almost obsessively, social conflicts that have a racial or racist overtone, thinking about the ways that the romanticized version of black history comes into play as a dynamic. I'm sort of intentionally vague right now. I think that's actually a strategy in a way in my work as to why I'm interested in the shadows. I am sometimes horrified by the thoughts that come to my mind and am occasionally blinded by them.

TG: So you struggle to confront the images you make yourself?

KW: Yes, I think that might be part of the conflict between the giddiness that I feel and at the same time the anger that other people feel.

TG: How did the character the "nigger wench" come to be? Who is she?

KW: I think in the time between undergraduate and graduate school I was really trying to figure out who I was as an artist—what is this little identity of mine? There was so much identity-based art, and I had not really taken stock of where I was and who I am and who it is I'm looking to define me. It was always coming from outside sources. That's how the nigger wench came to have a name. She didn't have a clear identity, but as I pursued literature and cultural studies and essays, reading everything pertaining to black women, this characterization became clear. My favorite reference is in Thomas Dixon's *The Clansman*.[1] There is a character, the "tawny vixen," black mistress to the white statesmen. The description is ambivalent in a way; the message is pretty clear. She is all catlike, trying to influence the powers that be with her wily ways. It's a persistent stereotype, the black woman whose powers overwhelm the "good" and the "just" white people.

TG: And who did you turn her into in your work?

KW: I think what happened is I began developing my work and analyzing the myriad of stereotypical black female figures out there and realized that the ones that I seem to feel most compelled to work with are those who were somewhat mischievous and evil. In graduate school, I started looking at work like Betye Saar's and other work of that era that resurrected the Aunt Jemima figure with a vengeance, but I was as interested in these overdetermined stereotypical figures. I tried to incorporate a pretty broad spectrum, perverse if you will, of racist stereotypes, but I always wind up back to this pickaninny, "nigger wench" figure.

TG: What would your response be to the simple question of what constitutes a positive image versus a negative image? That is, if there were a way to discuss this with you that was not, say, antagonistic, what would be your response to a sincere, heartfelt sense on someone's part that the work constituted what they might perceive as a negative image?

KW: It's complicated. Each one of the larger pieces I conceive as a kind of a dreamscape. It encompasses all of these different characters or elements that are all aspects of yourself or your psyche or some of the people in your life, manifested in different forms. I think that when I work out the large pieces, I'm half conscious of keeping a sort of balance, even if it starts off in a skewed place, so that if some of the actions are ugly or ambiguous or not in keeping with a progressive view of ourselves, then I try and at least make the gesture beautiful, and ultimately the form is beautiful.

TG: Well, I think that's the most powerful contradiction in your work—that it exists in a place of intense beauty. I think that you are one of the most significant artists consistently concerned with the notion of beauty and moving it out of this kind of trope and repositioning what might be a more radical approach to its use.

KW: It's a peculiar thing. I think since I started working this way, pretty much since graduate school, there is something about owning an image and owning a representation that is so liberating. I have always used historic picture files as references. Going into picture files and going to research an image, there was a moment that—and I can't say when it was—when looking at a racist representation stopped having that jarring feeling, that feeling when your skull hits the pavement, and it became something that I would approach the same way as art history. I started approaching these works as art historical. They are works that I could draw from as freely as I might a Delacroix or something . . .

TG: Did you feel you could own them?

KW: I could own them, and not just as representations of one's history but put them into the larger context of a subject that I study, a concept I inhabit as an artist making art.

TG: How do you feel your work is read in a contemporary context given the complex, recent history around race? How does the present affect how you consume and digest these images from the past?

KW: My work is all about the now. I approach this work the same way a Harlequin Romance novelist might approach it, all the history, the petticoats—it's all artifice, just a ruse to tantalize the viewer. One of the things, sort of grist for the mill, is the stuff of everyday situations. I remember when I was growing up, I had this cartoon strip that I was working on all the time. My mom was always impressed that any everyday situation would wind up in my cartoon. I was always just drawing my characters and reenacting the day-to-day situations in another form.

TG: So you were sort of transposing life into art. The past into the present.

KW: In most of my work, I work this out through images, but right now I've begun to work this out textually. In my last show, along with the paintings, I included a set of note cards. The note cards came about because I decided that I needed to readjust the way I was approaching my work. There are moments when it's too easy to become really diaristic right off the bat, so I thought that if I just start with a diary format, maybe art would occur in between instead of going the other way around—making the art and having it become diaristic. So that's how the textual insertions began. And it sort of happens automatically. Maybe it's another one of my evasive tactics to not really deal with the real—real life—and couch it in more familiar terms.

TG: That's an interesting idea because I wonder if, just for the sake of argument, we took one of your installations and recast all the figures in contemporary contexts, what then becomes the response? In many ways many of the sorts of actions get played out in popular culture all the time, so it would be a sort of interesting . . .

KW: In some ways it would be less interesting . . .

TG: It would be less interesting artwork . . .

KW: It would take on a different form somehow. I see the little stickers with sports club silhouettes on them all the time, and it just doesn't thrill me.

TG: Your work has always had a narrative impulse, narratives that come out sometimes in the way you contextualize the show in your own titling, labeling, show announcements, and now in your new work with the note cards. How does that writing happen? I imagine that there must be five hundred pages of some sort of parody of a slave narrative lurking in your studio somewhere if you put together some of this writing.

KW: Narrative is very important to my work. I appropriate from many sources . . . frontispieces for slave narratives, authentic documents, as well as a novel or a great sort of artistic spectacle. I was really apprehensive the first time I gave one of my large pieces a title. I had titled a show in graduate school, and I had given it a long title and I was very excited to do that, but it wasn't the same sort of a show. But I love historical paintings, and I also love the cyclorama and these other kinds of touring versions of art or non-art entertainment, and I love the language that goes with them. It's a little bit overblown, a little bit pompous, and I've been trying to acquire that sense of confidence. But at the same time, there is always a little backhanded slight. I think the first few titles or show announcements were really aimed at provoking the audience's sense of entitlement and superiority. "Ah, a black woman is doing this, she can sing, she can dance, she can paint, she can draw." What I wound up thinking about sort of midstream was the way, well . . . maybe the way self-promotion really works. If you say you are a person, a "Negress," of noteworthy talents, people believe it. I mean, I'm not quite capable of constructing the whole novel at once, the whole narrative. So I get these pieces, not even a whole chapter sometimes, a paragraph. If you could put together all of the works, all of the titles, it would still be this staccato stream of words. Each title repeats the thing before and never quite makes the kind of progress that you are set up for.

TG: A few formal things. You are moving toward projection, but let's go back to the silhouettes for a moment; I would like you to give a clearer sense of your working methods. You make sketches first of what you think or intend some of the images might be.

KW: Most of the time, yes.

TG: And then you sketch on the black paper and then cut?

KW: I usually draw them on the paper on the reverse side and then cut.

TG: So you cut basically freehand; there is no computer, no digital assistance, no overhead projector, and no tech assistance in any way. Your method is very simple, straightforward. What you create is coming from mind to eye to hand . . .

KW: Yes. I can't get my hands around technologically assisted fabrication. Not yet. It's a peculiar thing—at some point I decided that painting wasn't going to happen for me. After many years of studying and preparing to be a painter, I thought there must be some other way of getting out what I want to get out and it wound up being cutting.

TG: So it involves almost a painting-like gesture?

KW: Right. Or drawing, cutting feels more like drawing . . .

TG: Essentially the works are site-specific because they adhere directly to the wall. But they can have other lives beyond that initial presentation. How important is site specificity and ethereality?

KW: Ideas of site specificity and ephemerality just sort of developed. It is a sense I've been honing, in a way. I've sort of had to play catch-up around these issues of presentation after the work began to be widely shown. At the time of my first large wall installation, I was thinking it would be kind of interesting if I could make these kinds of archetypes, these stereotypes, and put them up there in this format that's easily destroyed . . .

TG: It conceptually goes against the reality of how they exist in the world. It's interesting; I've been working on a survey exhibition with Gary Simmons. His early erasure wall drawings also took on stereotypes from cartoons. The ephemerality issue is similar in both of your work. In theory, the way he makes the chalkboard drawings, a hand across the surface erases them, but the idea is that they never go away. Stereotypes persist.

KW: That's why the cutout installation remains interesting to me. But they are large and consuming, intellectually and physically. I have gone back to working small. The last pieces that I did that I was really happy with were the small gouaches that were presented in my exhibition in New York last fall.

TG: They were beautiful. Also a surprise in that they were so richly colored. How did these works come to be?

KW: Well, this was an outgrowth of the note card project I described earlier. I made three hundred note cards from last January to March that fueled a need to visualize. After making them, I congratulated myself for the effort by buying a really nice set of paints, gouache. I began painting the pictures on the kitchen table, which is very important to me for reasons I can't explain. I felt very crafty when I did them. The typewriter where I worked on the cards was right there. I needed to do something that was confinable, containable. More than anything, I wanted to make paintings. I knew that if I tried to be an artist about it, it wasn't going to work, but if I was just to be a person sitting at their table making landscapes, it might at least have a little bit of integrity. I just made landscapes that I imagined, and then I made small silhouettes that I cut out of tissue paper and put on the surface. They developed in very organic ways. It's kind of the way silhouette artists might have worked in the nineteenth century, with stock landscapes and then making cuttings of their sitters and choosing a sunny landscape as a background. Each painting was linked in a way to the original note cards.

TG: Were they intended to be shown together?

KW: I always saw them together, but I couldn't really justify putting them together for a while because I wasn't sure if I'd show the writings, but in the end I decided that I would show them.

TG: Is this similar to your earlier diaristic writing process?

KW: In some ways, but not always. It's hard to describe the writing from my diaries because there are moments when there are life changes going on and I start trying to mythologize, looking for a kind of symbol, archetype, or representative for me, a stand-in. So there are a few images like this, not all of them, but a group of the drawings where there is a Harriet Tubman–like figure, an ineffectual Harriet Tubman who can't remember which star is the North Star. And there is a small note card piece, something that I had written ten years ago but had forgotten that I had written it down then rediscovered it. It was a remembrance of a weird dream that I had about David Duke, which went on to inform some of the Klan images.

TG: It seems like there is a way in which you are the medium of your own work, taking on these various personas in order to speak for them, from them, and such speaking comes out in many ways.

KW: Sometimes, perhaps a little bit too much. I was attempting to tell this reporter from Maine the other day that there's an assumption I have about myself and, I guess, about the viewing audience, that there is a fair amount of African American history that has been absorbed and worked in strange ways. That's what I wind up drawing from in the popular consciousness. Not just contemporary black intellectual thought, but popular black thought. So at times I just have to take a step back and be reflective on how self-absorbed the work can get. But on the other hand, I am pretty aware that socially and politically I'm pretty ambiguous and there are times that I'm quite the old school painter, "Oh I don't need to talk about my work," which I actually don't believe, but I feel it somewhere in my heart. I've been thinking of this issue of voice since I started the note cards. Actually I've been thinking about the whole ancestor idea, of ghosts. My cousin has this joke which he transferred to me in which he tells the ghosts to "shut the fuck up while I'm working." But now I have decided to not let them be quiet and to engage the potential ghosts, so I'm not sure if it's just my own psychosis or if they actually hold the answer.

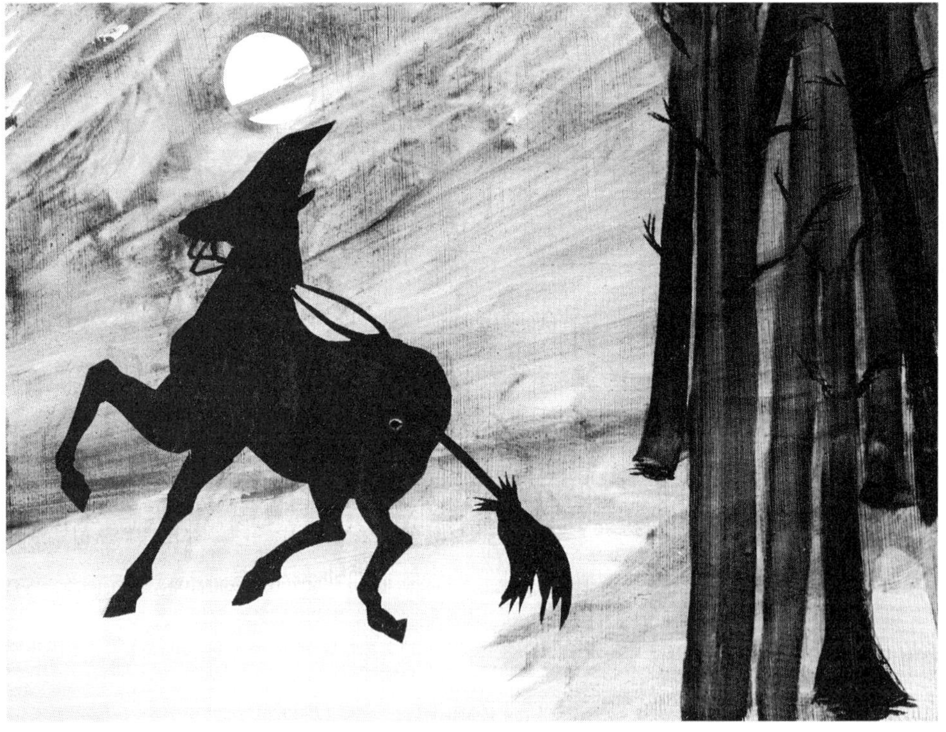

Kara Walker, *Familiar from American Primitives*, 2001. Paint, collage on board. 9 × 12 inches (22.9 × 30.5 cm). Artwork © Kara Walker, courtesy of Sikkema Jenkins & Co., New York; Sprüth Magers, Berlin.

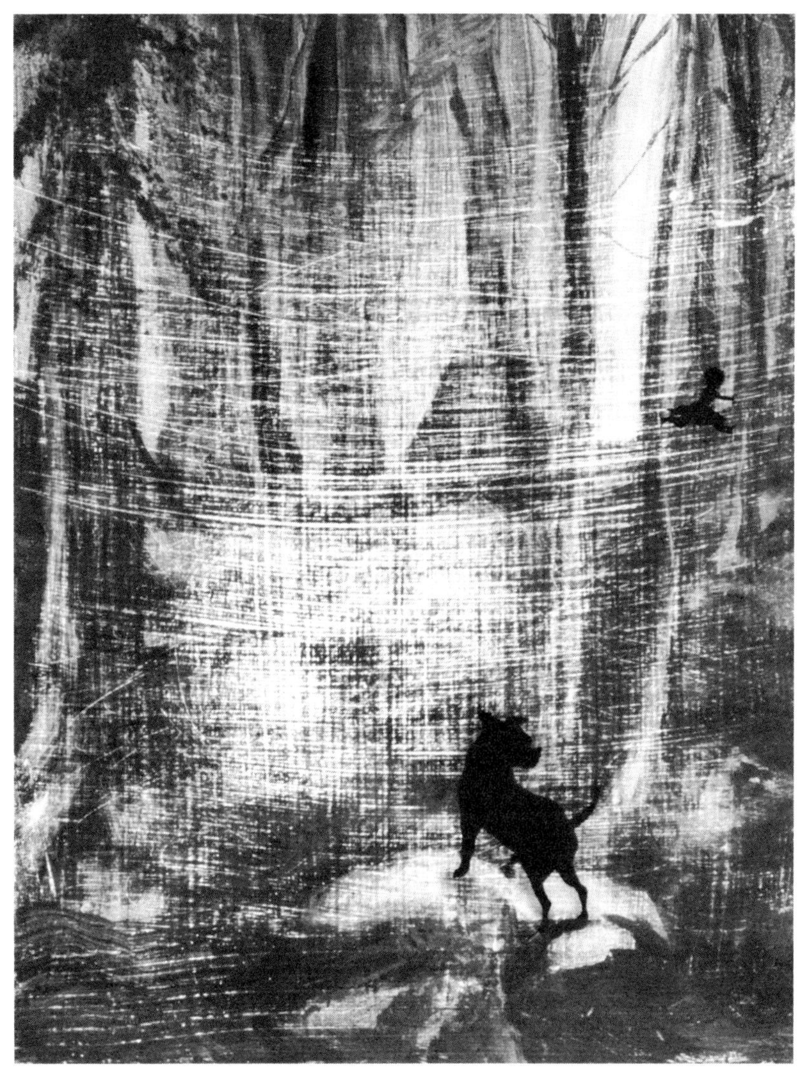

Kara Walker, *'Scape from American Primitives*, 2001. Paint, collage on board. 9 × 12 inches (22.9 × 30.5 cm). Artwork © Kara Walker, courtesy of Sikkema Jenkins & Co., New York; Sprüth Magers, Berlin.

Notes

[Editor's note: The two images from the *American Primitives* series did not appear with the original text of the interview, but it seemed important to include them here, as they are discussed by the artist and provide an insight into her pictorial approach.]

1. Thomas Dixon Jr., *The Clansman: An Historical Romance of the Ku Klux Klan* (New York: 1905; Lexington: University Press of Kentucky, 1970).

Kara Walker: "The Black-White Relation"

Anne M. Wagner

In Memory of Michael Rogin (1937–2001)

Silhouette

I am not the prisoner of history. I should not seek there for the meaning of my destiny.

—Frantz Fanon

This is an essay about race in representation, about blackness and whiteness as that fatal pairing takes visual form. In Kara Walker's work this happens when she uses black and white. The choice is polemical, though never cut and dried. Nor, we might say, is it ever simply "black and white." For all the graphic clarity and stark reductions of her cut paper characters, Walker's silhouettes neither illustrate nor simplify. Hers is a figural practice which, like many abstract or conceptual art-works, generates effects in wild disproportion to the elegant spareness of its technical means.[1] This essay aims to say how and why. In this I am not alone.[2] Kara Walker is one of the most visible of young African American contemporary artists, and one of the most successful. Not yet thirty-five, she has been given a whole string of museum and gallery exhibitions, awarded a MacArthur Fellowship, featured in a spate of interviews and articles, and targeted by a controversy which flared up over, among other issues, the extent to which white cultural institutions have embraced her work.

Walker's critics spoke from the heart of what inevitably gets called the "African American cultural community." In this case, for once, the label almost seems to fit. In 1997 her motives and morals were publicly challenged, most actively by the artist Betye Saar, who is among the most visible and best-established women of any skin color in American art today. What the protesters questioned, Saar via a letter-writing campaign calling for a boycott of the work, was its "negative images"—by which was meant the derogatory and regressive version of blackness they believed it displayed. In their eyes, Walker's version of blackness—its blackface—was a kind of pandering, a minstrel performance dishing out unmediated stereotype to whites who lap it up. But that's not all: for unlike other producers of "neo-black face art"—the artist Michael Ray Charles is a key case in point—Walker herself became as much of an issue as her imagery. While the "clean-cut, conservatively dressed, and soft-spoken" Charles was seen to lead "an upstanding life," one quite untarnished by his art, "the controversial Kara Walker" was "entirely dissimilar" as the source and voice of her work: variously "outspoken," "caustic," "dejected," "sassy," her personality, so readers of the *International Review of African American Art* were instructed, cried out for the "totally transforming" discipline of (her then-imminent) maternity.[3]

Black performer, white consumer, black critic: Who hasn't noticed that by these lights the old Bojangles formula, if now duly updated and transposed to the feminine, is with us still?[4] And the fracas also reminds us that black and white audiences have historically both responded to such "racial counterfeit"—as they do still. Think back to Frederick Douglass, writing in 1849 about his visit to Gavitt's Original Ethiopian Serenaders (a black minstrel show that performed in blackface): he was fully aware that some readers would disapprove, given "their dislike of everything that seems to feed the flame of American prejudice against colored people."[5] Among these worried readers surely would have figured Saar. Yet meantime, does the eager interest of today's white viewers in Walker (my own included) merely update and revitalize the means by which black popular culture has traditionally been both acknowledged and dispossessed by the powers that be? An affirmative answer can only mean that, despite one's best intentions, she is guilty as charged, with the blame then spreading from Walker, to me, to my white readers, and beyond. What we might well prefer to take as evidence, however limited and circumscribed, of the art world's belated integration becomes, in the eyes of some viewers, pandering, voyeurism, and worse. Business as usual, in other words, with Walker's cynicism in manipulating stereotypes only sustaining the base appetites she feeds.

How should current viewers respond to such haunting charges, not least given the evident credibility of their initial source?[6] Should they simply be dismissed as generational anxieties? (Back when I was young . . .) Or are they better understood as misguided symptoms of our ever-more-conservative times? (A falling tide lowers all boats . . .) Might it not be necessary to admit she is guilty as charged? Walker's work is both caustic and raunchy: remember that even Douglass—who maintained against his critics that black minstrels could help in "removing the prejudice against our race"—still declared that "industry, application, and a proper cultivation of their taste" were necessary for them to do the job.[7] Her industry notwithstanding, Walker keeps offering excess in lieu of refinement; even after five years of the discipline of motherhood, her posture is unchanged. Aggressively so: witness the intransigent title she chose for her latest show. *Kara Walker: American Primitive*—the phrase embraces all kinds of origins (dark and staid, authentic and primeval) as if thus to characterize both the artist's self and style.[8]

Alongside Walker's claim to the primitive, I want to set the sophistication of her use of black and white as metaphors for race. What is ambitious and programmatic about Walker's practice lies here; here too is found what Douglass might have learned to recognize as the "cultivation" of her art. For his part, Henry Louis Gates Jr. locates in her forms evidence of Walker's own "self-confidence, self-awareness, and control." Speaking of Walker's achievement as an artist, he writes that "the black object has become the black subject in a profound act of artistic exorcism."[9] Yet liberation into subjectivity clearly has its risks—or so the critical chorus seems to insist. Walker offers a staging of self and identity in which the chorus wants no part. Such reaction suggests that what Walker's art cultivates is the complex and discomfiting subjection of viewers to a radically destabilizing form of consciousness. And if white viewers value that experience, some reasons for such dubious pleasure clearly still need to be found.

Start, then, with black and white. The complexities begin at once, when we acknowledge that what is a trademark strategy is as much borrowed as original to her. Merely by making silhouettes, moreover, it is the artist herself who insists that we stage a comparison, the more odious the better, with her chosen source. Say we were to play an untitled 1995 work by Walker off against a late eighteenth-century example, the cut-paper portrait of Sara Hutchinson that William Wordsworth kept in his souvenir album, alongside his wife's, his sister's, and his own. Some such counterpoint is inevitable, because the practical resemblances are visually and technically strong enough to paper over the license Walker takes with her source technique. Like the family Wordsworth, Walker too uses black paper, but first draws in white chalk on its reverse side. Then she cuts. Still working on the back, she paints it with melted wax, so as next to burnish it onto another paper or a wall.[10] The silhouette product is enough like its historical prototype to compensate for what is usually a significant disjunction in scale: most of Walker's silhouette works are life-sized and multifigured. And they move in more-or-less sequential narratives that have little in common with the repetitive rhythm of portraits encountered one after another, as when, once upon a time, a viewer sat turning each scrapbook page. In fact, in its sheer variety and antic high-jinks Walker's customary parade looks less like a sentimental album and more like an illustrated book. It both recalls and exceeds the drolleries of turn-of-the-century illustration, from Rackham to Beardsley and beyond. Like them, she tells a story, though on a scale that aims less to entertain than overwhelm. In a Walker installation, both the figures and the spaces between them are big enough to stop you in your tracks.

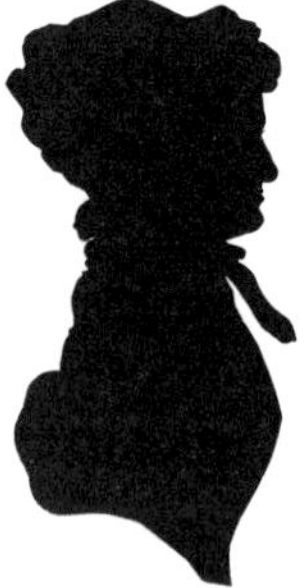

Miss Hutchinson, date and artist unknown. Silhouette, 4.5 × 3.75 inches (11.4 cm × 9.5 cm). Courtesy of the Wordsworth Trust.

Of course, silhouettes were always meant to be illustrative; the issue is what—how much and how little—they were devised to convey. One thing they initially circumvented was a reliance on artistic authorship. Not that we don't know the names of the main professional and amateur silhouettists who set to work in the mid-eighteenth century. Most were Northern Europeans: the Swiss Jean Huber and Johann Caspar Lavater, for example, or in Germany Philip Otto Runge, and even Goethe himself. (By the late nineteenth century, in America, many cutters were African American, a circumstance of which Walker, with her deep knowledge of the history of graphic communication, might well be aware.) But however anonymous or eminent its practitioners, the technique itself, given its reliance on the shadow—the "immediate expression of nature" in Lavater's words—always connoted both veracity and modesty.[11] And it was frugal to boot. The scene of its making—at least as Lavater showed it—need transport us nowhere more distant than a candlelit parlor, where it is never very late at night. There is satisfaction in learning that the silhouette took its name from an eighteenth-century French finance minister, a sometime reformer or perhaps, according to his opponents, merely an incompetent. His attacks on wealth and privilege soon made silhouette (the minister in question was called Etienne de Silhouette) stand for anything miserly or cheese-paring, from trousers without pockets to impromptu paper portraits.[12] This pedigree alone is enough to confirm the silhouette as a thoroughly bourgeois image, whose decent home- and handmade qualities help to compensate for its wholesale omission of even the merest hint of inner life—unless one believes with Lavater that outer and inner are one and the same. Silhouettes speak an economical language of substitution and erasure: Who could know, looking at Sara Hutchinson, what Wordsworth felt for her, or even if feeling was involved at all? Such an image trusts its viewers (their desires, their fantasies) to bring its blank blackness (back) to life.[13]

Only under these conditions can silhouettes do the work of portraits, answering desire and absence, but at a double remove. For such skiagrams derive their descriptions not from concrete and material beings, but from an ephemeral bodily substitute or byproduct, shadow. The silhouettist traces an outline, the edge of a pool of darkness as it was caught on some intervening vertical plane. From such a temporary effect comes a hard and fast distinction: black versus white. What is

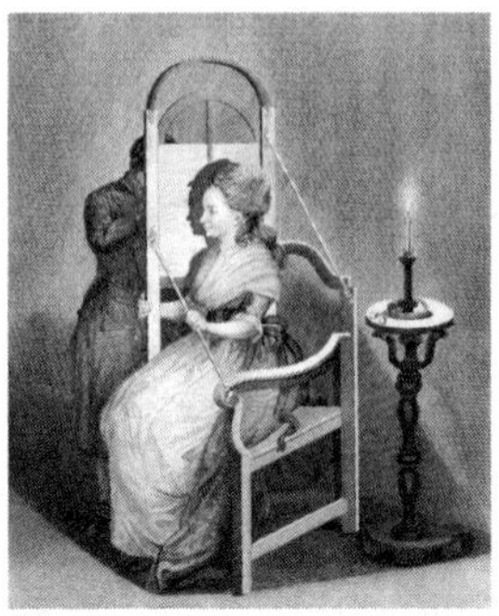

Thomas Holloway, *A Sure and Convenient Machine for Drawing Silhouettes*. Engraving, in *Essays in Physiognomy: Designed to Promote the Knowledge and the Love of Mankind* by Thomas Holloway et al. (London: J. Murray, 1792). Reproduced with permission of the National Galleries of Scotland.

shown is not a body, but how a body blocks the light. That the schema is reductive—that it conflates presence and absence—is overshadowed by the sheer drama of the forms which result: time and touch and the transitory yield to what Edmund Burke called the "power of black."[14] Flat dark shapes map a scheme for a paper-thin person the way the cartographer's meandering line divides sea from coastline; what Ernst Gombrich long ago termed our capacity for physiognomic perception, plus our inborn eagerness to resolve visual confusion, mean that we look past what is idiosyncratic and arbitrary—the swellings along the back of Hutchinson's profile, for example—to more or less effortlessly recognize a cap, its ribbons and the chin they tie under, with these same easy perceptions leading to some real measure of assurance, however misplaced, that the sitter is present as tangible material form.[15] Of course our certainty can sometimes be shaken: no one knows better than Gombrich (except maybe Walker) how swiftly, as our eyes move and refocus, a figure can become background, rabbit morph into duck. Yet most of the time, we are quite prepared to see the lineaments of a silhouette portrait as somehow typical, even characteristic; they can stand as a sign for a species or type as identifiable as the common crow or raven: remember that one other great use of the silhouette drawing lies in field guides, where they illustrate and make recognizable the defining attributes of families of creatures which, like very

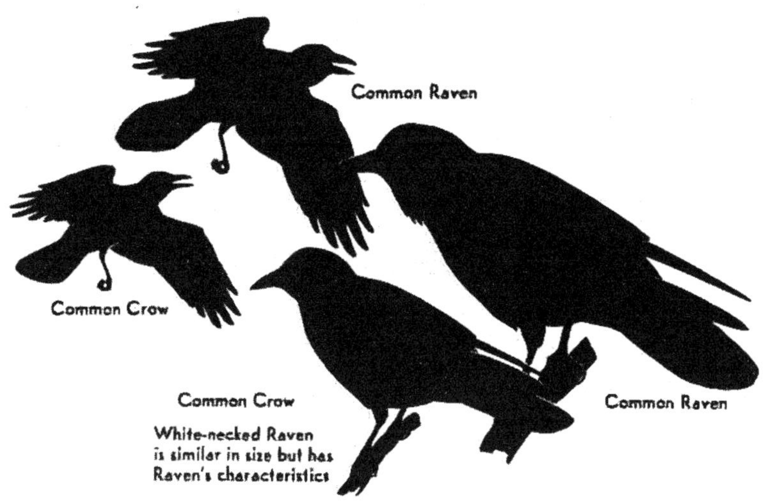

SILHOUETTES OF CROW AND RAVEN

Silhouettes of crow and raven. *A Field Guide to Western Birds*, 3rd edition, by Roger Tory Peterson (Boston: Houghton Mifflin, 1990).

black birds, are all too easy to confuse. Such uses both remember and domesticate the infinite pains taken by Lavater and his followers to separate degradation from beauty, degeneration from morality, "them" from "us."[16]

The silhouette's deep origins in bodily absence and sentimental memory, as well as its long connection with often prejudicial tasks of description, illustration, and identification, are why my introductory comparison is worth pursuing, and why, I think, Walker so clearly insists that it be staged. She wants us to see her mimicry, and its distortions; it's hard not to recognize how often she contaminates her models with what is the visual equivalent of the *idée reçue*. The lass she portrays in *Untitled* (1995), for example, has a pert nose and saucy hairstyle that are romantic, though not in the manner of Wordsworth—this is romance, Harlequin brand. Yet Walker's imitations still aim to be faithful enough to force us to spell out what she is doing differently. The difference is this: Walker's silhouettes aim to suggest they capture the outlines of flesh-and-blood models—they work like the silhouettes they imitate, in other words. Sometimes, in the case of the opening image, they are almost direct imitations. *Almost*: in Walker's hands the very idea of the silhouette portrait begins to leak, from its most vital and volatile points. Yet it still keeps alive the metaphorics of clarity and simplicity while being anything but. Take the bust: the word names a portrait type, while euphemizing a body part; in my chosen example a nimble female with pigtails climbs like a pirate up the dripping flow. Do we need this tiny invader to remind us that unlike Lavater, Goethe, or Huber (though like Runge, interestingly enough), Walker had no sitters; thus, they cast no shadows, they had no bodies. Each of her characters is both an invention and a citation: each is cut from a freehand drawing into shapes whose sheer vitality and obscenity reanimate and darken racial stereotypes.

Darken: "to grow clouded as with gloom or anger."[17] My dictionary definition is apposite, though it doesn't go far enough. Darken: "to grow clouded as with gloom or anger" or with, I now add, the unspeakable. For Walker's shadowy figures are more than simply bodily: they drip sweat, saliva, shit, sperm, and milk; they copulate, masturbate, and explode. They are often bestial in their bodily conduct, and sometimes bestial in bodily form. None of these activities or bodies would be acceptable in a drawing room at any time of day or night. Here is where the gloom and anger lie. We might term Walker's repertoire of figures invented imitations, whose sheer recognizability and simultaneous obscenity set us adrift in time and space. We are lost somewhere in a scatological shadow play set in a nightmare of the slave-owning South. No field guide exists to this particular habitat, nor, despite the period costumery, do its inhabitants necessarily seem to have died out with the waning of minstrelsy and Jim Crow. They are too active to seem moribund, and too recognizable to be dismissed as safely part of the past. Instead they cross-breed past with present: Hollywood travels south to Tara and knocks at the slave cabin door. In walk Josephine Baker and Al Jolson; they pull up a chair beside Uncle Tom, and everyone gets carried away. Each figure, that is to say, epitomizes and conforms to some generally legible, culturally available formula for black identity, while contaminating it with violent and erotic fantasy. Somewhere in this process, a transformation occurs. Black paper changes, becomes animated, and starts to carry a special rhetorical weight. It stands not only for the black body as flattened into a single especially scandalous,

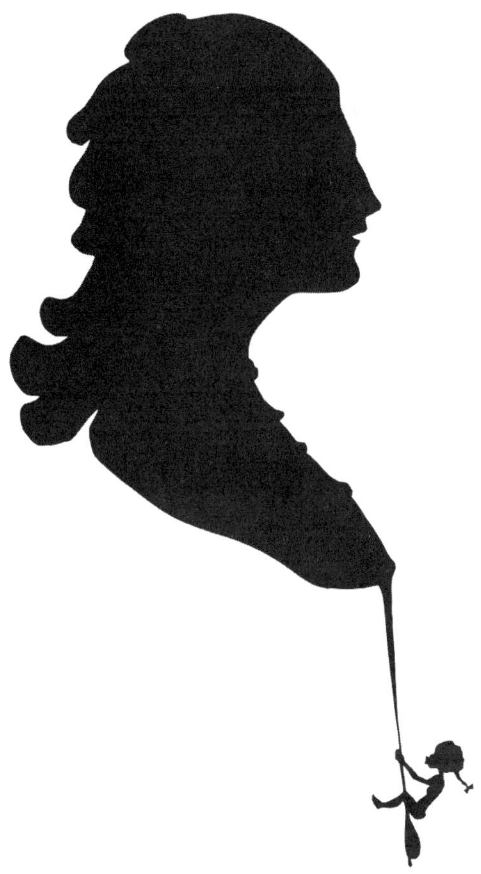

Kara Walker, *Untitled (Profile with Little Girl)*, 1995. Cut paper on paper. 50 × 38 inches (127.3 × 81.3 cm). Artwork © Kara Walker, courtesy of Sikkema Jenkins & Co., New York; Sprüth Magers, Berlin.

often erotic, dimension, but also for black skin as the quintessence of that body. Black skin turns to blackface, in other words: blackface as the hyperbolic performance of scripted identity. Walker, we might say, is "corking up." The phrase names the backstage ritual of generations of minstrel performers, including, let it be said, those of African descent, like Manny in Spike Lee's *Bamboozled*, who weren't born black enough (as if anyone could be!) to fill their stereotyped roles.[18]

For Walker, this masquerade is a means her art uses to address "blackness" as construct, as an idea or sign asserted rhetorically, in disembodied, almost spectral guise. "Blackness" has little to do with living, breathing bodies; it refers to something more and other than skin or surface, and it is this complex process of figuration and reference that we are aiming to describe. I want to suggest that in Walker's skiagrams blackness stands for what Michael Rogin has called, in a recent essay on Ralph Ellison, "imaginary Negroes"—projections of a long history, shadows that play across the screen of the American consciousness.[19] This may be part of what Walker's critics find so disturbing: her work insists that the shadow of "blackness" has cast darkness (my dictionary's "gloom and anger") within every viewer's mind and self. Yet it also demonstrates, in ways that extend its force and polemic, that "blackness" is only visible in and against the "whiteness" of its containing ground.

Epidermalization

> . . . assaulted at various points, the corporeal schema crumbled, its place taken by a racial epidermal schema.

What is blackness, if it is not—or not only—some attribute or quality of skin? Is it a "fact" of color, or a coloristic relation? Does it have anything to do with skin and its color at all? Surely it is clear that in Walker's work blackness and whiteness are concepts or constructs: their pairing emerges as the key relation—relentlessly, even tendentiously so.[20] Most viewers, I trust, cannot help but think of counterproposals to her polarizing imagery, especially the various multiculturalist answers to a world seen in black and white. Such artworks play off and to wider shifts along the fault line of difference, from the effort to forge a rainbow coalition to simultaneous shakeups in the marketplace, when product stylists at long last discovered the profits to be had in trading on the diversity of skin. We need only remember a few symptomatic innovations of the last two decades: some corporate innovator somewhere finally realized it might make sense to produce a transparent Band-Aid, while at Crayola, the "flesh" colored crayon was tardily rebaptized "peach."

One of the most ambitious efforts to image these changes is Byron Kim's *Synecdoche* (1991–1992). The title alone is enough to signal both figurative and rhetorical aspirations, though from the word alone we don't learn much about how to read the artist's tone. Kim assembled a number of 10 × 8-inch panels, each an abstract monochrome painted in oil and wax. I say "a number" not to fudge the question, but to convey that "number" is an issue for the work: *Synecdoche* was conceived as intentionally open-ended; it is unfinished and meant to stay that way. In 1993 it was exhibited at the Whitney Biennial with 204 panels; in a slightly later incarnation the number had grown to 275. All this becomes relevant when you learn that each swatch reproduces the skin color of someone the artist has met. While Kim mixes pigments to match pigmentation—he studied each sitter from life—the wax additive is what quickens the color and gives it a vital glow. When the grid is assembled, however, its panels find their place not by hue or date, but alphabetically, according to the first name of the person portrayed. It should be clear that each patch of color stands, yes, synecdochally, for the absent body it indexes and aims to match. Yet that endless chain of bodies—Kim's stream of acquaintances—is itself part of some larger, still less visible (and still unfinished) whole.

The programmatic aspect of the piece makes it clear why, for all the work's apparently abstract logic, its maker considers *Synecdoche* "representational, even figurative":[21] Kim figures skin and color as vehicles for endless variation, even while seeming to suggest that such

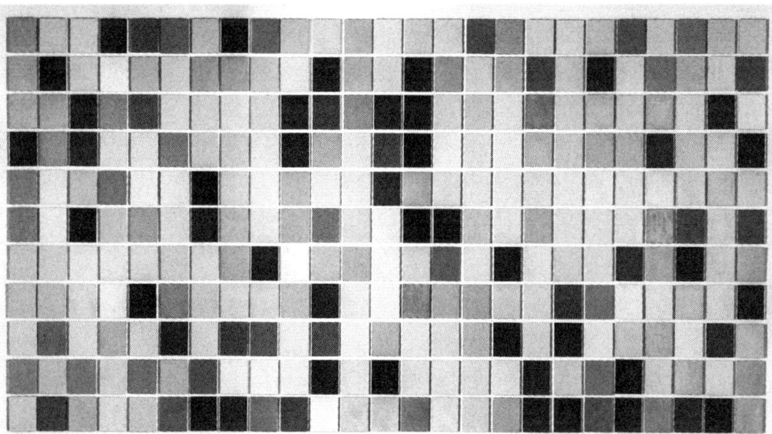

Byron Kim, *Synecdoche*, 1991–1992. Oil and wax on panels. Dimensions variable. © Byron Kim 2021. Images courtesy of the artist and James Cohan, New York.

multiplicity has no real determinant weight in the underlying structure of the whole. The result is that *Synecdoche* functions visually as a field for something like the proverbial "play of differences," without those differences doing much to determine the strict pattern it observes. I think the work's sheer orderliness—its conceptual program—is key to its complexity of tone. For Kim sets up a schema where what ends up as really decisive is not a programmatic claim for the inexhaustible differences of skin. What matters more is the radical arbitrariness of the alphabetic grid; within it a single letter, the first letter of a first name, is the law.[22] Whose skins, whose colors, are these? We *can* learn the relevant names, and match them to colors—this much is true. Look for example at Kim's study for the Sylvester Rodney panel—its variations in tone are eliminated in the final lush wax panel (so much for the studies from life that Kim so carefully prepared!). The study of Leslie Roberts looks pale by comparison—this is part of the point. Yet in *Synecdoche*'s final arrangement could where the Ss fall, or the Ls, or the Ws, ever be thought to matter a lot? Because Kim used first names to define the final schema—hence linking all seven of the Lisas, say, but breaking up the family Rodriguez—coloristic randomization was made complete. What results is a potentially endless field of meaningless comparison. The grid may conjure paint chips or makeup samples (Kim is mimicking both), yet it offers its colors in such profligate chaos that even the most competent "taste professional" would be hard pressed to know which is which. Or who. And what would you use these samples for? The more we look, the more mute and monstrous each specimen becomes. The piece assembles a deathly museum in which both skin and color simultaneously end up archiving and cataloguing samples of a social and political phenomenon before it is well and truly dead. Skin and color become premature specimens, artifacts that their collector seals off from the culture from which they stem. Behind his pluralist protocol lies a pessimism of which its maker is entirely aware: if the modernist grid is made newly carnal, skin itself, in all its diversity, is sapped of vital life.

I need *Synecdoche* as part of my argument because as a metonym for open-ended difference, it can serve as a foil to the metaphorical commitments evident in the artwork I began with. Looking back at it, I imagine Walker taking issue with Kim's chief idea. I am even prepared to suggest that her main objection would work more or less along the same lines as mine. For her the issue of color may be radically restricted, but it is far from dead. In her hands the play of difference dances hectically back and forth along a single axis, the divider between black and white. Even Kim has on occasion insisted on the same stark opposition: in a 1993 piece produced in collaboration with Glenn Ligon, black announces itself as plural yes, but also univocal and unmodulated: it stands as the single antithesis to a whole palette of subtle variations in hue.[23] Easy to guess the ironic title: of course, they named it *Black and White*. Here metaphor and metonymy are made to join hands. Walker, I wager, would never forge that link; for her neither black nor white can be tied back to some observable epidermal real. Nor can either ever be entirely isolated, abstracted, or given self-contained form. On the contrary, the two are always mutually contingent, their boundaries shared, the one policing and invading the other, even while the very idea of boundary comes under considerable visual stress. We first read black on white, but we come eventually to realize that it is white that makes black coalesce in bodies the more antic and outrageous for the visual games they play.

We are back again to the question of what is contentious in Walker's work. The scandal does not lie in her ventriloquizing of conventions, or her reiterations of stereotype: there is by now a long history of such rebellious and diagnostic appropriations. One of its touchstones is *The Liberation of Aunt Jemima*, an assemblage made in 1973 by Betye Saar. This anti-heroine, a commercial trademark and a commercial object, is shown shaking off her servitude: no points for noticing that she has already grabbed her gun. But who is Aunt Jemima: Can a trademark really rebel? Would it matter if she did? Does it go without saying that Walker's strange characters—her banana-clad exotic dancers and famished savages—take stereotype into a whole new objectified realm? What is outrageous about such figures is not merely their eroticism, but the out-and-out perversity of their bodily gestures and forms. Walker lets loose the stock characters of myth and history and mass entertainment: she really gives them their head. I realize my choice of metaphor is unfortunate, given these particular images: in one work are creatures simultaneously so desperately hungry and fecund and perversely erotic that they suckle, give suck, and self-suckle: Is this onanism, or pederasty, or nurture? The odd overlay is obvious when I try to name the result: What sort of speech act is it to say "her black banana dick"?[24] In two linked bodies are efficiently telescoped and exploded several

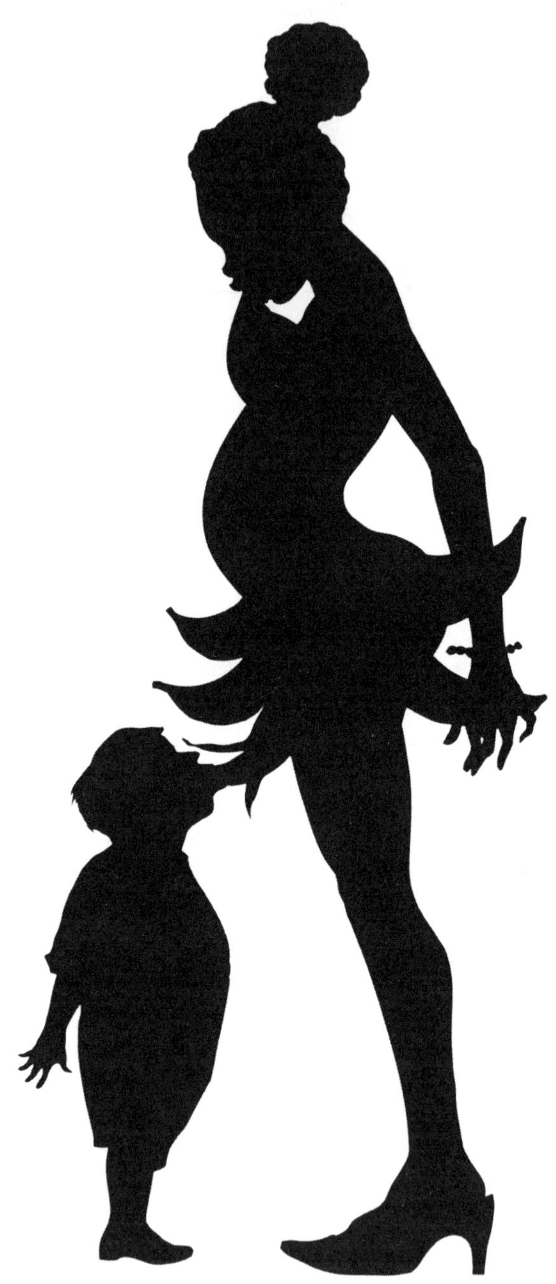

Kara Walker, *Consume*, 1998. Cut paper and adhesive on wall. 69 × 32 inches (175.3 × 81.3 cm). Artwork © Kara Walker, courtesy of Sikkema Jenkins & Co., New York; Sprüth Magers, Berlin.

stock black roles. The other image takes up the drama—or perhaps I should say melodrama, given each figure's parodic pose—of birth: no sooner does a baby drop from the womb than, howling, it is set upon as the main dish in an adolescent cannibal's meal. Both images dwell obscenely on female identity and its links to bodily function, with the result that Walker's black comedy blurts out what for Saar seems an unspeakable admission: these black and white tableaux declare that the artist's own imagination has drunk deeply at a tainted well. Here is history fully desublimated, its imaginary actors made to cavort in ways for which Aunt Jemima, like her "liberator" Saar, would have no words.

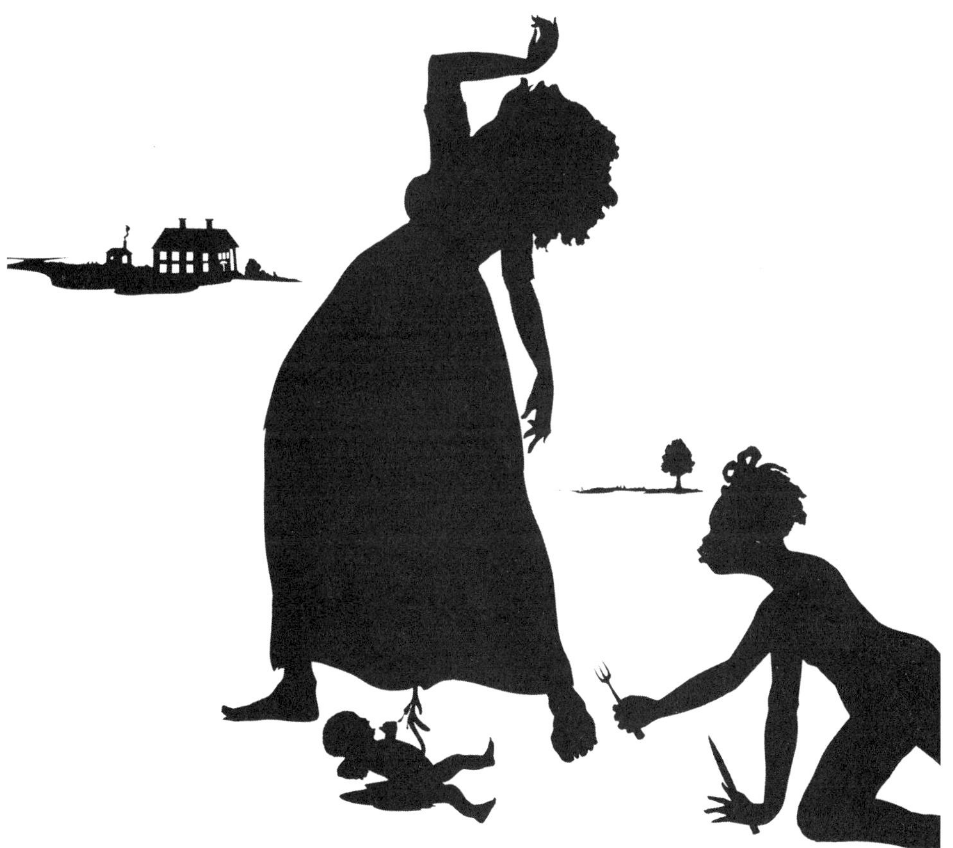

Kara Walker, *Untitled*, 1994–1995. Cut paper on canvas. 48 × 54 inches (121.9 × 137.2 cm). Artwork © Kara Walker, courtesy of Sikkema Jenkins & Co., New York; Sprüth Magers, Berlin.

Black and White

> My life should not be devoted to drawing up the balance sheet of
> Negro values.

Of course, Walker is not entirely alone in her insistence that black artists and imagery stake a claim to cultural pathologies. Nor is she isolated
when she suggests that such symptoms leave their mark on the shape
of identity and self. In this, her greatest ally and precursor may well be
Frantz Fanon—hence Fanon's usefulness in understanding what and
how black and white mean when Walker uses them, and why they
might reasonably, necessarily, be deployed to such extreme and painful
effect. The connection lies in how both approach "The Black-White
Relation." The phrase, like the other citations punctuating this essay,
refers us to *Black Skin, White Masks*, first published in French in 1952,
then in English in 1967, two years before Walker's birth.

What is painful about Fanon's investigation of subjectivity and
alienation starts with his insistence on the pervasive and deforming
impact of black and white. Remember his stark formula: "The white
man is sealed in his whiteness. The black man in his blackness." Again,
the two terms inevitably make a pair. Though Fanon, like Walker,
dwells most on blackness, he too insists on blackness as impacted by
whiteness, blackness as "crushing objecthood." And, to quote Fanon
still further, "Not only must the black man be black, he must be black
in relation to the white man." For the black subject, this knowledge
comes as an annihilating revelation, which, in a knowing echo of Freud
on gender, Fanon dramatizes as a defining moment of sight. "Mama,"
says the child to his mother, "Mama! See the Negro! I'm frightened!"
Seeing himself thus seen, Fanon writes, "I made up my mind to laugh
myself to tears, but laughter had become impossible. . . . My body was
given back to me sprawled out, distorted, recolored, clad in mourning
in that white winter day."[25]

Fanon's text bespeaks his professional commitment to addressing,
and ameliorating, the psychopathology of colonialism. Yet his diction
is far from clinical: rather than stand at a safe distance from his subject,
he instead mobilizes what Homi Bhabha has called "an agonizing performance of self-images." The phrase alerts us to Fanon's structuring of
his book around a first-person narrator, a vehicle for insistent stagings

of what is a historically specific and simultaneously mutable black male self. That self, though sometimes emerging as a psychiatric professional, is hardly exempt from the very pathologies he aims to diagnose and cure. Bhabha, to his credit, is alert to these and other shadows in Fanon's work; it is Bhabha who acknowledges Fanon's radicalism as of the sort "that never dawns without casting an uncertain dark."[26] The shadows in Fanon's text collect most deeply around the uncertain issues raised by black male subjectivity and sexuality, not least the objectification of both men and women that black male desires court and convey. Fanon enters the colonized bedroom, and what he finds there, in its occupant's fantasies of virility and abjection, evidences—perhaps even epitomizes—a fatal absence of self.

In lieu of a fully authorized subject, a black man (not a woman) is "forever in combat with his own image," because it exists only in appropriated and colonized forms: black is (only) the "protean imaginary other" to white.[27] Elsewhere in the text, however, "Fanon" himself—as subject, as author—claims his "own" voice and subjecthood. In fact the book is at its most vehement, calling out with the rhythmic repetitions of the pulpit, when its author declares the need—his own need?—to put this painful history behind him. "My life should not be devoted to drawing up the balance sheet of Negro values." "I am not a prisoner of history. I should not seek there for the meaning of my destiny." "I am not the slave of the Slavery that dehumanized my ancestors." The salvo of declarations comes quickly, the next on the heels of the last: "I am a man, and what I have to recapture is the whole past of the world. I am not responsible solely for the revolt in Santo Domingo."[28] All these pronouncements come from the manifesto with which *Black Skin, White Masks* concludes. Yet to declare freedom from history Fanon must simultaneously conjure its outlines and shadows. Tom-toms, cannibalism, racial defects, slave ships, Uncle Remus, Br'er Rabbit, "sho' good eatin": the litany is as familiar as it is inevitable. It is clear that the only way for Fanon to refuse the inheritance is to call its specters to mind. Nor can we ever really be sure whether the "I" who writes his way toward exorcism is the same or different from the book's other main object and quantity, the shattered black male.

What happens when Walker invokes the same legacy is that she willingly courts the same confusion, surrendering the historical distance Fanon dreamt of refusing but could not maintain. For rather than

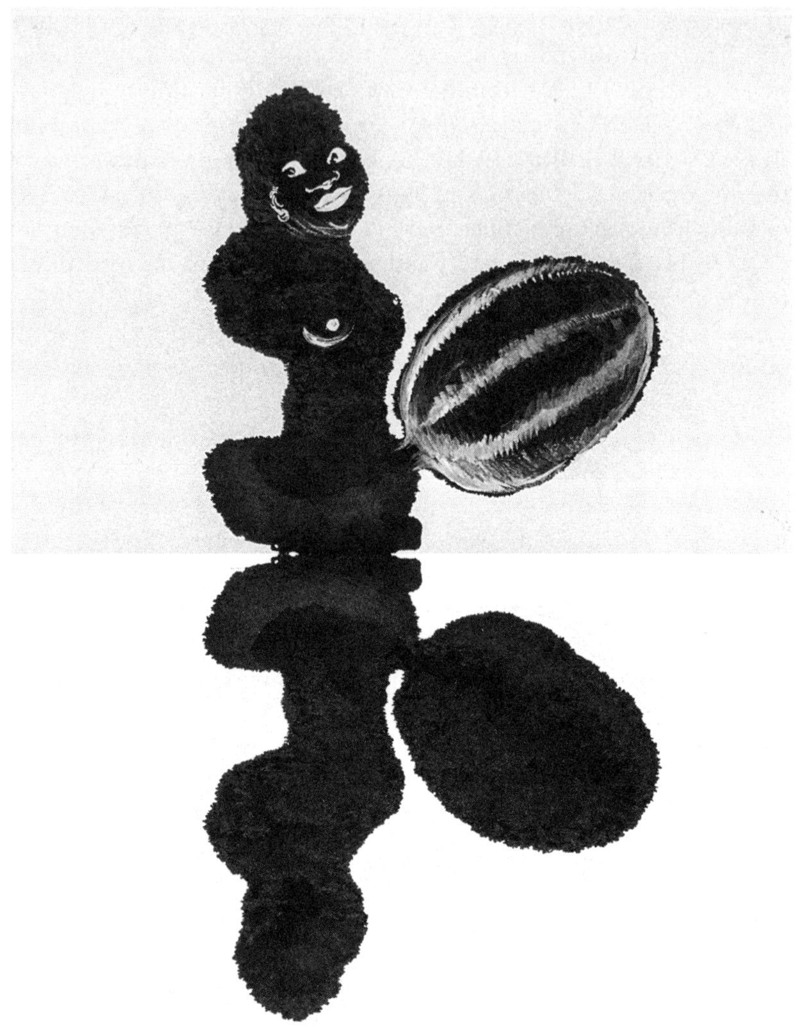

Kara Walker, detail from *Untitled*, 1995. Ink, pencil, and gouache on paper. 9 parts: 8.75 × 12 inches (22.2 × 30.5 cm) each. 10 parts: 12 × 8.75 inches (30.5 × 22.2 cm) each. Artwork © Kara Walker, courtesy of Sikkema Jenkins & Co., New York; Sprüth Magers, Berlin.

wishing to refuse stereotype, she insists that it peoples her imaginative and fantasy life. She even employs a means of representing that insistence which a clinician like Fanon might otherwise use to heal. I am thinking in particular of a set of untitled inkblot drawings begun in 1995. In all of them ink is poured and paper folded, à la Rorschach; she then finds the faces hiding in the stains. Sambos, pickaninnies: out they jump, grinning and claiming their due. Of course, these experiments are less spontaneous than polemical; they propel associations that are anything but free. Walker may be mimicking a diagnostic exercise, but diagnosis is still the result. It is important, in this context, that when speaking of her subject matter, Walker asserts, pace Rorschach, a posture of carefully studied control: "It seems like I had to actually reinvent or make up my own racist situations so I would know how to deal with them as black people in the past did. In order to have a real connection with my history I had to be somebody's slave. But I was in control. That's the difference."[29] Walker means what she says: for a contemporary African American woman, laying hold of history necessarily means following a genealogy that leads back from racism to slavery as a matter of course. "The disaster of the man of color," writes Fanon, "lies in the fact that he was enslaved."[30] But if recovering (from) the past demands feeling a way into its bodily and psychic dimensions, might not the silhouette, with its built-in requirement for desire and projection, risk unleashing (or flattening) both? It is just this instability that her detractors seem to fear. Whose fantasies do control these works? Do her works not put the lie to her own confident assertion, by enacting exactly the uncertainty about who or what—what histories, visions, and appetites—might be playing the master's role? The sexual antics of Walker's black figures beget a new history, one written by both maker and viewer; the shadowy antic couplings of her cutouts reanimate the stereotypes of primitivism and degeneracy in ways that demonstrate that they are still alive and well in our minds.[31]

It is time for this essay to reach its conclusion. At best it can only be provisional, for no other reason that Kara Walker is not only still working, she has not stopped addressing these questions herself. One way of ending, given the lack of an ending, is to turn to her 1999 installation in Oakland at the California College of Arts and Crafts. Here, quite literally, is where my own interest in Walker began: in a long white gallery, filled end to end with a gray-painted, purpose-built wall. Along it, left to right, marched a procession of figures; Walker has said that she was thinking of nineteenth-century mass entertainment—particularly the panorama[32]—and she gave the piece a title, printed on a handbill, that aimed to press the revivalism home: *No mere words can Adequately reflect the Remorse this Negress feels at having been Cast into such a lowly state by her former Masters and so it is with a Humble heart that she brings about their physical Ruin and earthly Demise.* No mere words: the title seems all the more apposite when you try to spell out exactly what you see.

The story begins with a black swan and a young black woman who takes out her eye—it is white—and hands it to a child: above her hovers the tracery of a woven snare or net. Next to them struts a black man whose white swan-headed cane seems to pull him quickly along. White and black swans keep on returning throughout the narrative, but on all the white swans save one, new heads have been grafted: they are heavy, black, and human, and have an oddly pugilistic force. Past the pool of swimming swan hybrids are several figures lost in perverse and excessive sex. Half-eaten drumsticks—they must be swan parts— litter the ground. After sex comes revolution: a young Liberty has mounted the barricade, her hand on a swan-headed gun. Yet the whole long sequence ends with the flash of a photograph, not a gunshot, as a new young woman—or she may be a battle-scarred Liberty (she has a wooden leg)—takes the picture of a misshapen black veteran who sits his battered body on a stump. Walker has said of this installation that it represents a revolution that "feeds on itself." Shall we take her at her word? The remark makes the work a parable of misdirected blackness, a blackness that loses its force and its way. Walker does not say why. All we learn is that in this particular world (is it so far distant?) white stands for sex and vision, trophies and beauty and perversion, all this against a sea of gray. Here the newly made hybrid—the white swan awkwardly fitted with its black head—may swim for a moment, yet cannot survive.

This allegory comes to no real conclusion: it ends with a photo-graph no one will see. Nor is it easy to parse: my condensed narrative elides much of what happened during my time in the gallery as I tried to take in precisely what mere words must struggle to address. How to convey the wild visual energy of figures and background, or tease out their rhymes and repetitions and puns? In the sky the exploding cannon ball looks like a flower and a cotton boll, while cut black clouds float like a kind of remainder, what is left when the cutting is done. To tell

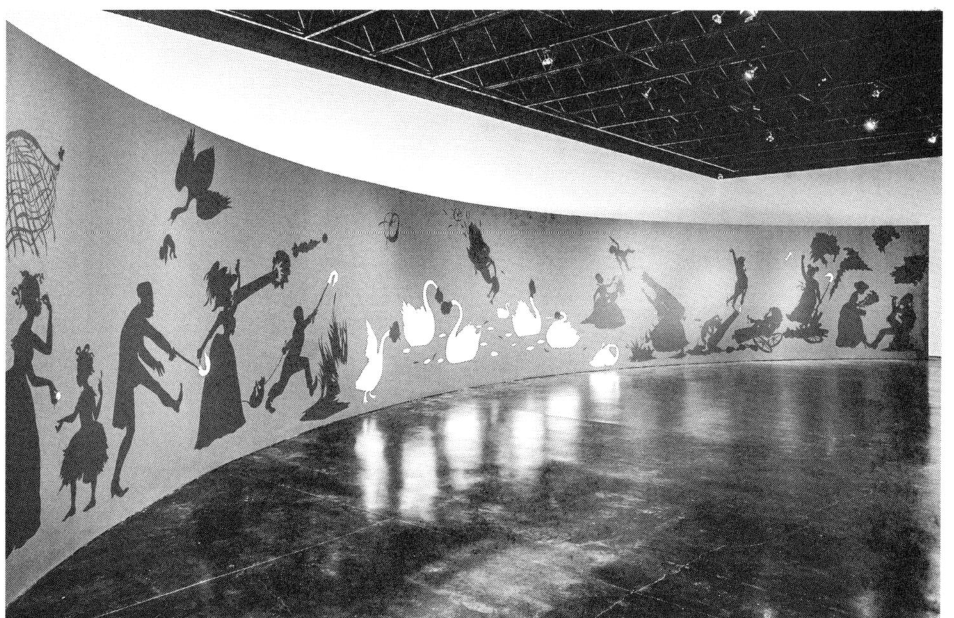

Installation view: Kara Walker, *Kara Walker: No mere words can Adequately reflect the Remorse this Negress feels at having been Cast into such a lowly state by her former Masters and so it is with a Humble heart that she brings about their physical Ruin and earthly Demise*, 1999. Installation using cut paper and adhesive on wall. Overall size approximately 132 × 780 inches (353.3 × 1981.2 cm). California College of Arts and Crafts (CCAC), Oakland, CA, 1999. Photo: Ian Reeves. Artwork © Kara Walker, courtesy of Sikkema Jenkins & Co., New York; Sprüth Magers, Berlin.

a story about these figures is to decide who and what these figures are and do—as if that were an easy task. It is not. My narrative surely says as much about me and my history as it does about Walker and hers. And so together artist and viewer conspire in telling the story of race.

With its final photographic motif, *No mere words* sparked a new departure. It seems to have propelled her work and its field of reference ever closer to the present. The vignette, like the panorama format itself, stands for mass entertainments that turn away from the domestic sphere of album and silhouette and toward another, more public image world. There Walker clearly found it necessary to begin to operate with at least one shade of gray.

Gray is the color of doubt and thought: gray area, gray matter. It is clear that with the Oakland installation Walker's language of color likewise began to point in a new direction—one that continues to expand. In her most recent work lights and gels bathe the walls in colors worthy of the burning of Atlanta, while projected shadows conjure the landscape of the South. In this newly spectacular setting the old cutout characters look blacker than ever before. And the contrast is the greater given yet another new element in the wild shadow play. The hot lighting means that flesh and blood viewers, whatever their color, cast their outlines upon the wall, in the process becoming even more active players in the racial melodrama of Walker's invented South.

Drama or melodrama? It makes a difference which word we choose. I think it is worth insisting on the latter term, for it better explains the risky extremism of Walker's work. Why choose hyperbole as the vehicle to address slavery's wound, when there is no exaggerating that wound's seriousness and depth? Melodrama, as the mode of convention and excess, leads Walker straight from popular visual culture through fantasy, and on into a bodily quagmire where polite convention is sullied in aid of a larger moral truth. Yet as with silhouette and stereotype, to work within melodrama as a category is again to enlist the viewer's own assumptions and fantasy, sponsoring that active complicity no one among us can pretend to evade. Standing in a Walker installation, physically elided with it, we become part of the play. This is what is best about Walker's work: its strength is an inclusiveness that intends to let no one off its outrageous hook. Inclusiveness, though not diversity: she still refuses any truck with pluralist ideas. Next to her work Kim's smart and ironic rerouting of abstract paintings risks looking numb. I think such numbness counts among her greatest fears. She is dead set on remembering, so as to show that the outrages of the past have had inescapable consequences for the content and formation of present-day selves. And the task of remembering has something to say about the artist's own self-scrutiny as a black woman in America today. Here one final quotation may be apposite: "There are times," Walker recently said to an interviewer, "there are times when . . . you're not thinking about race for a brief moment. Then suddenly the entire history of the whole United States of America or the American South or post-Reconstruction comes crashing down on you and you say to yourself, 'Hmm, this reminds me of something. I'm not sure what it is, but it is vaguely familiar.'"[33] Melodrama? Hardly: surely Walker suggests that forgetting is only a pretense. There is no eluding racism's routinely shattering erasures, those yawning gaps and everyday absences which her art's blackness is aiming to fill.

Notes

1. David Batchelor has pointed to a deep-seated devaluation of color within the Western tradition ("Chromophobia: Ancient and Modern, and a Few Notable Exceptions," *Art & Design* 12, nos. 7–8 [1997]: 12, 30–37), yet similar prejudices subordinate black to white.

2. Among other responses to Walker's art that I have found helpful are the three essays in *Parkett* 59 (2000): Gwendolyn DuBois Shaw, "Final Cut," 129–132; Elizabeth Janus, "As American as Apple Pie," 139–140; and Hamza Walker, "Nigger Lover or Will There Be Any Black People in Utopia?," 152–159. See also Dan Cameron, "Kara Walker: Rubbing History the Wrong Way," *Art on Paper* 2, no. 1 (September–October 1997): 10–14 (my thanks to Sarah Evans for alerting me to this essay).

3. The details offered here concerning the response to Walker's work are taken principally from Juliette Bowles, "Extreme Times Call for Extreme Heroes," *The International Review of African American Art* 14, no. 3 (1997): 2–16, 64, and Karen C. C. Dalton, Michael D. Harris, and Lowery Stokes Sims, "The Past Is Prologue but Is Parody and Pastiche Progress? A Conversation," *IRAAA* 14, no. 3 (1997): 17–29. The latter is a conversation between Lowery Stokes Sims, then curator of twentieth-century art at the Metropolitan Museum of Art, New York, and the artist Michael D. Harris; the discussion was moderated by Dalton, director and curator of the Image of the Black in Western Art Research Project and Photo Archive, Harvard University. Bowles, for her part, wrote as an editor of the *IRAAA*. As Gwendolyn DuBois Shaw elaborates ("Final Cut," 131–132 n. 1), Bowles was later moved to explain some of the more extreme terms of the discussion initially offered in the IRAAA in an "Editor's Response," *IRAAA* 15, no. 2 (1998): 50–51. In the IRAAA conversation, Stokes Sims proved herself to be more tentative than both Saar and Harris, her interlocutor, in directly attacking Walker.

4. According to Michael Rogin, "minstrelsy was an all-male entertainment form, combining racial and gender cross-dressing, male bonding and racial exclusion, misogyny and drag." See his *Blackface, White Noise: Jewish Immigrants in the Hollywood Melting Pot* (Berkeley: University of California Press, 1996), 28.

5. Frederick Douglass, "Gavitt's Original Ethiopian Serenaders," *North Star*, June 29, 1849, as cited in Eric Lott, *Love and Theft: Blackface Minstrelsy and the American Working Class* (New York: Oxford University Press, 1993), 36–37.

6. Saar's construction *The Liberation of Aunt Jemima* (1973) has become a paradigm for the ways in which "African-American artists in the 1960s and 1970s confronted these insidious images [stereotypes] by depicting them in their art but by changing their attributes or surroundings" (Sharon F. Patton, *African-American Art* [Oxford: Oxford University Press, 1998], 202). Note that, ironically enough, it is in the context of her discussion of Saar's work that Patton warns that "such tactics must be played out carefully because the use of these images risks perpetuating that which the artist wants to destroy."

7. Lott, *Love and Theft*, 37.

8. The show was on view at Brent Sikkema Gallery, September–October 2001.

9. Henry Louis Gates Jr., as quoted in Bowles, "Extreme Times," 5.

10. This brief description of Walker's procedures draws on a letter to me from Trevor Schoonmaker, former Assistant Director, Brent Sikkema Gallery, March 14, 2000.

11. J. C. Lavater, *Essays on Physiognomy*, as quoted in Victor I. Stoichita, *A Short History of the Shadow* (London: Reaktion Books, 1997), 157.

12. For basic information and further bibliography on the silhouette, see the entry by Garry Apgar, *Grove Dictionary of Art*—Online, Jane Turner, ed. (Basingstoke: Macmillan, 1998), s.v. "silhouette." See also Stoichita, *Short History*, especially chap. 5. Sarah Evans has drawn my attention to the recent revival of silhouette portraits in the society practice of Elliott Pickett.

13. The silhouette might usefully be thought of as sharing a mythical origin with drawing—in particular, with the tale of Dibutades, daughter of the potter, who traces with a stylus the outline of her lover's shadow on the wall. Jacques Derrida is at pains to insist that even such an immediate effect as a shadow is at a double remove from the body that makes it: "Detached from the present of perception, fallen from the thing itself—which is thus divided—a shadow is a simultaneous memory and Butades' stick . . . goes back and forth between love and drawing" (*Memoirs of the Blind: The Self-Portrait and Other Ruins*, trans. Pascale-Anne Brault and Michael Naas [Chicago: University of Chicago Press, 1993], 51).

14. See Edmund Burke, *A Philosophical Enquiry into the Origin of Our Ideas of the Sublime and the Beautiful*, ed. Adam Phillips (Oxford: Oxford University Press, 1998), 113.

15. See Ernst H. Gombrich, "On Physiognomic Perception," in *Meditations on a Hobby Horse and Other Essays on the Theory of Art* (London: Phaidon Press, 1963), 45–55. On human visual tendency and capacity to seek visual pattern and order, see idem, *The Sense of Order: A Study in the Psychology of Decorative Art*, 2nd ed. (Ithaca, NY: Cornell University Press, 1979).

16. For a range of studies on Lavater and physiognomics, see Ellis Shookman, ed., *The Faces of Physiognomy: Interdisciplinary Approaches to Johann Caspar Lavater* (Columbia, SC: Camden House, 1993); note in particular the essay by Judith Wechsler, "Lavater, Stereotype, and Prejudice," 104–125. The artist Matthew Buckingham has produced an exhibition and book, both titled *Subcutaneous* (Murray Guy Gallery, New York, October–November 2001; volume published by Shark Books and Murray Guy, 2001), on the theme of the contentious relationship between J. C. Lavater and Georg Christoph Lichtenberg.

17. *The Random House Dictionary of the English Language*, unabridged ed. (1967), s.v. "darken."

18. On the practice of corking up, not least as practiced by black performers, see Lott, *Love and Theft*, 26ff. and passim. Rogin provides a history of "burnt cork" that extends from its origins, but more profoundly aims to situate minstrelsy on the field of power; see *Blackface, White Noise*, 19–44.

19. Michael Rogin, review of *Juneteenth*, by Ralph Ellison, *London Review of Books*, March 2, 2000, 12–15.

20. There are also works that, like Walker's art, insist on the relevance and mutual dependency of black and white, even while adopting very different means to do so. The range includes the conceptualism of Joseph Kosuth, whose 1966 *White and Black* (from the Art as Idea as Idea series) uses an identical format—a square photostat panel with

white letters on a black ground—to render the two opposing terms, as well as the figuration of Edward Kienholz, whose *It Takes Two to Integrate, Cha Cha Cha* (1961) opposes two black and white baby dolls, each of which is imprinted with a diamond design in the opposite hue. The effect conjures tire tracks, or perhaps the weave of a chain link fence around a schoolyard, against which it is easy to imagine both figures pressing.

21. Byron Kim, as quoted in Thelma Golden, "What's White . . . ?," in *1993 Biennial Exhibition*, by Elisabeth Sussman et al. (New York: Whitney Museum of American Art, in association with Harry N. Abrams, 1993), 28. I am also grateful for a telephone conversation with Kim in March 2000, which greatly helped to clarify my sense of his work's procedures and aims.

22. The use of alphabetical schemes was a mainstay of 1960s conceptualism, beginning with Robert Morris's *Card File* (1962), not least for the ways such a system could be used to expose the role of chance.

23. [Editor's note: The author did not imply that the "black" paintings in *Black and White* all share the exact same hue; she was aware that they were all subtly different. Rather, she sought to underscore the tension between the verbal component of the painting ("Black and White") and the visual. The irony of the work lies in the fact that "Black" comprehends an array of subtle chromatic variations, while "White" encompasses a range of easily differentiated hues.]

24. This question was fruitfully raised for me by Caroline Arscott, in response to an earlier version of this essay presented in a session of the Association of Art Historians, Edinburgh, April 2000. I am grateful to Briony Fer and Tamar Garb for the invitation to speak on that occasion.

25. These four quotes are from Fanon, Frantz Fanon, *Black Skin, White Masks*, trans. C. L. Markmann (New York: Grove Press, 1967; reprint, with an introduction by Homi K. Bhabha, London: Pluto, 1986), 11, 109, 109, and 113, respectively.

26. Homi K. Bhabha, introduction to Fanon, *Black Skin, White Masks*, xi, ix. I have also found helpful Bhabha's "Interrogating Identity: Frantz Fanon and the Postcolonial Prerogative," in *The Location of Culture* (London: Routledge, 1994), 40–65; Diana Fuss, "Interior Colonies: Frantz Fanon and the Politics of Identification," *Diacritics* 24, nos. 2–3 (1994): 20–43; and Gwen Bergner, "Who Is That Masked Woman? or, The Role of Gender in Fanon's *Black Skin, White Masks*," *PMLA* 110, no. 1 (1995): 75–88. Bergner has criticized Bhabha for minimizing, even while acknowledging, the problems of Fanon's treatment of gender ("Who Is That Masked Woman?," 84).

27. Fanon, *Black Skin, White Masks*, 194; my discussion here relies on the approach taken by Fuss, "Interior Colonies."

28. Fanon, *Black Skin, White Masks*, 229, 229, 230, and 226.

29. James Hannaham, "Pea, Ball, Bounce: Interview with Kara Walker," *Interview* 28, no. 11 (November 1998): 119.

30. Fanon, *Black Skin, White Masks*, 281.

31. My formulation relies on, and paraphrases, Bhabha's analysis of Fanon's response to the "loaded question [of] where cultural alienation bears down on the ambivalence of psychic identification" (Introduction, xi). To cite the key passage, which continues (xii) following Bhabha's own citation of Fanon's description of his alienation under the white man's gaze: "From within the metaphor of vision complicit with a Western metaphysic of Man emerges the displacement of the colonial relation. The Black

presence ruins the representative narrative of Western personhood: its past tethered to treacherous stereotypes of primitivism and degeneracy will not produce a history of civil progress, a space for the *Socius*; its present, dismembered and dislocated, will not contain the image of identity that is questioned in the dialectic of mind/body and resolved in the epistemology of 'appearance and reality.' The White man's eyes break up the Black man's body and in that act of epistemic violence its own frame of reference is transgressed, its field of vision disturbed."

32. Walker declared her interest in the history of the panorama as mass entertainment in the printed text and handout, prepared by then-curator Lawrence Rinder, which accompanied the CCAC show.

33. Hannaham, "Pea, Ball, Bounce," 116.

Maladies of Power: A Kara Walker Lexicon

Yasmil Raymond

The following lexicon identifies a number of key elements—character types, objects, bodily fluids, environments, and events—that appear repeatedly or occasionally in Kara Walker's art and, when considered together, illuminate certain allegorical meanings, philosophical associations, and visual references between and beyond the works. The contradictions inherent in positions of power and acts of brutality are the underlying subject in this glossary of visual symbols and, I would argue, in Walker's imagery as a whole. Put simply, the artist exposes the impossibility of moral absolutes within the dynamics of domination, a predicament that applies as well to art that deals with such subject matter. In his study on the visual representation of slavery, Marcus Wood argues that "art which describes or responds to trauma and mass murder always embodies paradox." He adds, "How can aesthetic criteria be applied to describe the torture and mass destruction of our own kind? How is it possible to make something beautiful out of, and to perceive beauty within, something which has contaminated human values to such a degree as to be beyond the assumed idealizations of truth and art, beyond the known facts and beyond the manipulations of rhetoric?"[1] Human slavery, the cruelest of capitalist systems, has yet to be, and may well never be, accurately described either verbally or visually. It is this impossibility, however, that has served as the impetus for Walker's work over the past decade.

Appropriating preconceived ideas about the antebellum South, she has given visual form to the unimaginable acts, unspoken testimonies, and unanswered questions from that period in American history that continue to resonate today. As the artist has explained,

> I don't know how much I believe in redemptive stories, even though people want them and strive for them. They're satisfied with stories of triumph over evil, but then triumph is a dead end. Triumph never sits still. Life goes on. People forget and make mistakes. Heroes are not completely pure, and villains aren't purely evil. I'm interested in the continuity of conflict, the creation of racist narratives, or nationalist narratives, or whatever narratives people use to construct a group identity and to keep themselves whole—such activity has a darker side to it, since it allows people to lash out at whoever's not in the group. That's a constant thread that flummoxes me.[2]

This lexicon of symptoms, tools, weapons, and ordeals attempts to articulate this conception of the amorphous nature of power and of morality, which drives Walker's efforts to visualize the histories of injustice that plague our past and continue to feed our present conscience.

Hoop Skirts

Among the best-known portrayals of the antebellum South are Margaret Mitchell's 1936 novel *Gone with the Wind* and its equally popular 1939 film adaptation. Set in 1861, Mitchell's mythologized depiction of the period as a genteel and benevolent agrarian society permanently fixed in the American psyche a distorted account of the American South. The broad cultural influence, popularity, and sheer longevity of both the novel and the film give evidence to a continuation on some level of white-supremacist values in popular culture and an implicit justification, long after manumission, of slavery and segregation.

Depictions of the horrors of slavery and plantation life—slave hunts, mutilation, rape, and murder—became, starting in the late eighteenth century, the focus of slave narratives and abolitionist campaigns but rarely were the subject of literature and visual art.[3] During the first half of the nineteenth century, paintings occasionally centered on scenes of life in the South, as in Eastman Johnson's *Old Kentucky Home—Life in*

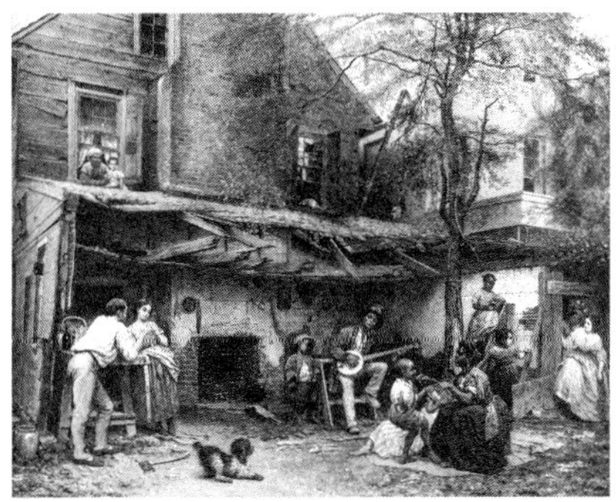

Eastman Johnson, *Old Kentucky Home—Life in the South (Negro Life at the South)*, 1859. Oil on canvas. 36 × 45.5 inches (91.4 × 114.9 cm). The Robert L. Stuart Collection, the gift of his widow Mrs. Mary Stuart, New-York Historical Society, S-225. Photo credit: Glenn Castellano/ New-York Historical Society.

the South (Negro Life at the South). Made before the outbreak of the Civil War, it perpetuated the myth of a harmonious rural life while disguising the inhumane treatment endured by slaves—some four million of them in the United States alone.[4]

In 1994, Walker exhibited her first cut-paper silhouette mural, *Gone, An Historical Romance of a Civil War as It Occurred between the Dusky Thighs of One Young Negress and Her Heart*, a tableau some 50 feet long and 13 feet high that was unprecedented in form, scale, and subject matter.[5] The figures, slightly larger than life-size, were first drawn with white chalk on black paper and then cut with an X-ACTO knife and adhered to the wall to create a panoramic mural reminiscent in scale to the *tableaux vivants* and cycloramas that emerged in the late eighteenth and early nineteenth centuries. Flanking the pastoral scene are two large trees covered in Spanish moss that evoke the warmer climate of the American South. A total of thirteen figures, four objects (a sword, a bust, a pumpkin, and a broom), and one dead duck are rendered in the reductive fashion of caricatures and with the idealized, well-proportioned, and eternally youthful features of fairy-tale illustrations. The full moon above concedes the clandestine nature of the events unfolding in front of our eyes: in the left foreground, a female figure wearing an overflowing hoop skirt leans forward to kiss her lover while revealing the legs of someone else, a young female lover, hiding beneath her garment.

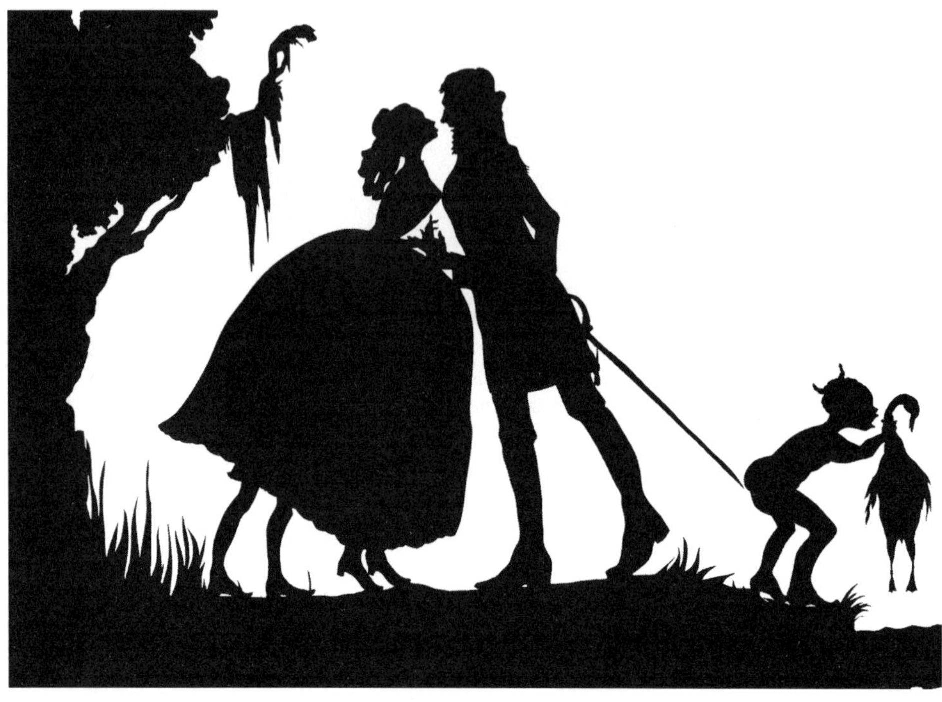

Kara Walker, detail from *Gone, An Historical Romance of a Civil War as It Occurred between the Dusky Thighs of One Young Negress and Her Heart*, 1994. Cut paper on wall, 156 × 600 inches (396.2 × 1524 cm). Artwork © Kara Walker, courtesy of Sikkema Jenkins & Co., New York; Sprüth Magers, Berlin.

The hoop skirt, a symbol of morality and the quintessential fashion statement of southern women before the Civil War, is an ever-present motif in Walker's imagery; both mistresses and slave women don such garments not to protect their virtue but to disguise their own repressed desires. In *Gone*, the breaching of the hoop skirt unleashes a series of lustful events, including a scene in which a toddler girl sucks the penis of a boy her junior. Above, in the sky, a naked boy rises up with the help of his balloon-like penis while below, a young black woman lifts her leg to give birth to twins (see also the section below on "Birth").

The mural's scale insists that the viewer participate in the experience by walking across the periphery of the landscape as if spying on the events taking place. Despite the surrealism of the actions, the veracity of the figures—which exhibit human proportions and traits—incites us, whether consciously or unconsciously, into an unexpected interaction. We are drawn into role-playing and time travel in a manner that recalls a passage from Octavia E. Butler's 1979 novel *Kindred*. The modern-day protagonist and narrator, Dana, has been suddenly thrown back in time to come to the aid of her white ancestor Rufus, now a young boy; when she asks him what year it is, he replies:

> "It's . . . eighteen fifteen."
> "When?"
> "Eighteen fifteen."
> I sat still, breathed deeply, calming myself, believing him. I did believe him. I wasn't even as surprised as I should have been. I had already accepted the fact that I had moved through time. Now I knew I was farther from home than I had thought. And now I knew why Rufus's father used his whip on "niggers" as well as horses.
> I looked up and saw that the boy had left his chair and come closer to me.
> "What's the matter with you?" he demanded. "You keep acting sick."
> "It's nothing, Rufe. I'm all right." No, I was sick. What was I going to do? Why hadn't I gone home? This could turn out to be such a deadly place for me if I had to stay in it much longer.
> "Is this a plantation?" I asked.
> "The Weylin plantation. My daddy's Tom Weylin."[6]

The antebellum plantation in this first experiment of Walker's and in subsequent depictions constitutes not only a historical and geographical reference but also a psychological terrain in which the cast shadows of masters and slaves embody the repressed prejudices, desires, and obsessions that the contemporary American collective consciousness refuses to acknowledge, visualize, and reconcile. Like Dana, viewers of Walker's work are metaphorically and emotionally transported to the plantation of their own racial and gender prejudices, superiority and inferiority complexes, and anxieties and fetishes. By its very nature, the identity exorcism present in Walker's imagery is a paradox in that its potential is dependent solely on viewers' consciousness of their own body, race, and ancestry while at the same time engaging a third-person consciousness that reinforces Frantz Fanon's verdict, "It is the racist who creates his inferior."[7]

Boots and Shoes

Like clothing, footwear carries symbolic potency and poetry in Walker's imagery, helping to expose complex connections and reveal hidden plots and desires. From the sturdy knee-high boots of the plantation masters to the pointed-toe ankle boots of the mistresses, shoes appear selectively on the feet of Walker's characters, primarily to differentiate nonslaves from slaves. But in instances when slaves are shown wearing shoes, Walker interrogates not only the status that such articles granted the wearer but also the symbolism they impart about the power dynamics between masters and slaves.

In the 1995 mural *Look Away! Look Away! Look Away!*, a slave child, identified by her ripped skirt, wears an oversize male boot on her right foot. The left counterpart can be found on the foot of a naked toddler in the mural *The End of Uncle Tom and the Grand Allegorical Tableau of Eva in Heaven*, also from 1995. Apart from the master's children, the rest of the figures in both murals are depicted without shoes. This deliberate absence problematizes the nature of the object and assigns it a specific symbolic value and desire. A child wearing oversize shoes as if "dressing up" suggests an affectionate relationship with the owner of the footwear. In this sense, if a slave child is wearing the boots of the master, the implication is that the child has access to the residence and may in fact be the offspring of the master and a domestic slave. Such a relationship did not necessarily correspond to a privileged position vis-à-vis the field slaves, but it did inevitably afford greater accessibility to material possessions. As Orlando Patterson contests in his analysis of the conditions of slavery, "Proximity to the master also carried enormous risks and disadvantages. The slave was under the constant supervision of the master and therefore subjected to greater and more capricious punishment and humiliation than those housed elsewhere."[8] Walker knows that it is unlikely that slave children were permitted to wear the master's shoes, and so the unsettling question remains: How did they get their hands on these objects?

In these two early murals, the children share the trophies of their master's affection while crippling the boots' potential use value. This

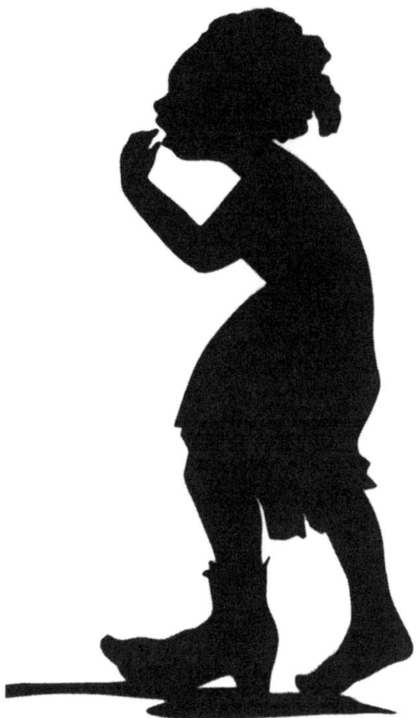

Kara Walker, detail from *Look Away! Look Away! Look Away!*, 1995. Cut paper on wall and adhesive on wall. 156 × 420 inches (396.2 × 1066.8 cm). Artwork © Kara Walker, courtesy of Sikkema Jenkins & Co., New York; Sprüth Magers, Berlin.

splitting of the object's functionality renders each individual boot an icon of love, of accessibility to the master's property and "heart," granting the boots sentimental value and thus instilling the scene with an underlying fear of what would happen if these objects were lost. Furthermore, by being oversize—of having room to "grow into"—the shoes themselves propose the terrifying fate that awaits the children, who will eventually grow up and be put to work or sold and, in the case of the girls, most likely be raped. This horrendous scenario is articulated in the gasping gesture of one young girl in *Look Away! Look Away! Look Away!* who holds her hand close to her mouth as she witnesses another slave girl nearby accepting a gift from an adult male figure who is naked from the waist down. From his beard and pince-nez, we take him to be the master.

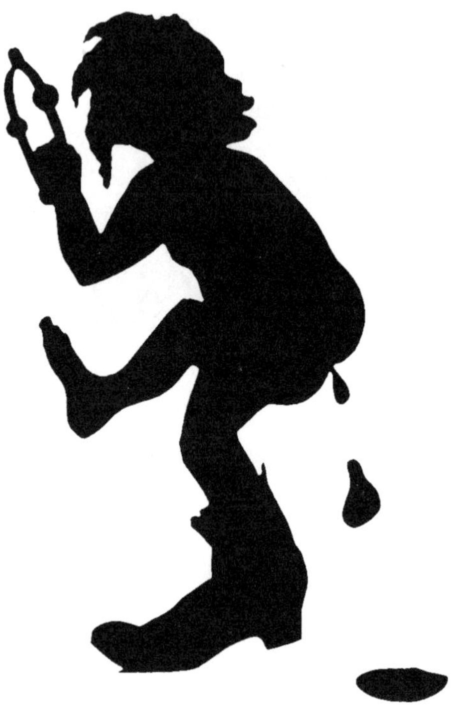

Kara Walkerd, detail from *The End of Uncle Tom and the Grand Allegorical Tableau of Eva in Heaven*, 1995. Wall installation. 156 × 420 inches (396.2 × 1066.8 cm). Artwork © Kara Walker, courtesy of Sikkema Jenkins & Co., New York; Sprüth Magers, Berlin.

In 1996, the image of a child wearing a pair of oversize female ankle boots appeared in the mural *African't*. The mural, which spans some 60 feet, depicts various scenes of torture and subversion as a bare-chested girl wearing a banana-leaf skirt tries to set a palm tree on fire. The young slave girl, identified by the iron piece around her neck, approaches the grass at the foot of the tree with an air of defiance and a sense of purpose that contrast with the innocence and imbedded symbolism of children playing dress-up in the earlier examples. Furthermore, here the boots—a complete pair, even if slightly oversize— have real use value as protective covering for the feet and for running away from terror. They stand as a symbol of mobility and insubordina- tion. Still, the correspondence between function and desire, sign and

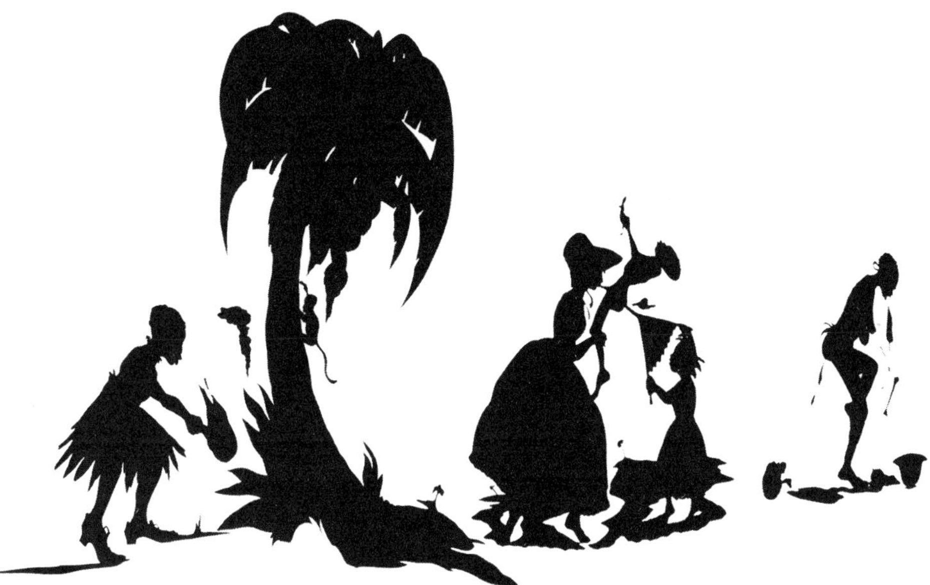

Kara Walker, detail from *African't*, 1996. Cut paper and adhesive on wall. 144 × 792 inches (365.8 × 2011.7 cm). Artwork © Kara Walker, courtesy of Sikkema Jenkins & Co., New York; Sprüth Magers, Berlin.

sentiment, introduces yet another level of dependency, which in turn transforms the boots into a different kind of fetish, one that embodies the promise of freedom.

This correlation between shoes and autonomy/mobility becomes more apparent in the 1997 mural *Slavery! Slavery! Presenting a GRAND and LIFELIKE Panoramic Journey into Picturesque Southern Slavery or "Life at 'Ol' Virginny's Hole' (sketches from Plantation Life)" See the Peculiar Institution as never before! All cut from black paper by the able hand of Kara Elizabeth Walker, an Emancipated Negress and leader in her Cause.* Consisting of more than twenty figures rendered slightly larger than life-size, this monumental piece, measuring 12 × 85 feet, is installed in a circular room that recalls historical cycloramas. The title is infused with Walker's sense of irony, and the imagery explicitly quotes scenes from Johnson's pastoral painting *Old Kentucky Home* (p. 83). An example of antebellum genre painting, *Old Kentucky Home* is an ambiguous depiction of idleness and interracial interactions in which a white mistress enters the yard of the slave quarters and finds a slave man playing the banjo while a slave child dances with his mother. In Walker's version, the picturesque scene of afternoon leisure is rendered as a carnivalesque nightscape in which unsettling events take place under a crescent moon. The composition is divided into three vignettes: around the fountain, under the moon, and outside the slave quarters. In the latter, the majority of the adult slaves are depicted in motion—some are walking, others dancing—and all of them, with the exception of one, are wearing shoes that, even in their various states of wear and tear, enable mobility and hence the possibility of escape (see p. 215). Starting at the right, a male slave wearing a pair of torn old ankle boots bends down cautiously to hide from someone. Nearby, a quartet of figures dances to the rhythm of a drum while a decapitated boy, holding tightly with both hands the severed head of a chicken, strides along in oversize pointed-toe shoes. Ahead of him, an older man prepares his family to escape by hiding the children inside a wagon filled with hay. Holding a pitchfork, he seems to have pitched the boy who flies above, dropping his makeshift bag. Leading the procession is a young woman eating an apple and carrying an infant strapped to her back. Though her path is blocked by a pile of feces, her ankle boots will allow her to trudge through it toward an uncertain destiny.

In Walker's art, shoes are encoded with property issues. Their absence or presence, especially on the feet of slave figures, not only provides an immediate visual cue as to a character's gender and race but also introduces allegorical elements to the compositions. In her fantastical revisioning of power relationships and ownership, material possessions help to set the terms of a character's personality, role, and destiny. In her examination of the unending network of inhumane tortures that defined the plantation slavery system in the South, Walker relies on specific objects—hoop skirts, footwear, utensils, brooms, weapons, cotton bolls—to signify power dynamics within ethical, sexual, and fetishistic scenarios.

Knives, Razor Blades, and Ropes

Mutilations, murders, and suicides are common occurrences in Walker's fantasized version of the antebellum South, where masters, mistresses, and slaves alike inflict their deepest internal conflicts upon one another. Western art history is replete with images of torture and death, from the crucifixion of Christ and the martyrdom of the saints to the brutalities of war. One memorable example is the gory *Judith Slaying Holofernes* by the Baroque painter Artemisia Gentileschi. The disparity of scale between the bodies emphasizes the brute violence of the act: while Judith's accomplice uses both arms to push down on Holofernes's muscular body, the Hebrew heroine presses his head to the side and slices his neck with the heavy sword in her right hand. The slaying Judith is incarnate in the body of a child slave in Walker's 2000 light installation *Mistress Demanded a Swift and Dramatic Empathetic Reaction Which We Obliged Her.*[9] Using both hands to wield a machete as big as she is, her body arched to gather strength and her head tilted slightly to avoid looking, the petite girl pierces the abdomen of the mistress. Behind the small heroine an adult male slave with his hands and feet chained and wearing a punishment collar looks on, stunned by the action unfolding before his eyes.[10] The figures are rendered in black cut-paper silhouettes, and the blue and purple light cast by the overhead projector frames the scene, which takes place outdoors at night, under an oversize tree dripping with Spanish moss. The lighting lends an element of secrecy and danger to the setting.

When Walker depicts children as executioners, she speaks to the manner in which their unspoiled frankness absolves them from maliciousness. In this way, their acts of murder take on the spontaneity of an accident or the inevitability of self-defense. In *Look Away! Look Away! Look Away!* the master's young daughter slices off her left hand with a butter knife. This violent act of self-mutilation is muted by the calm demeanor of the child and the absence of blood spills from the scene. In a second mural, *The Battle of Atlanta: Being the Narrative of a Negress in the Flames of Desire—A Reconstruction*, also from 1995, a naked slave child runs holding an amputated hand while behind her an older girl, perhaps her sister, follows with the dismembered leg of the master, signified by the knee-high boot attached to it (see p. 19).[11] Adding to the horror of the image is the evocation of serenity and the ease with which they hold onto the mutilated limbs, as if they were fresh-picked flowers. In both instances, we are inclined to believe that these are either acts of self-preservation or delirious visions of innocent children "playing" revolt.

Violence, which under slavery was the master's mechanism to impose total control over the slaves, is meticulously depicted in Walker's

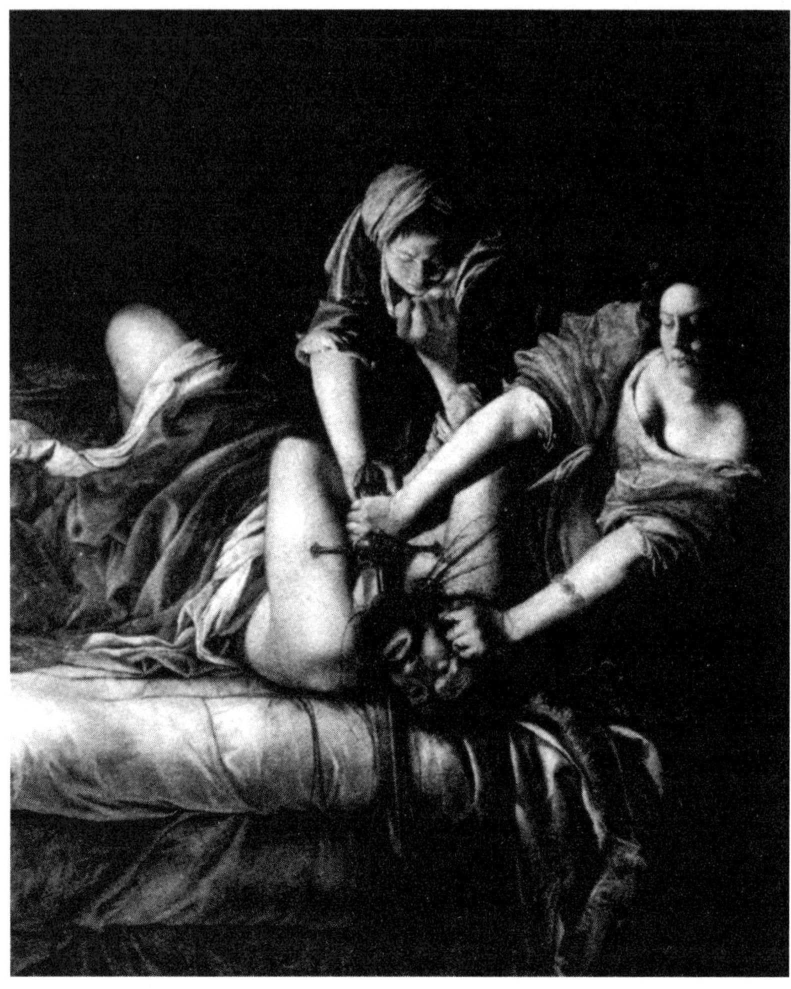

Artemisia Gentileschi, *Judith Slaying Holofernes*, ca. 1620. Oil on canvas. 6 feet 6 inches × 5 feet 4 inches (2 × 1.6 m). Collection Uffizi Gallery, Florence.

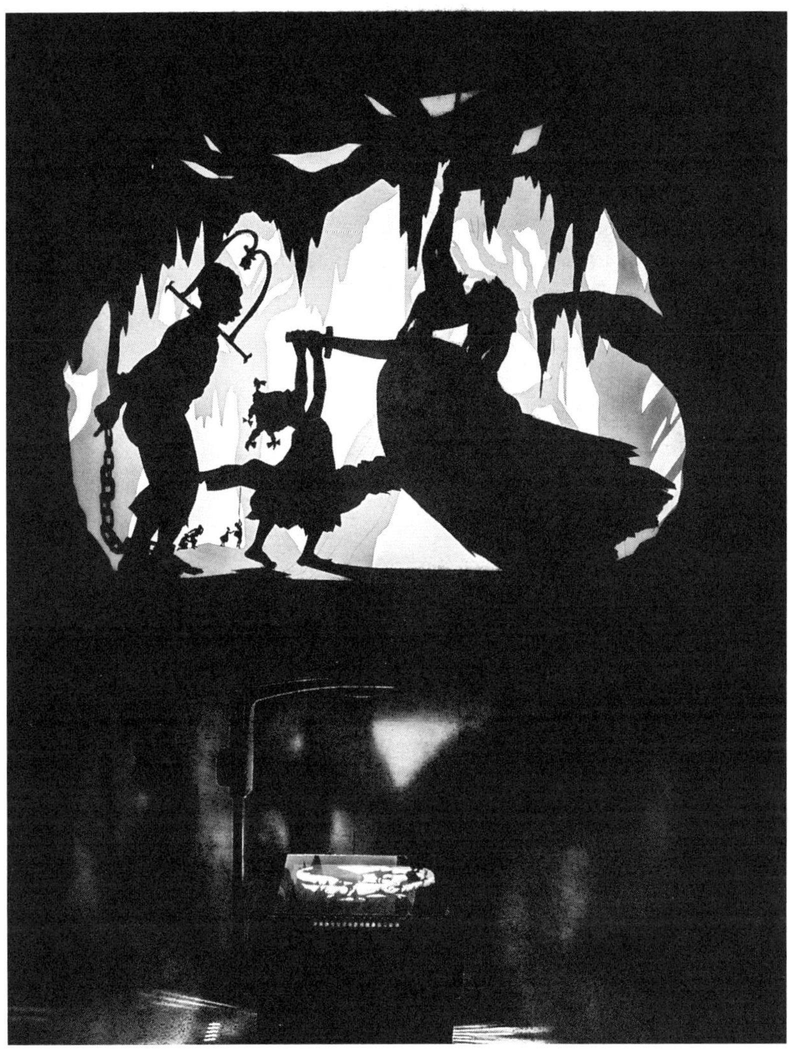

Kara Walker, *Mistress Demanded a Swift and Dramatic Empathetic Reaction Which We Obliged Her*, 2000. Cut paper and projection on wall. 114 × 204 × 300 inches (289.5 × 518 × 762 cm). Artwork © Kara Walker, courtesy of Sikkema Jenkins & Co., New York; Sprüth Magers, Berlin.

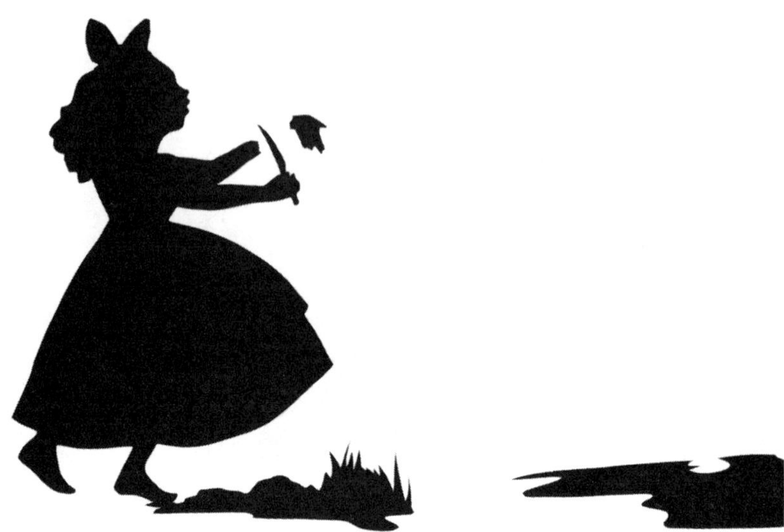

Kara Walker, detail from *Look Away! Look Away! Look Away!*, 1995. Cut paper on wall. 13 × 45 feet (4 × 13.7 m).

work. Her visual strategy, which she has previously defined as "two parts research and one part paranoid hysteria,"[12] consists primarily in visualizing a tragicomedy of plantation slavery that demystifies the history of the Old South and plays out with sardonic humor an imaginary counteraction. Violence and murder are often accompanied in her work by extreme absurdity, whereby shocking juxtapositions of random and premeditated actions lead to vicious results. In *The End of Uncle Tom and the Grand Allegorical Tableau of Eva in Heaven*, the young Eva is depicted swinging an oversize axe with the blade toward her own head while nearby an obese male figure with a peg leg balances himself with the help of his sword as he rapes a young slave girl and the tip of his blade pierces the chest of a slave child on the ground. Walker establishes her characters as potential assassins who are infected with what Michel Foucault called "the disease of power," and she is eager to show us what happens when an object of torture is applied to a human being.[13] This model of representation based on dominance and human bestiality is, above all, a caricature of power.

The objectification of power is the rhetorical position informing all of Walker's characters as the plantation master and the slave are equally capable of inflicting corporal violence on the other. Suicide in these scenarios is the slave's ultimate revenge. A slave committing suicide was viewed as an assault on the master's property, and those who attempted it but did not succeed were severely punished. In Walker's few renderings of slaves taking their own lives, the act is often presented as a fable of martyrdom, as in two single-image silhouettes, *Cut* and *Burn*, both from 1998. In each instance, the female victim resorts to extreme measures, the first by cutting her wrists with a razor blade and the second by setting her dress on fire. However, their gestures are defiant in tone and symbolism. In *Cut*, a slave woman, having just cut off both her hands, jumps in the air and swings her arms back over her head. Rather than depicting her as a collapsed victim awaiting her death, Walker directs our attention to the woman's shameless gesture of bliss and defiance, which suggests that her suicide stands as an act of transgression and empowerment.[14]

In *Burn*, a prepubescent girl tosses to the ground the tin can that held the starter fluid. Her eyes are closed and she holds her arms out in a wide-open gesture as large flames rise up around her, transforming her skirt into a burning bush. To her left we see a large cloud of smoke, which along one side outlines the profile of a woman, a Latin cross, and a cemetery filled with obelisks and tombstones. What is initially striking about this piece is the stoicism of the young woman who, in her determination not to endure a life of captivity, is compelled to bear one final pain. The youthful promise of the girl's body is at odds with her disheartened detachment from life and affirms her absolute rebellion against those who hold power over her body and life. Both *Cut* and *Burn* resonate with a passage in Butler's novel *Kindred* in which the suicide of the slave girl Alice articulates this question of autonomy for the protagonist, Dana, who has returned, for one last time, to the Weylin plantation:

> [Rufus] stopped at the barn door and pushed me through it. He didn't follow me in.
>
> I looked around, seeing very little at first as my eyes became accustomed to the dimmer light. I turned to the place where I had been strung up and whipped—and jumped back in surprise when I saw that someone was hanging there. Hanging by the neck. A woman.

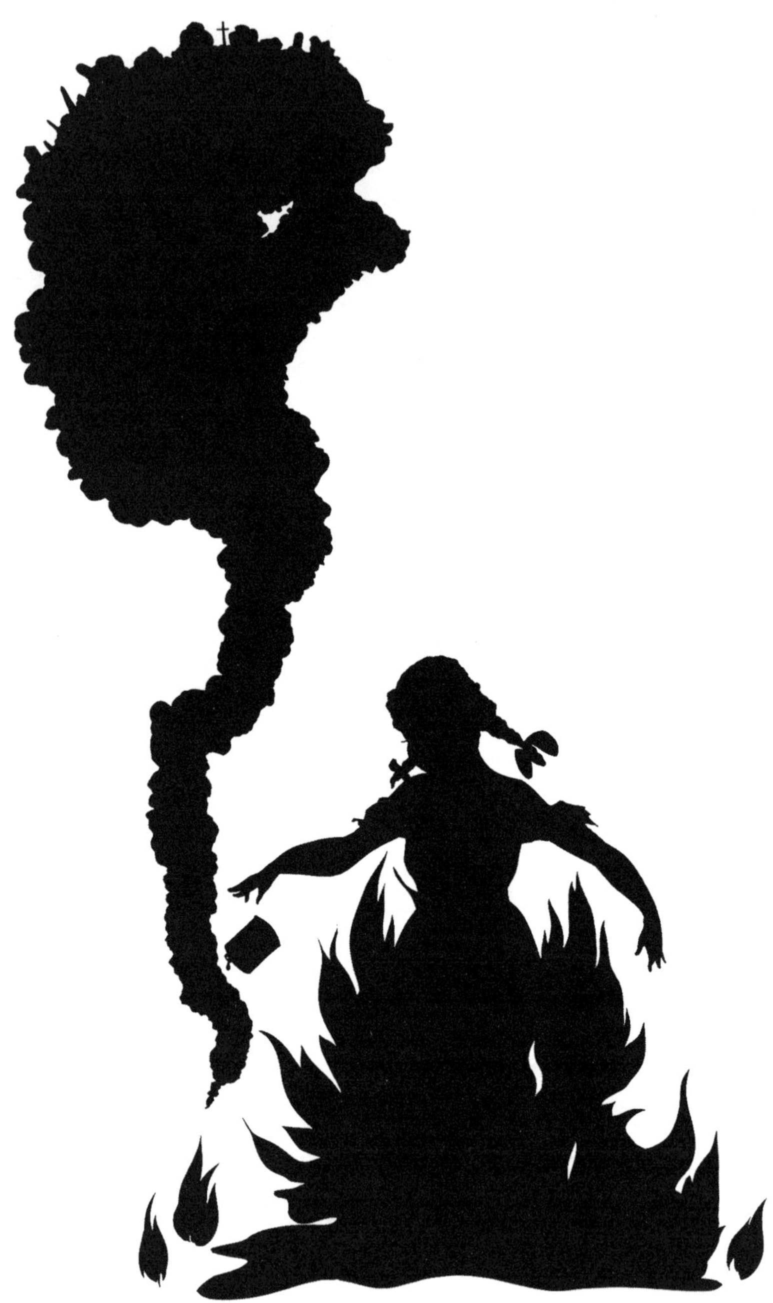

Kara Walker, *Burn*, 1998. Cut paper and adhesive on wall. 92 × 48 inches (233.7 × 121.9 cm). Artwork © Kara Walker, courtesy of Sikkema Jenkins & Co., New York; Sprüth Magers, Berlin.

Alice.

I stared at her not believing, not wanting to believe. . . . I touched her and her flesh was cold and hard. The dead gray face was ugly in death as it had never been in life. The mouth was open. The eyes were open and staring. Her head was bare and her hair loose and short like mine. She had never liked to tie it up the way other women did. It was one of the things that had made us look even more alike—the only two consistently bareheaded women on the place. Her dress was dark red and her apron clean and white. She wore shoes that Rufus had had made specifically for her, not the rough heavy shoes or boots other slaves wore. It was as though she had dressed up and combed her hair and then . . .

I wanted her down.[15]

Alice and the suicides in Walker's silhouettes share an understanding of the violent and porous nature of power dynamics. In both cases, there is a refusal of ethics in their calculated acts of rebellion, as the ownership of their death is their main concern. Walker's pantomimes have nothing to do with historical guilt or innocence; there is no doubt about whose hand held the whip. The concern is rather with the living effects of the trauma of slavery and how to materialize, characterize, and visualize this abstract condition, which Fanon poignantly described in the following paradox: "The disaster of the man of color lies in the fact that he was enslaved. The disaster and the inhumanity of the white man lie in the fact that somewhere he has killed man."[16]

Water

Images of ships, tidal waves, washtubs, and sea monsters in Walker's work reference the transatlantic encounters between Europeans and Africans and the traumatic diaspora that is estimated to have brought nine to twelve million Africans to North and South America and the Caribbean to work as slaves.[17] In Freudian theory, the appearance of water imagery in dreams signifies birth, and Walker has described the cleansing property of water in relation to her work (see the section below on "Birth"); but more often than not, her scenes of flowing water are infused with feelings of loss, fragmentation, and mystery. The sea and watery creatures have populated her work since 1994, when she

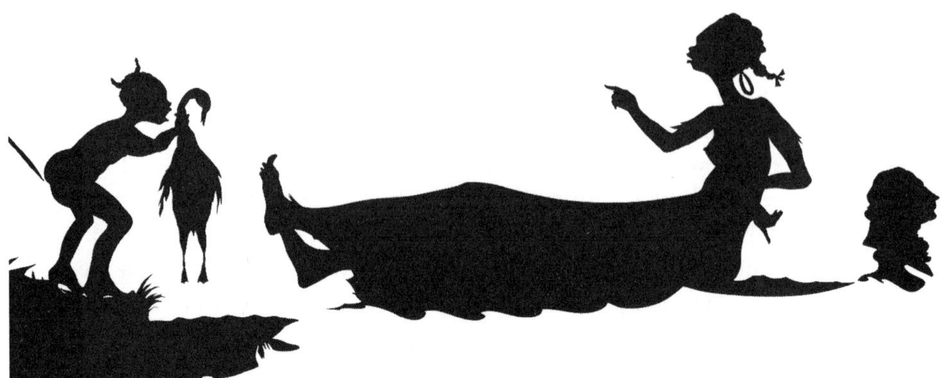

Kara Walker, detail from *Gone, An Historical Romance of a Civil War as It Occurred between the Dusky Thighs of One Young Negress and Her Heart*, 1994. Cut paper on wall. 156 × 420 inches (396.2 × 1066.8 cm). Artwork © Kara Walker, courtesy of Sikkema Jenkins & Co., New York; Sprüth Magers, Berlin.

created *Gone, An Historical Romance of a Civil War as It Occurred between the Dusky Thighs of One Young Negress and Her Heart*, which includes the image of a ghostly half-woman, half-boat figure drifting across a body of water, literally embodying the arduous journey of Middle Passage.

The association between the brutal violence of the transatlantic slave trade and the dangers of deep waters is generated in Walker's depiction of the ocean as a paradigm of contested ideas about origin and racial authenticity. Departing from the "ethnic absolutism that currently dominates black political culture," sociologist Paul Gilroy, in his influential work on the Atlantic slave trade, daringly considers the history of the slave routes as a network of reciprocal influences and hybridization among Europe, Africa, and the Americas.[18] Questioning the very notion of racial purity, Gilroy focuses on the routes of the Middle Passage, European colonial expeditions, and the circulation of people, before and after slavery, within this triangular network to propose a history of transcontinental entanglement of ideas and cultures that "provides a different sense of where modernity might itself be thought to begin in the constitutive relationships with outsiders that both found and temper a self-conscious sense of western civilization."[19] Walker charts the implications of this historic encounter in her renderings of water, which takes on numerous forms: a turbulent and traumatic path, a sentimental shore of romantic departures, an underwater cemetery filled with ancestors, or the yearning nectar of thirsty beings unsure of their own needs and desires.

Endless Conundrum, an African Anonymous Adventuress, made in 2001, delineates the concept of the Atlantic Ocean as a fluid force guiding this exchange of cultural codes, influences, and appropriations between the European trespassers and the indigenous Africans. At the bottom of the tableau, a naked toddler stands in a washtub, restrained by a ball and chain. Her head is lowered in sadness and perhaps resignation, and the hopelessness of the girl's physical bondage is amplified by her lack of arms. In the upper right, a coastal scene shows a reclining female figure on the shore with her arm stretched out, finger pointing at her colonial admirer, who seems to be disappearing into the sea. Different from her treatment of the female bodies of her antebellum characters, Walker's African counterparts are anatomically disproportionate and bear the traits, including cone-shaped heads and elongated faces, of African masks. This objectification of their bodies undoubtedly is meant to evoke the types of traditional African ceremonial objects that were sold widely in Europe in the early twentieth century as "fetishes" from the colonies and subsequently ended up in the glass vitrines of museum displays, stripped of their social and cultural context. The ideological degradation of African forms and subject matter was further pathologized in the studios of modernist artists such as Brancusi, Matisse, and Picasso, who imitated the forms of these artifacts and mythologized them for embodying primal urges and power, especially in the realm of sexuality.

In Walker's allusions to water, the Atlantic Ocean is the original sacrificial site where her characters engage in psychological and physical abuse in order to exorcize the horrors of the contaminated waters that feed the collective ancestry of Europeans, Africans, and Americans. The relationship between water and thirst as both a bodily need and a historical drive is exemplified in the central vignette of *Grub for Sharks: A Concession to the Negro Populace*, made in 2004, which shows a naked woman drinking water that drips from a fantasy-induced cloud. With knees bent and head titled back, the figure reaches with caution toward a single drop of water melting from a group of nebulous forms above her head, where a coastal scene of a village floats in the

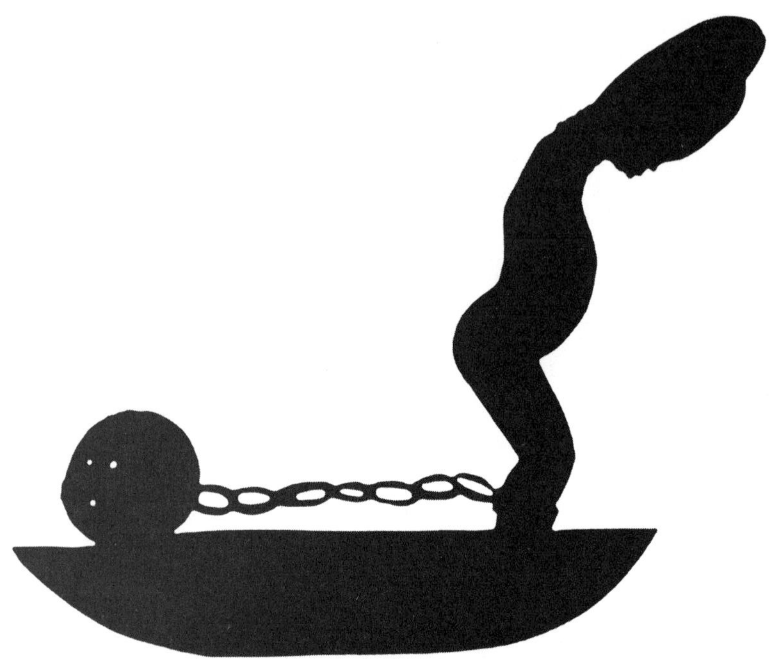

Kara Walker, detail from *Endless Conundrum, An African Anonymous Adventuress*, 2001. Cut paper and adhesive on wall. Includes original exhibition set, template, and artist certificate. 191 × 453 inches (485.1 × 1150.6 cm). Artwork © Kara Walker, courtesy of Sikkema Jenkins & Co., New York; Sprüth Magers, Berlin.

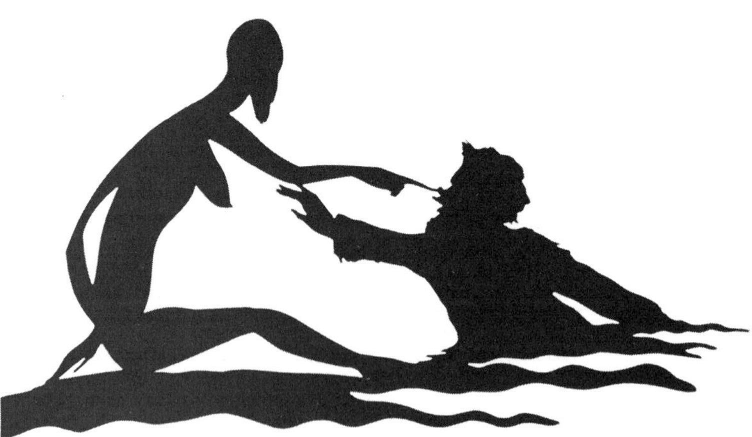

Kara Walker, detail from *Endless Conundrum, An African Anonymous Adventuress*, 2001. Cut paper and adhesive on wall. Includes original exhibition set, template, and artist certificate. 191 × 453 inches (485.1 × 1150.6 cm.) Artwork © Kara Walker, courtesy of Sikkema Jenkins & Co., New York; Sprüth Magers, Berlin.

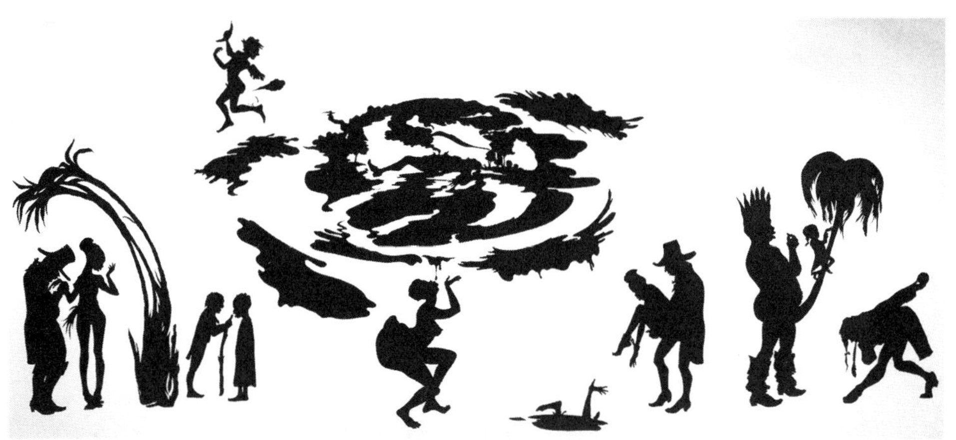

Kara Walker, detail from *Grub for Sharks: A Concession to the Negro Populace*, 2004. Cut paper and adhesive on wall. Installation variable. Artwork © Kara Walker, courtesy of Sikkema Jenkins & Co., New York; Sprüth Magers, Berlin.

distance. The object of desire, the water, contains the memory of that distant landscape—a fetishized memory that transmutes into a drop of water intended to satiate the character's immeasurable longing for her place of origin. The figure's protruding backside echoes the physiognomy of Saartjie Baartman, a Khoisan woman from South Africa who was brought to Europe in the nineteenth century as a colonial curiosity for her steatopygia, or voluptuousness of buttocks. Also known as the "Hottentot Venus," she was the victim of the colonial drive for racial superiority that designated black females as subhuman.[20] Walker's Baartman is a visual trap, revealing a double image in which she is both an archetype of the original mother and a grotesque Other, both a symbol of authenticity thirsty for her origins and a fetishized being. Most recently, Walker returns to this dual figure in the 2005 film animation *8 Possible Beginnings or: The Creation of African-America, a Moving Picture by Kara E. Walker* in which a giant, black, female sea creature consumes the floating dead bodies of the slaves thrown overboard from the slave ships during the transatlantic journey only to excrete them into a formless mass from which a male figure is born. In this sense, the Middle Passage in Walker's work becomes a birthplace where modernity comes into existence and where the concepts of Africa and America merge.

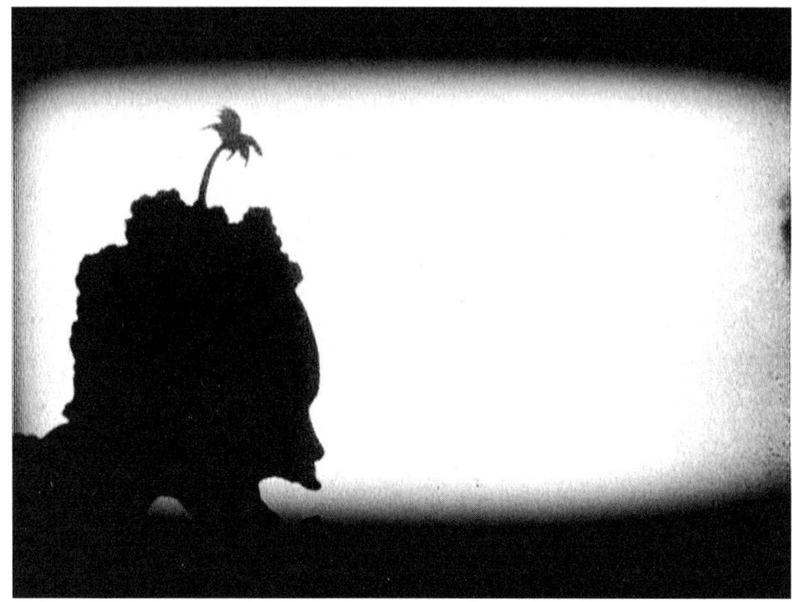

Kara Walker, still from *8 Possible Beginnings or: The Creation of African-America, a Moving Picture by Kara E. Walker*, 2005. Video (B&W with audio). 15:57 minutes. Artwork © Kara Walker, courtesy of Sikkema Jenkins & Co., New York; Sprüth Magers, Berlin.

Birth

Infants and toddlers appear in a variety of vulnerable situations in Walker's work: falling lifeless to the ground, dangling from delicate umbilical cords, or clinging to a mother's breast. A fetus hanging from an umbilical cord underneath the skirt of a female figure was the subject of one of the artist's earliest cut-paper silhouettes on canvas, an untitled work made in 1994–1995 (see p. 69). Birth is also the central theme of her most recent animated film, *8 Possible Beginnings or: The Creation of African-America, a Moving Picture by Kara E. Walker.*[21] Walker's creation myth was the result of a series of experiments with light and video projections, cut-paper marionettes, and live performance that began in 2001 and continued in 2004 with her first film animation, *Testimony: Narrative of a Negress Burdened by Good Intentions.*[22] Shot in black-and-white film and video, *8 Possible Beginnings* consists of eight grim fantasies that hypothesize the genesis of the black experience in America. For Walker, the past is both the poison and the antidote for contemporary social ailments: "One theme in my artwork is the idea that a Black subject in the present tense is a container for specific pathologies from the past and is continually growing and feeding off those maladies. . . . Murky, toxic waters become the amniotic fluid of a potentially new and difficult birth, flushing out of a coherent and stubborn body long-held fears and suspicions."[23]

The inspiration for *8 Possible Beginnings* was Walt Disney's highly patronizing 1946 animated film *Song of the South*, itself based on Joel Chandler Harris's book *Uncle Remus: His Songs and His Sayings* (1881). In Walker's version, however, there is no happy ending. The film opens with a title card announcing the name of the film and its creator, in the style of D. W. Griffith's infamous film *Birth of a Nation*.[24] The first story, titled "Along a Watery Road," unfolds at sea. As the waves part, a ship emerges, and the sound of strong winds alerts us to the approaching danger while intertitles foretell the fate of several bodies,

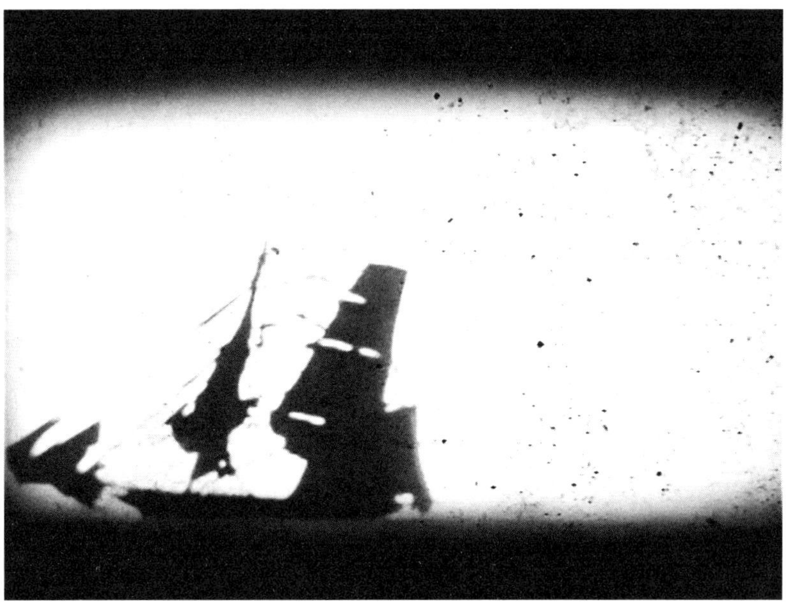

Kara Walker, still from "Along a Watery Road," *8 Possible Beginnings or: The Creation of African-America, a Moving Picture by Kara E. Walker*, 2005. Video (B&W with audio). 15:57 minutes. Artwork © Kara Walker, courtesy of Sikkema Jenkins & Co., New York; Sprüth Magers, Berlin.

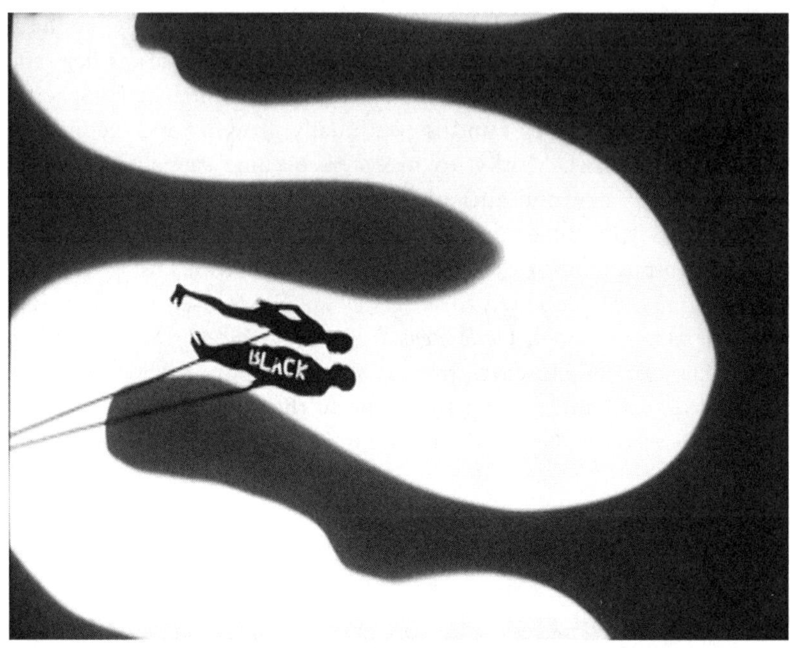

Kara Walker, still from "Motherland," *8 Possible Beginnings or: The Creation of African-America, a Moving Picture by Kara E. Walker*, 2005.

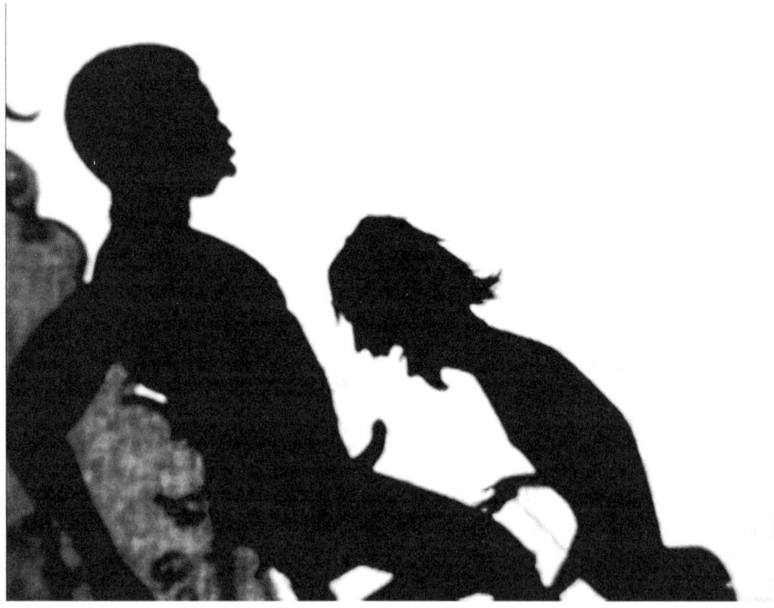

Kara Walker, still from "The New World," *8 Possible Beginnings or: The Creation of African-America, a Moving Picture by Kara E. Walker*, 2005.

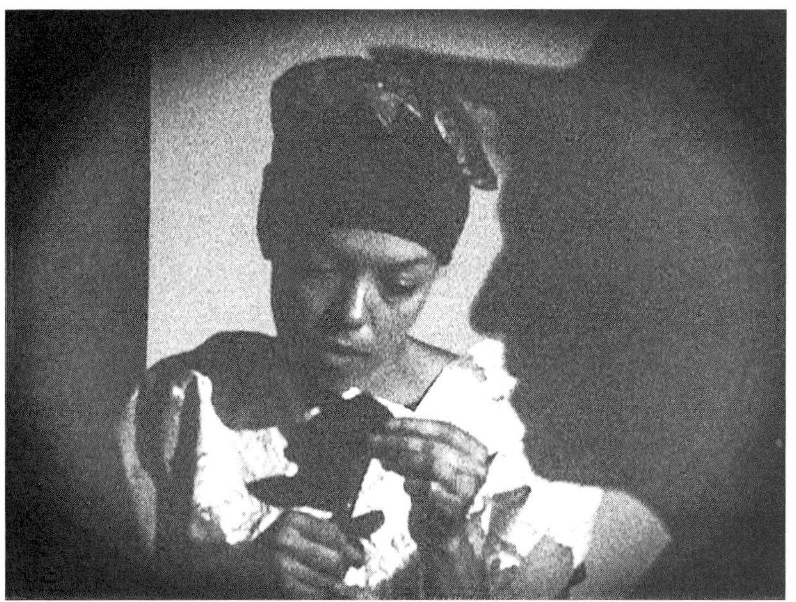

Kara Walker, still from "Interlude," *8 Possible Beginnings or: The Creation of African-America, a Moving Picture by Kara E. Walker*, 2005.

which are labeled with various aphorisms for blackness: "AFRICAN," "AUTHENTIC," "BLACK," "ONE FAKER," and "A WANNABE." As the bodies are thrown overboard and carried away on the waves, a mysterious palm tree appears floating on the horizon, which segues into the beginning of the second story, titled "Motherland." As the camera focuses on the palm tree, it emerges from the water as part of the head of an enormous sea creature, a female monster who feeds on the dead bodies of the Africans. We follow the bodies as they enter the monster's mouth and travel down through her intestines until they are defecated. Our attention is now directed away from the sea and to the land in the third scene, titled "The New World," in which a robust male figure is born from the pile of feces. His name is King Cotton, and he rises up from the ground and admires the cotton plants in the landscape around him. As he dances in the field, he encounters an ill-looking skinny master among the bushes, has a sexual encounter with him, and becomes pregnant. At this point, the cut-paper animation changes into live footage for a short "Interlude" during which a

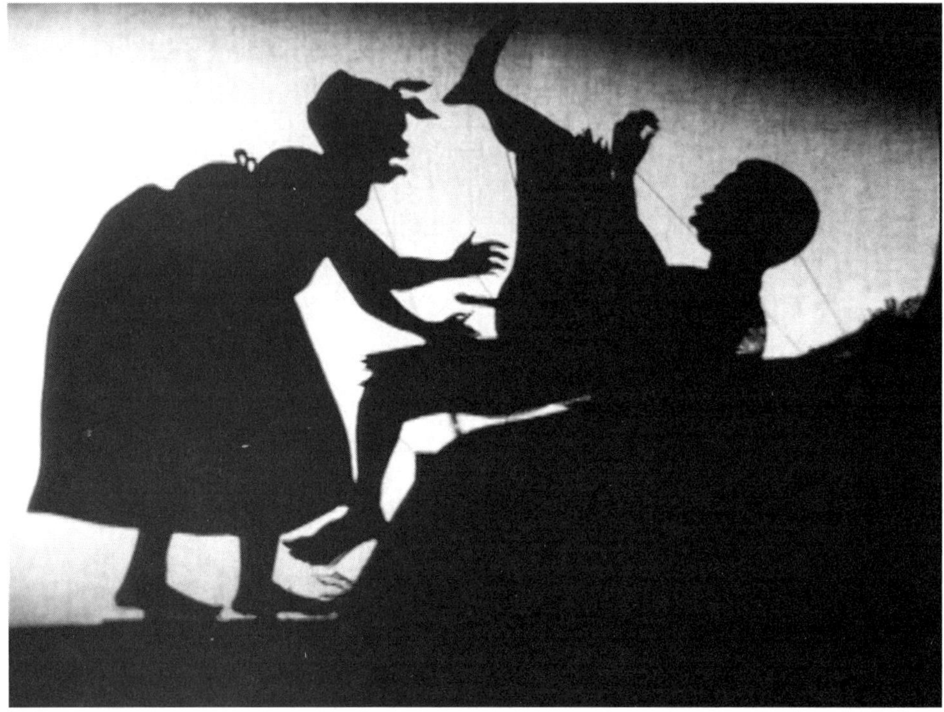

Kara Walker, still from "New Labors," *8 Possible Beginnings or: The Creation of African-America, a Moving Picture by Kara E. Walker*, 2005.

young woman dressed up as a maid creates a cut-paper silhouette of her master. In the fifth story, "New Labors," a midwife helps King Cotton give birth to a black cotton plant. The sixth story, "A Darkey Hymn: 'All I Want,'" unfolds inside a cave, where a young girl walks in darkness, stalked by the cast shadow of her master; she recites a monologue, echoed with a slight delay in the voice of an adult woman, that reveals her desire to "be white." Suddenly, we are transported back to the plantation, in a scene titled "Plantin' Time," where we see King Cotton gently watering the newborn plant. In the final segment, "The Story of Br'er Rabbit, Br'er Fox, and How Briar Patch County Come to Be Called That," Walker introduces Harris's original characters. The segment opens with Lil' Timmy, the master's grandson, begging Uncle Remus to tell him a story. Fearing the whip of his master, the old man complies and recounts a gruesome tale in which Br'er Rabbit and Br'er

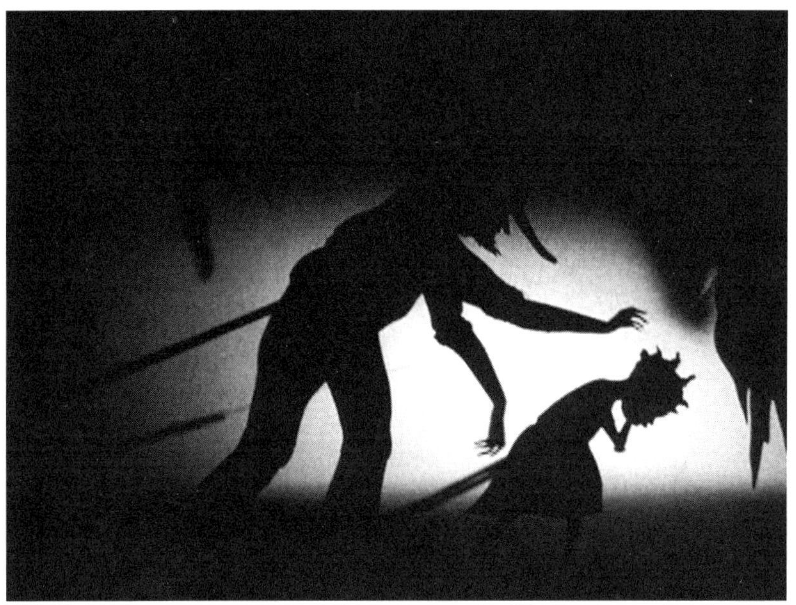

Kara Walker, still from "A Darkey Hymn: 'All I Want,'" *8 Possible Beginnings or: The Creation of African-America, a Moving Picture by Kara E. Walker*, 2005.

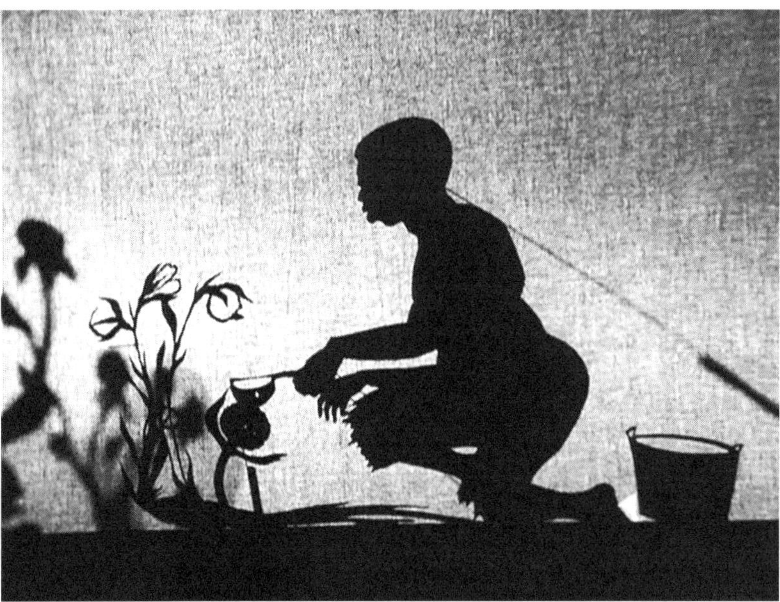

Kara Walker, still from "Plantin' Time," *8 Possible Beginnings or: The Creation of African-America, a Moving Picture by Kara E. Walker*, 2005.

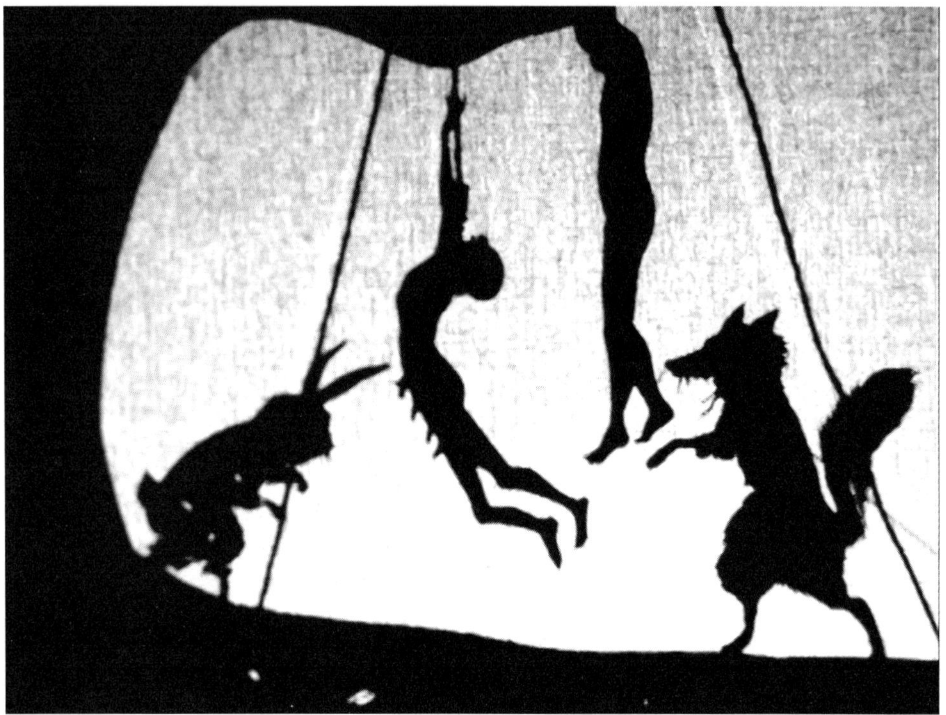

Kara Walker, still from "The Story of Br'er Rabbit, Br'er Fox, and How Briar Patch Country Come to Be Called That," *8 Possible Beginnings or: The Creation of African-America, a Moving Picture by Kara E. Walker,* 2005.

Fox discover the lynched bodies of three black men hanging from a tree. The animation ends with little Timmy strolling joyfully past the bodies accompanied by the song "Zip-a-dee-doo-dah," the lyrics of which intoxicate the setting with bitter sarcasm.

Walker's *8 Possible Beginnings* is a visual riddle that poses many questions as it unearths the malignant roots of the black experience in the United States. Walker is not in favor of a generalized anguish. She grants no accusatory voice to any of the characters, nor does she disguise the victim from the victimizer. Instead, she proposes eight hypotheses from which we might glean an ontological explanation for the origin, extent, and depth of racism. Like Uncle Remus, her role is that of a trickster who occasionally pulls the weak strings that awaken the despair of our collective memory and mute the question of absolution.

Symbolically, birth connotes origin. In Walker's work, the representation of birth encapsulates not only self-preservation but also self-destruction. During slavery, breeding became the most insidious method of control; for the slave women forced to breed, abortion was a powerful gesture of revolt against the system.[25] It is no accident that images of childbirth and of infants in Walker's work epitomize the suffering and sacrifice of slaves while simultaneously alluding to the disturbing and conflictive role that motherhood played in the lives of female slaves. In literature, this dilemma is keenly personified in the character of Sethe in Toni Morrison's novel *Beloved*. Sethe is a runaway slave who, in order to prevent the slave-catchers from taking her children, kills them with her own hands. The description of her tragic solution reveals the redemptive intent of her actions:

> Right off it was clear, to schoolteacher especially, that there was nothing there to claim. The three (now four—because she'd had the one coming when she cut) pickaninnies they had hoped were alive and well enough to take back to Kentucky, take back and raise properly to do the work Sweet Home desperately needed, were not. Two were lying open-eyed in sawdust; a third pumped blood down the dress of the main one—the woman schoolteacher bragged about, the one he said made fine ink, damn good soup, pressed his collars the way he liked besides having at least ten breeding years left. But now she'd gone wild, due to the mishandling of the nephew who'd overbeat her and made her cut and run.[26]

To further complicate matters, Walker's portrayals of childbirth transgress the very boundaries of gender. In *The End of Uncle Tom and the Grand Allegorical Tableau of Eva in Heaven*, Walker first conceived the motif of a man giving birth. Toward the end of this 35-foot-long mural, the character of Uncle Tom, from Harriet Beecher Stowe's 1852 novel *Uncle Tom's Cabin*, is depicted with curls receding from his bald head, his arms raised to the sky in a gesture of clemency, his pants pulled down, and an umbilical cord connected to a fetus trailing off behind him. In Walker's hyperbolic, feminizing interpretation of Stowe's ideal house slave, Uncle Tom is rescued from the Victorian desexualized stereotype of the cuddly, big black man and rendered instead as a surrogate mother experiencing a hellish childbirth. Both Tom and

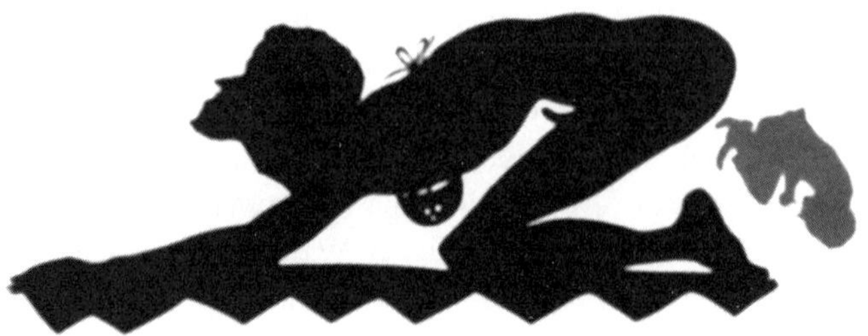

Kara Walker, detail from *Endless Conundrum, An African Anonymous Adventuress*, 2001. Cut paper and adhesive on wall. Includes original exhibition set, template, and artist certificate. 191 × 453 inches (485.1 × 1150.6 cm). Artwork © Kara Walker, courtesy of Sikkema Jenkins & Co., New York; Sprüth Magers, Berlin.

Eva—the latter a reference to Stowe's Evangeline, the blond girl who taught Uncle Tom to read the Bible and upon her deathbed gave locks of her hair to her slaves—were primary figures in Walker's early imagery, notably in a series of drawings from 1995, collectively titled *Negress Notes*, in which the couple is depicted in sexually charged scenarios and Tom breastfeeds Eva (see also the section below on "Mother's Milk").

In *Endless Conundrum, An African Anonymous Adventuress*, the act of a slave man giving birth is depicted as defecation. This exchanging of parental roles—transferring the gestation function from mother to father—transforms the male slave into a surrogate mother who, lacking a vagina, must discharge his baby from the anus, making the association between excrement and enslavement explicit (see also the section below on "Feces and Semen"). Indeed, there is an unsettling lifelessness to the newborns, even when they are attached to umbilical cords and especially when they are falling onto the ground. The body language of the surrogates communicates surrender, evoking the forced denial of parenthood and family ancestry under slavery.

Walker's allegorical figures of men giving birth and of fetuses permanently attached to their umbilical cords are variations on her larger creation myth, relative to the black experience, that seems to permeate her art. For black Americans, the question of one's origin is not about ancestry so much as language and speech—about who is labeled and by whom, as well as what those labels mean. I would argue that this ontological question has also driven Adrian Piper's work from early on, as she examines the construction of racial identity through dialectical

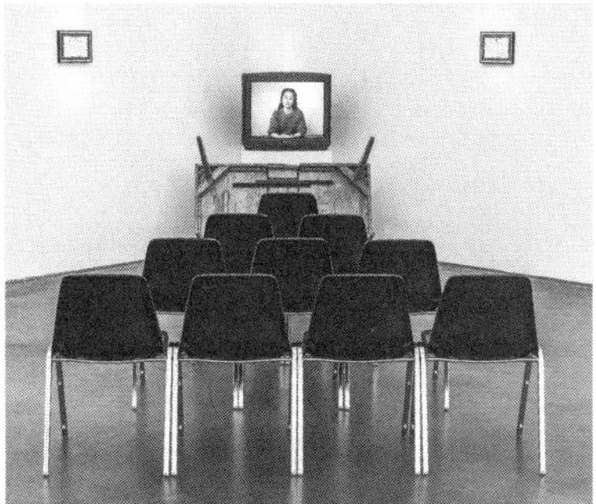

Adrian Piper, *Cornered*, 1988. Video installation. Video (color, sound); with table, chairs, monitor, two framed birth certificates for Adrian Piper's father Daniel R. Piper, and lighting. Dimensions variable. Collection of the Museum of Contemporary Art Chicago. © Adrian Piper Research Archive Foundation Berlin. Photo: Nathan Keay.

arguments that combine her own autobiographical facts, eugenics theories, and identity politics. As part of her 1988 video installation *Cornered*, Piper is seen on a monitor speaking to the camera in the typical monotone voice of a news reporter. She engages in a monologue that begins with the self-labeling statement "I am black" and continues with a series of impersonations of rhetorical questions related to her light-skinned complexion. On the wall hang two birth certificates for Piper's father, also a light-skinned African American, one of which categorizes him as white and the other as "Octoroon." Piper's rhetoric of race is not a strictly circular argument. Nor is the content strictly autobiographical. Like Walker, her concern is to debunk conventional ways of seeing blackness, to critique the stereotypical notion that black Americans desire to be white, and to expand the discussion of race and representation beyond affirmations of difference and essentialized arguments of cultural identity. In both cases, the quest for identity is a quest for one's true origin.

Feces and Semen

Ten puddles of excrement mark the path of a naked toddler in *The End of Uncle Tom and the Grand Allegorical Tableau of Eva in Heaven*. Oblivious to the vulgarity of her actions, the young girl, playing her tambourine, marches past a group of children. Aside from her breaking of the social taboo against defecating in public, what is disturbingly precocious and symbolically relevant in this picture is the girl's refusal to stop her march to take care of her business. Her unnerving procession is a mockery of good manners and self-discipline. The absurdity of the scene is highlighted by the abnormal ratio of body waste to the child's actual size. But such disproportion also alludes to the proliferation in the postslavery era of racialized images and ephemera that objectified physical blackness in ridiculous, condescending, and outright hateful ways.[27] Drawing on the vicious humor of racial stereotypes, Walker finds in such imagery the potential to disrupt and challenge dehumanizing depictions of the black body, the very kind at play in the unruly behavior of the young girl. As the artist has noted, "Every time I enter a flea market, I see something like a pickaninny with its head in a toilet. This association of blackness with excrement conjures up a very early memory . . . wondering what the color of my white friends' shit was. Whoever made the original toy literally employed a toilet to his or her humor, ha ha. I find these bawdy/body associations extremely important, though. I relate through it as well . . . this black body . . . jiggling around and representing everything but itself."[28]

Like many scenarios in Walker's art that suggest infantile lack of restraint, the images of figures defecating are encoded with messages about obscenity, disobedience, and defiance. In *World's Exposition*, a silhouette mural from 1997, a half-human, half-monkey figure hangs by her tail from the branch of a tree while painting the foliage and casually defecating. An allegorical figure of an artist, or perhaps even a self-portrait, the image points to the ways in which the racist imagination parades artists of color, particularly women artists, as exceptional species whose primal instincts and creative talents are intended to amuse and delight bourgeois audiences. For her part, Walker's hybrid creature is acting in accordance with racist objectification of the black female body—"the naked image of Otherness," as bell hooks contests, when speaking of this body being put on display for entertainment. As hooks notes, "Objectified in a manner similar to that of black female slaves who stood on auction blocks while owners and overseers described their important, salable parts, the black women whose naked bodies were displayed for whites at social functions had no presence."[29] And yet, Walker's surrogate Josephine Baker, even though she is put on display like a caged animal at the fair, daringly shows off her "gifts" with

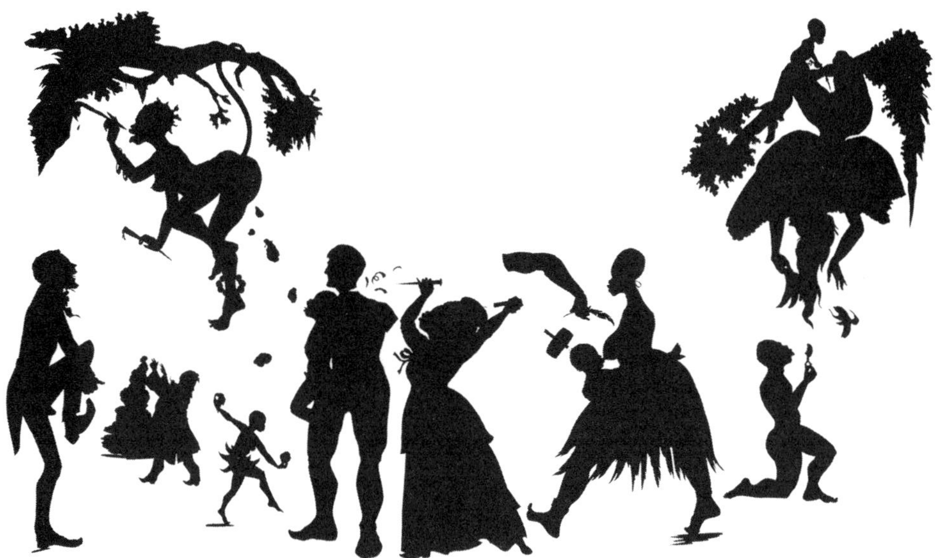

Kara Walker, *World's Exposition*, 1997. Wall installation of cut paper and adhesive on wall, 21 elements. 120 × 192 inches (304.8 × 487.7 cm). Artwork © Kara Walker, courtesy of Sikkema Jenkins & Co., New York; Sprüth Magers, Berlin.

double irony as she reveals herself to be both the artist's muse and the artist. In both of the examples discussed above, the figures are engaged in infantile abandon and sensual defiance while exposing a heightened awareness of their bodies that is alienated not from reason but from obedience to prudish social constrictions.

In Christian symbolism, defecation is associated with dirtiness, indulgence, and greed. In the panel painting known as *Hell*, part of Hieronymus Bosch's triptych *The Garden of Earthly Delights* (ca. 1504), a human figure defecating coins into a bottomless pit represents the deadly sin of avarice. "We know that the gold which the devil gives his paramours turns into excrement after his departure," Freud wrote in "Character and Anal Eroticism," adding that "the devil is certainly nothing else than the personification of the repressed unconscious instinctual life."[30] In his discussion of the child's erotic interest in defecation, Freud concludes by noting that this original excitation is destined to be extinguished in later years only to be replaced by a new interest in material possessions and money. Walker plays off these

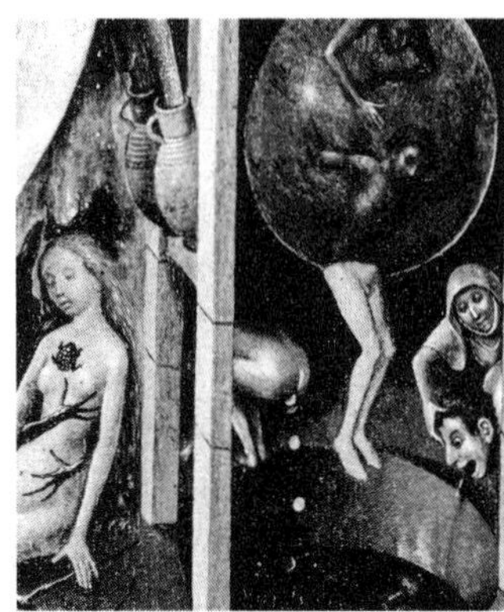

Hieronymus Bosch, *Hell*, detail of right panel of *The Garden of Earthly Delights*, ca. 1504. Triptych plus shutters. Oil on panel. 86 5/8 × 38 inches. Collection Museo del Prado, Madrid.

associations between material possessions and fecal matter in *Presenting Negro Scenes Drawn Upon My Passage Through the South and Reconfigured for the Benefit of Enlightened Audiences Wherever Such May Be Found, By Myself, Missus K. E. B. Walker, Colored* from 1997, which shows a naked slave woman defecating on top of a pile of more excrement. Buried up to her knees, she reaches out to eat from the mound. Nearby, a suspicious-looking male figure, wearing a broad hat and long jacket and carrying a large bag, bends down to take some of the soft material. The juxtaposition of the clothed and the naked emphasizes the divergence of their desires: whereas the man reaches out to hoard new possessions, the woman seems to be in a state of desperation. Eating dirt, after all, was a way for a slave to commit suicide;[31] the woman's vulnerable situation, stuck inside the pile of feces, seems to confirm the inevitable outcome of her destiny.

If Walker's scatological images can be interpreted as symbolizing slaves' resistance to absolute domination, then her depictions of slave characters in unconditional submission to their bodies' sexual desires can be interpreted as symbolizing their human weakness and vulnerability. In displaying emotional fragility and sexual abandon, Walker attempts to evoke the amorphous nature of moral authority, or, to borrow a phrase from theorist Achille Mbembé, "the banality of power," where neither oppressor nor oppressed is ethically superior.[32] Like

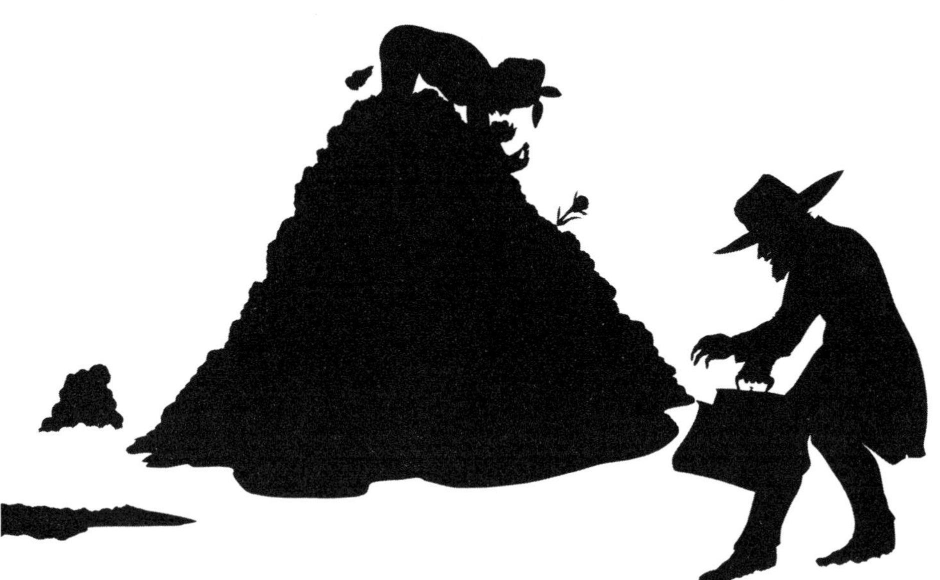

Kara Walker, detail from *Presenting Negro Scenes Drawn Upon My Passage Through the South and Reconfigured for the Benefit of Enlightened Audiences Wherever Such May Be Found, By Myself, Missus K. E. B. Walker, Colored,* 1997. Cut paper and adhesive on wall. 144 × 1860 inches (365.8 × 4724.4 cm). Artwork © Kara Walker, courtesy of Sikkema Jenkins & Co., New York; Sprüth Magers, Berlin.

Mbembé, Walker questions the notion of power based in traditional binary oppositions—good/evil, moral/immoral—and instead considers the impotence of power. This approach is openly disclosed in her nihilistic depictions of sexual encounters between masters and slaves, in which she strategically manipulates the codes and taboos of sentimentality, sexual desire, and miscegenation that remain prevalent in contemporary American culture.

The artist's first film, *Testimony: Narrative of a Negress Burdened by Good Intentions*, from 2004, is a black-and-white silent puppet animation that tells the story of the lynching of a plantation master by his slave lover. For this piece, Walker created small-scale renditions of her most famous characters: the Auntie, the master, the master's son, and the Negress mistress.[33] The story takes place on a cotton plantation and is narrated through a series of intertitles that recount how the men, in their "longing for fulfillment," temporarily relinquished their bodies to the slave women. Of course, the problem is that power has no conscience, and as viewers are quickly told, the women refused "to revert to the old order" and instead they "rounded 'em up" and murdered their masters/lovers. Driven by opposing passions, the young antiheroine of the story is shown in the last scene sucking the penis of her dead lover and getting her face splashed with an enormous amount of semen in what can be interpreted as the one last gesture of her power, which is also her weakness: her affection, which is also her selfishness; her pride, which is also her shame; and her sublimation, which is also her freedom. A tragicomedy, Walker's fable, presented in the spirit of slave testimonials, delves into the flaws of assigning any kind of moral superiority in the realm of human emotions. As in her life-size silhouettes, the characters in Walker's animation—both masters and slaves—cannot be viewed through a moral lens, as it is precisely the impossibility of escaping an immoral and corrupt system that leaves no room for benevolence from either side. In *Incidents in the Life of a Slave Girl*, Harriet Jacobs describes this conundrum:

> You may believe what I say; for I write only that whereof I know. I was twenty-one years in that cage of obscene birds. I can testify, from my own experience and observation, that slavery is a curse to the whites as well as to the blacks. It makes the white fathers cruel and sensual; the sons violent and licentious; it contaminates the daughters, and makes the wives wretched. And as for the colored race, it needs an abler pen than mine to describe the extremity of their sufferings, the depth of the degradation.[34]

Mother's Milk

Slave narratives and testimonial writing from the eighteenth and nineteenth centuries tell us of women sold at auction while still breastfeeding their newborns. Some slave women served as nursemaids to the mistress's children, and some as birth mothers of the master's illegitimate offspring. Procreation was crucial in the mechanisms and calculations of plantation slavery in the South, with particularly harsh implications for women (see also the section above on "Birth"). As a natural extension, perhaps, of her birthing imagery, Walker's work includes several depictions of breastfeeding that inspire

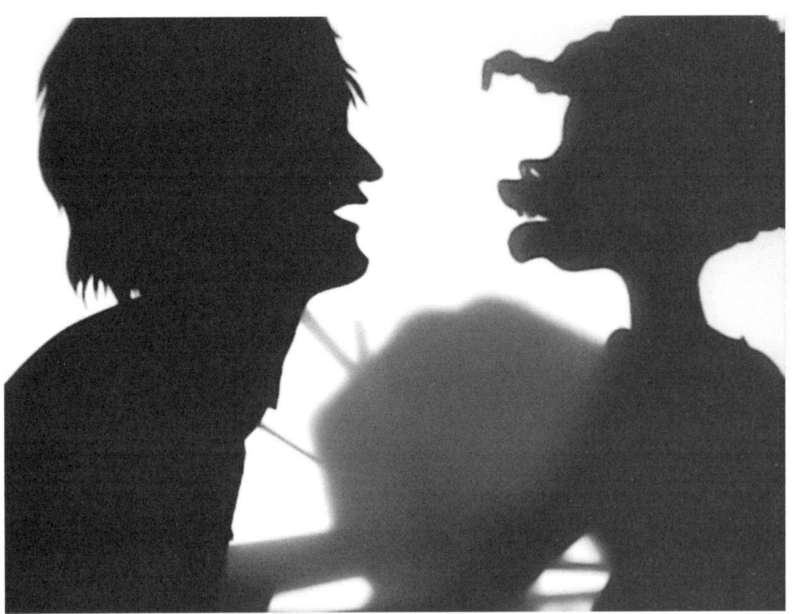

Kara Walker, still from *Testimony: Narrative of a Negress Burdened by Good Intentions*, 2004.

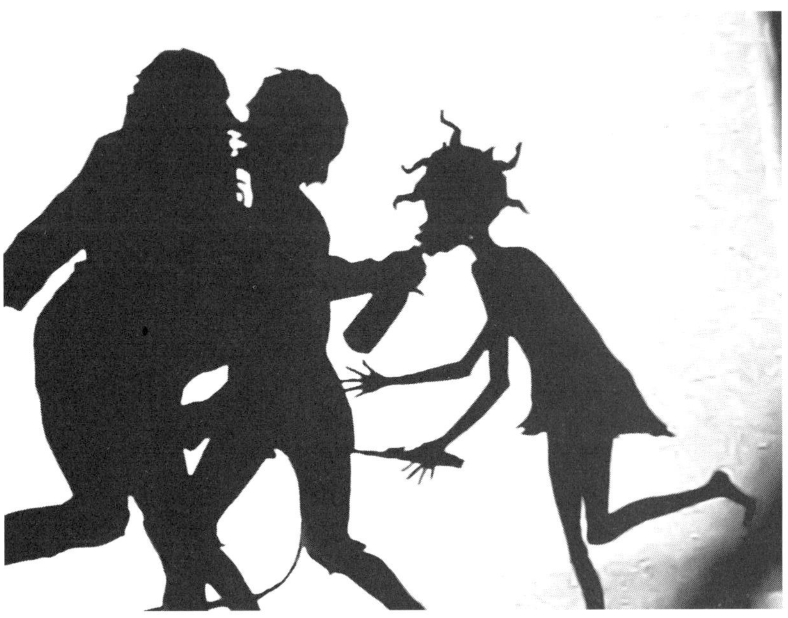

Kara Walker, still from *Testimony: Narrative of a Negress Burdened by Good Intentions*, 2004.

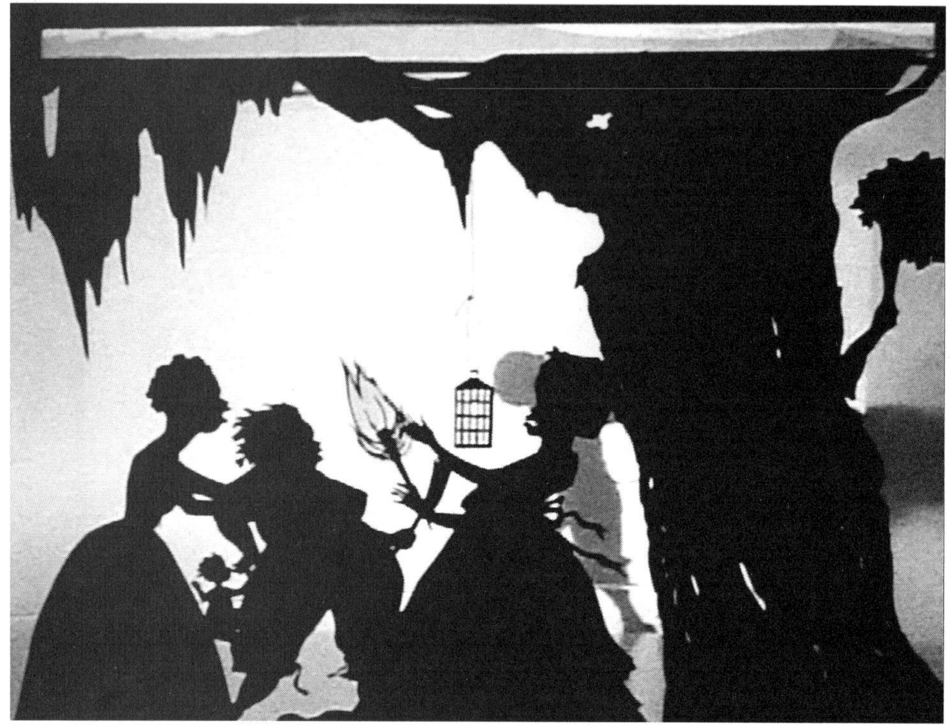

Kara Walker, still from *Testimony: Narrative of a Negress Burdened by Good Intentions,* 2004.

associations with nourishment and motherhood or, in some cases, fatherhood, as well as symbolically affirming the lineage that slaves were denied.

An early example of the allegorical figure of the nursemaid in Walker's work can be found in the first image of the five-part print *A Means to an End . . . A Shadow Drama in Five Acts* made in 1995. Here, a young slave woman, with one hand resting on her hip, is shown balancing a white boy in the air while he sucks from one of her breasts. A later conception of this balancing act, in *The End of Uncle Tom and the Grand Allegorical Tableau of Eva in Heaven* (see p. 23), brings more physical tension and metaphorical implications to the initial motif. In this vignette, rendered as a pyramid of bodies, a young woman crouches to balance on her knees an infant whose mouth is aiming for her bare

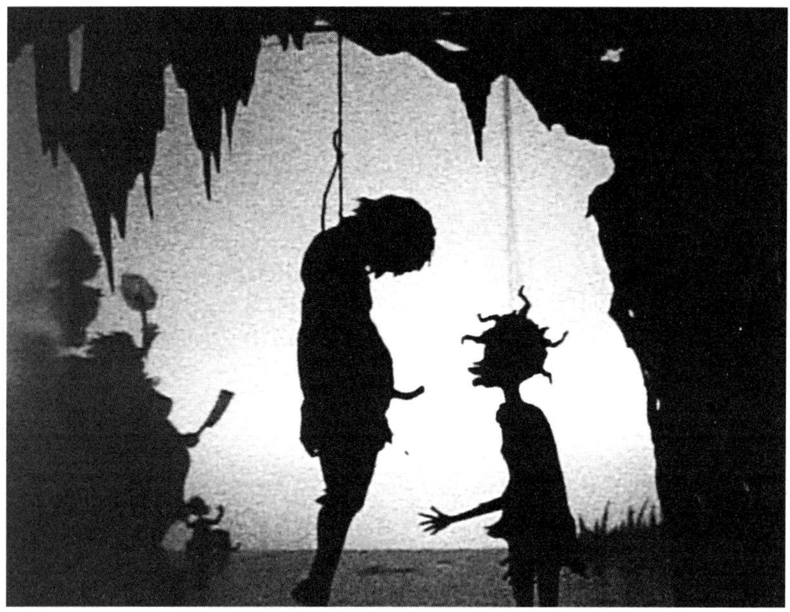

Kara Walker, still from *Testimony: Narrative of a Negress Burdened by Good Intentions*, 2004.

nipple; she herself sucks the breast of a second female figure, in front of her, who in turn, while holding a large watermelon behind her back as a counterweight, stands on her tiptoes and leans forward to suck the breast of a third woman (balancing in part on the back of the first). This fantasy arrangement holds great emblematic meaning as the child reaches impatiently with both hands and mouth for her mother's nipple while the women, as they thrust out their necks, seem to be hurrying to satiate their thirst. The portrait is striking for its unsentimental tone and sense of urgency. The women seem to be seeking from one another the nourishment not of milk but of a richer nectar that affirms their shared heritage. Stripped of its biological function, the maternal act of lactation is rendered as an oral transfusion that is simultaneously sensual and repulsive, empowering and repressive, whereby ancestral lineage is both dished out and consumed by so many nameless mothers, sisters, daughters, and granddaughters.

Ancestry is the fluid that flows in Walker's breastfeeding imagery. Under slavery, the denial of birthright served to support the master's

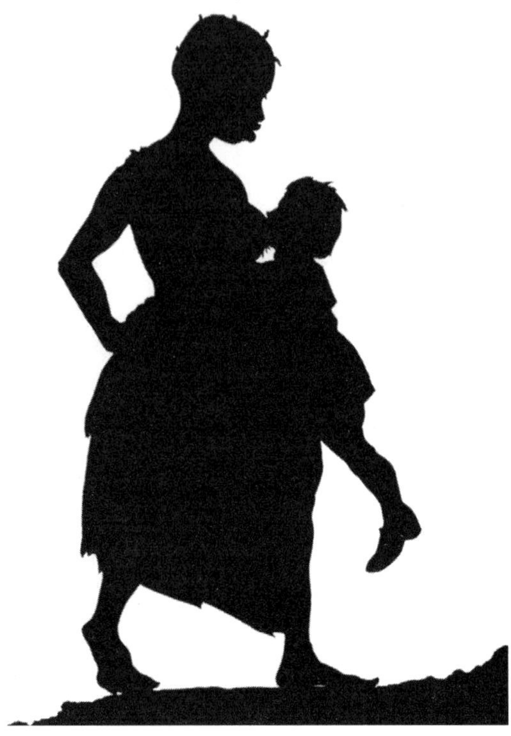

Kara Walker, detail from *A Means to an End . . . A Shadow Drama in Five Acts*, 1995. Etching, aquatint. 34.75 × 115.5 inches (88.27 × 293.4 cm). Artwork © Kara Walker, courtesy of Sikkema Jenkins & Co., New York; Sprüth Magers, Berlin.

totalitarian rule. As Patterson points out in his introduction to *Slavery and Social Death*, "Not only was the slave denied all claims on, and obligations to, his parents and living blood relations but, by extension, all such claims and obligations on his more remote ancestors and on his descendants. He was truly a genealogical isolate. Formally isolated in his social relations with those who lived, he also was culturally isolated from the social heritage of his ancestors."[35] In this scene of uninterrupted milking, the women in Walker's quartet, so mythical in their weightless bodies, reclaim their birthright not only by drawing in the nourishment of their ancestors but also by drawing out the venom of slavery.

Intimate scenes of breastfeeding appear sporadically in Walker's work, alternating between genders. In an early watercolor drawing from *Negress Notes*, an elderly male slave, an Uncle Tom/Uncle Remus stereotype, is depicted nursing a young slave girl from a nipple that has metamorphosed into an elongated penis. The gender and age differences add ambiguity and sexual tension to the scene as the male figure leans down toward the child and gazes in the distance as if on alert for an unwanted intruder. This image of paternal lactation is further displaced in the gouache drawing John Brown, made a year later. Here, the abolitionist leader, who was executed by hanging for his involvement in the 1850 raid at Harpers Ferry, Virginia, is shown barechested with his arms behind his back. Next to him, a slave woman holds a naked toddler in her arms as the child pulls with his teeth at one of Brown's dry nipples. Brown's stoicism is emphasized by the stiff posture of his torso, which does not yield to the child's forceful pulling. Turning a cold shoulder to the pain—metaphorically speaking, to parenthood—he looks away from the child and the mother. John Brown is frequently depicted as a martyr sacrificed for the abolitionist cause; however, Walker's portrayal of him as a dry father figure, a "failed patriarch," brings into question his authority and entitlement in the pantheon of African American idols.[36]

The mouths depicted in these compositions are guided not only by penury and hunger but also, certainly, by libidinal desire. The appetites seem to be driven by a deep longing for something that extends beyond food and warmth to comfort and pleasure, beyond sexual pleasure to a lust for life. Walker gives form to this desire in her characters' oral fixation with the mother/father nipple, which proposes that their "fetishism" originates from their enslaved condition.[37] In this sense, these allegorical figures are imagined in a permanent state of infancy, constantly searching for nourishment, sucking endlessly but never fulfilling their old thirst. This condition is vividly captured in *Consume* (see p. 68), a cut-paper piece from 1998 in which a bare-chested, pubescent girl wearing oversize high-heeled shoes and a banana-leaf skirt sucks on her own breast while a toddler boy, most likely the master's son, mimics her by sucking on one of the bananas dangling from her skirt. In this sexual fantasy scene the young woman, in a gesture of autonomy and self-preservation, has discovered in her own body a way to appease her needs and desires while the infant, too young for self-recognition, pacifies his desire with a surrogate nipple.

Milk as a euphemism appears in a suite of sixty-six works on paper titled *Do You Like Creme in Your Coffee and Chocolate in Your Milk?*, from 1997. These drawings, made with diaristic spontaneity in response to the letter-writing campaigns organized against her and her work by a handful of artists and critics in 1997, record a private universe inhabited by subjects real and imagined, occasionally accompanied by sour observations on xenophobia. Both the images and the text are infused with satire, occasional comic twists, and explicit sadistic sexual drama. The double rhetorical question of the work's title carries a double meaning, quoting, as the artist has explained, the well-known American joke that begins with the statement "I like my coffee like I like my women" and to which is added "any number of combinations, 'hot, black and sweet,' 'Black with a touch of cream,' etc."[38] Playing off sexual innuendos, Walker alludes explicitly to the unspoken word in the racial conflict in America: miscegenation. For not only is she underlining the "inner plantation" that perpetuates racial segregation some fifty years after *Brown v. Board of Education*, the 1954 Supreme Court decision dismantling segregation in public schools; she is also alluding to Fanon's "infernal circle" of race: "When people like me, they tell me it is in spite of my color. When they dislike me, they point out that it is not because of my color."[39]

Precedents for Walker's bold interracial commentaries had been set by artists such as Adrian Piper and Robert Colescott, both great influences in her work. Colescott's sense of irony is evident in *Rejected Idea for a Drostes Chocolate Advertisement*, from 1974, which depicts a couple ice-skating hand in hand. The woman, who is black, wears a traditional Dutch white nurse's bonnet; her white lover, who is tall and blond, looks at her lustily, as evidenced by his exposed erection. Like Walker's double question, Colescott's pun is two-tiered, referring both to the legendary weakness among the Dutch for the exotic drink of the Olmecs and to the country's infamous colonial past. The black female body as both subject and repository of sexual fantasies, phobias, and taboos prevails as the locus of a major portion of Walker's work, exposing age-old maladies, analyzing their roots and effects, and possibly, in the process, diminishing their menacing power.

The Merits of Arguing over
Representation:
I mean - you cant please everyone and why
should you anyway!?
          Pindell's argument - that
This (my) WORK is not accepted by ALL Black people
    is Right - (she smirks - intending to Deflate
      the Issue) What ARTWORK actually Does that?
      And what does this imply? - That
    ART's function to Black people is to
    VERIFY the TRUTH all the time and to.
    express Collective experience (which grows increasingly fractured)
    The veiwer is expected to nod and turn in "MM HUM!"
    appreciation of the facts and
    NOT (as I want wif my work) to question
    the way we Muddle up the facts (DAILy)

          — Repeat Repeat Repeat

    I DO Manage to write (i say)
    The Same things over i over
    using slightly differnt
          language.

Kara Walker, *Do You Like Creme in Your Coffee and Chocolate in Your Milk?*, 1997. Watercolor, colored pencil, and graphite on paper. 66 parts: 11.75 × 8.25 inches (29.8 × 21 cm) each. Artwork © Kara Walker, courtesy of Sikkema Jenkins & Co., New York; Sprüth Magers, Berlin.

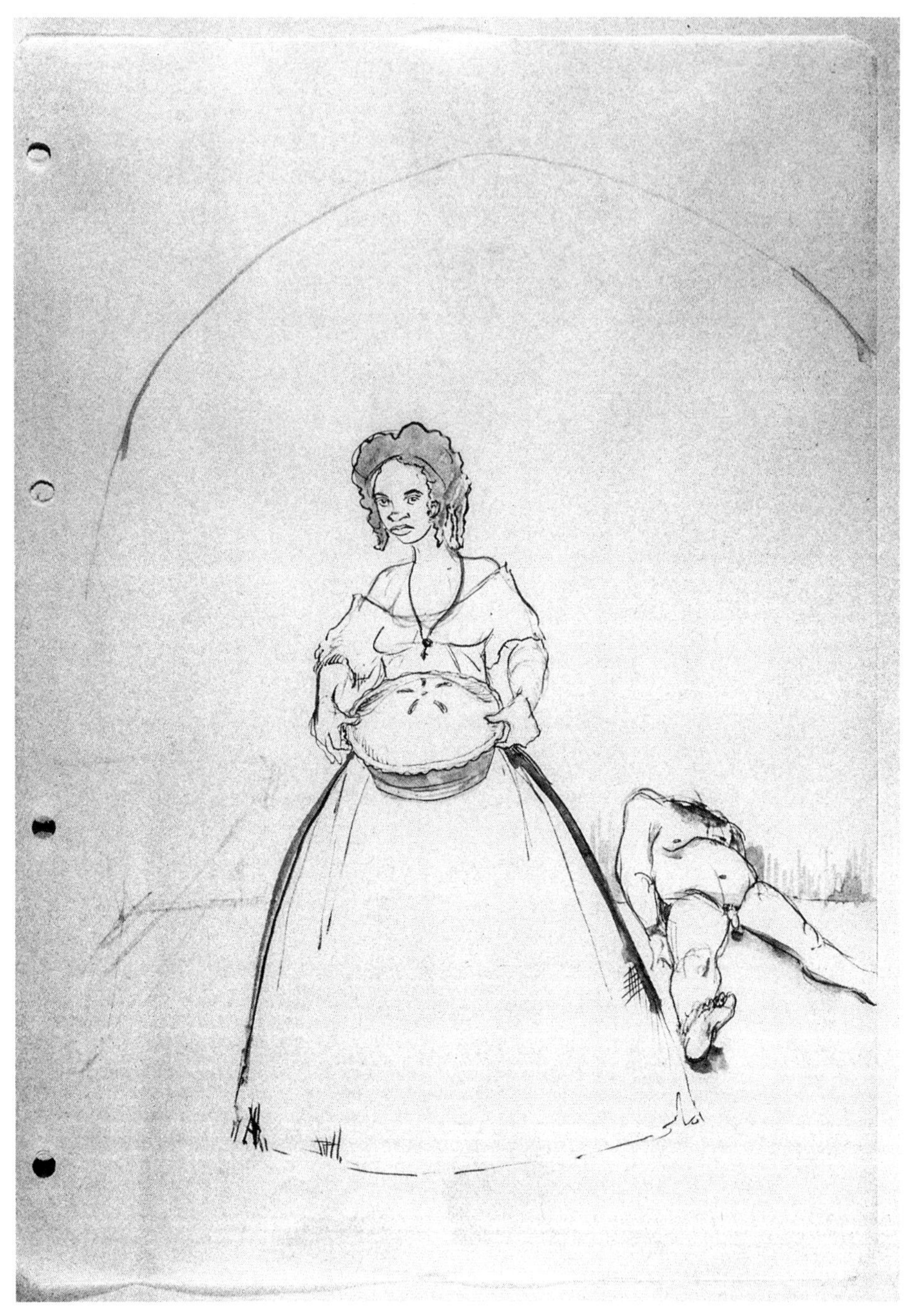

Kara Walker, *Do You Like Creme in Your Coffee and Chocolate in Your Milk?*, 1997.

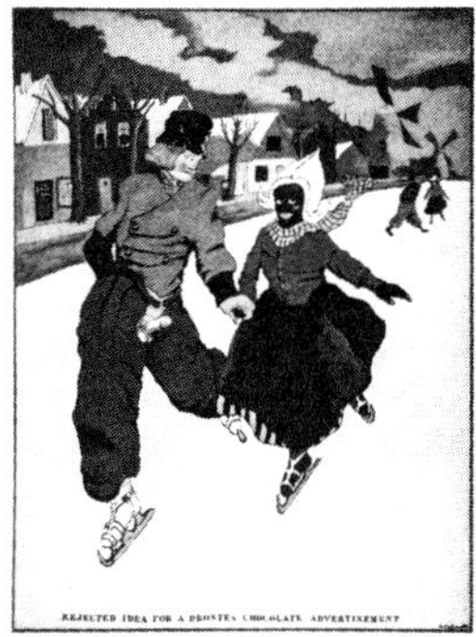

Robert Colescott, *Rejected Idea for a Drostes Chocolate Advertisement*, 1974. Acrylic on canvas, 80 × 59.5 inches. Estate of Robert Colescott/ADAGP, Paris, 2022.

Notes

1. Marcus Wood, *Blind Memory: Visual Representations of Slavery in England and America, 1780–1865* (New York: Routledge, 2000), 7.

2. Walker quoted in David D'Arcy, "The Eye of the Storm," *Modern Painters* (April 2006): 59.

3. In Europe, J. M. W. Turner's 1840 painting *Slavers Throwing Overboard the Dead and Dying—Typhoon Coming On*, also known as *The Slave Ship*, is probably the best-known work of art devoted to the subject of slavery, but it is a rare example. For an extended account of this work, see Wood, *Blind Memory*.

4. See Orlando Patterson, *Slavery and Social Death: A Comparative Study* (Cambridge, MA: Harvard University Press, 1982), 483.

5. This work was shown in the 1994 group exhibition *Selections 1994* at the Drawing Center, New York.

6. Octavia E. Butler, *Kindred* (Boston: Beacon Press, 1979), 27.

7. Frantz Fanon, *Black Skin, White Masks*, trans. Charles Lam Markmann (1952; New York: Grove Weidenfeld, 1967), 93.

8. Patterson, *Slavery and Social Death*, 177.

9. This light installation was exhibited for the first time in 2000 at the Centre d'Art Contemporain in Geneva along with three other light pieces: *Insurrection! (Our Tools Were Rudimentary, Yet We Pressed On)*; *Why I Like White Boys. An Illustrated Novel by Kara E. Walker, Negress*; and *Emancipated, and On Tour*. In these works, Walker combined, for the first time, cut-paper silhouettes and overhead light projections.

10. Steel rods were welded onto punishment collars to enforce a submissive posture and bells were hung to prevent slaves from running away. For further analysis of the representation of torture and other methods of punishment, see Marcus Wood, "Representing Pain and Describing Torture: Slavery, Punishment and Martyrology," in *Blind Memory*, 215–291.

11. Both of these murals were part of an installation that included *The End of Uncle Tom and the Grand Allegorical Tableau of Eva in Heaven*, also from 1995, as part of Walker's solo exhibition *From the Bowels to the Bosom* at Wooster Gardens/Brent Sikkema, New York, in 1996.

12. Walker interviewed by Susan Sollins in the video documentary *Art:21—Art in the Twenty-First Century*, season 2, VHS and DVD (New York: PBS, 2003).

13. Michel Foucault, "The Subject and Power," in *Power: Essential Works of Foucault, 1954–1984*, vol. 3, ed. James D. Faubion, trans. Robert Hurley et al. (New York: New Press, 1994), 326–348.

14. For further analysis of this work, see Gwendolyn DuBois Shaw, "Final Cut," in *Seeing the Unspeakable: The Art of Kara Walker* (Durham, NC: Duke University Press, 2004), 125–151, and Darby English, "This Is Not about the Past: Silhouettes in the Work of Kara Walker," in *Kara Walker: Narratives of a Negress*, ed. Ian Berry, Darby English, Vivian Patterson, and Mark Reinhardt, exhibition catalog (Cambridge, MA: MIT Press, in association with the Frances Young Tang Teaching Museum and Art Gallery at Skidmore College and Williams College Museum of Art, 2003), 140–167.

15. Butler, *Kindred*, 248.

16. Fanon, *Black Skin, White Masks*, 231.

17. See Orlando Patterson, "The Transatlantic Trade," in *Slavery and Social Death*, 159–164.

18. Paul Gilroy, "The Black Atlantic as a Counterculture of Modernity," in *The Black Atlantic: Modernity and Double Consciousness* (Cambridge, MA: Harvard University Press, 1993), 5.

19. Gilroy, *The Black Atlantic*, 17.

20. See Sander L. Gilman, "The Hottentot and the Prostitute: Toward an Iconography of Female Sexuality," in *Race-ing Art History: Critical Readings in Race and Art History*, ed. Kymberly N. Pinder (New York: Routledge, 2002), 119–138.

21. This work was created after her 2005 solo exhibition *Kara E. Walker's Song of the South* at REDCAT, Los Angeles, which consisted of three film animations projected onto cut plywood silhouettes of trees and two live performances staged by the artist at the opening and closing of the show. Afterward, in her studio, Walker revised and restaged sections of the initial animations and performance and conceived a new storyboard for *8 Possible Beginnings*, which premiered in her spring 2006 solo exhibition at Sikkema Jenkins & Co., New York.

22. Walker's first use of video and performance in her work took place during her 2004 solo exhibition *Fibbergibbet and Mumbo Jumbo: Kara E. Walker in Two Acts* at the Fabric Workshop and Museum, Philadelphia.

23. From Walker's introductory panel to her 2006 solo exhibition *Kara Walker at the Met: After the Deluge* at the Metropolitan Museum of Art, New York.

24. Walker's piece is the antithesis of Griffith's malicious attempt to provide historical justification for segregation. Griffith's 1915 film was inspired by Thomas Dixon's racist novel *The Clansman: An Historical Romance of the Ku Klux Klan*, published in 1905.

25. For more on this topic, see Orlando Patterson, "Enslavement by Birth," in *Slavery and Social Death*, 132–135.

26. Toni Morrison, *Beloved* (New York: Plume, 1987), 149.

27. See P. J. Gibbs, *Black Collectibles: Sold in America* (Paducah, KY: Collector Books, 1987).

28. Walker quoted in Alexander Alberro, "Kara Walker," *Index* 1, no. 1 (February 1996): 27.

29. bell hooks, "Selling Hot Pussy," in *Black Looks: Race and Representation* (Boston: South End Press, 1992), 62.

30. Sigmund Freud, "Character and Anal Eroticism" (1908), in *The Standard Edition of the Complete Psychological Works of Sigmund Freud*, ed. and trans. J. Strachey with A. Freud, A. Strachey, and A. Tyson, 24 vols. (London: Hogarth, 1955–1974), vol. 9, 174.

31. See Wood, *Blind Memory*, 226.

32. See Achille Mbembé, "The Aesthetic of Vulgarity," in his *On the Postcolony* (Berkeley: University of California Press, 2001), 102–141.

33. *Testimony* is reminiscent in form and technique of Lotte Reiniger's fantastical animation *Adventures of Prince Achmed*, from 1926. In her second animation, *8 Possible Beginnings*, Walker names Reiniger in her list of acknowledgments.

34. Harriet Jacobs, *Incidents in the Life of a Slave Girl* (1861; New York: Dover Publications, 2001), 46.

35. Patterson, *Slavery and Social Death*, 5.

36. On the "failed patriarch," see Gwendolyn DuBois Shaw, "The Lactation of John Brown," in *Seeing the Unspeakable*, 67–101. Shaw presents an incisive study of this particular work.

37. See W. J. T. Mitchell, "Drawing Desire," in *What Do Pictures Want? The Lives and Loves of Images* (Chicago: University of Chicago Press, 2005), 57–75. Mitchell offers insightful examination of Freud's theories of the pleasure principle and the death drive and how they are manifested in images.

38. Walker interviewed by Hans-Ulrich Obrist, "All Cut from Black Paper by the Able Hand of Kara Elizabeth Walker . . . ," in *Safety Curtain: Kara Walker*, ed. Johannes Schlebrügge, exhibition catalog (Vienna: Museum in Progress, in cooperation with Vienna State Opera House and P & S Wien, 2000), 15.

39. Fanon, *Black Skin, White Masks*, 116.

A Performative Turn: Kara Walker's *Song of the South (2005)*

Lorraine Morales Cox

In the fall of 2005, artist Kara Walker premiered *Song of the South*, a comprehensive installation, film, and performance piece exhibited in the gallery at the Roy and Edna Disney/CalArts Theater (REDCAT) in Los Angeles.[1] The multimedia work reflects Walker's ongoing desire to seek out conceptual and emotive strategies for confronting the historical trauma of slavery and contemporary racial and sexual oppressions. In considering the trauma of the past and the failure of emancipation in relation to the self, Ron Eyerman writes, "Slavery formed the root of an emergent collective identity through an equally emergent collective memory, one that signified and distinguished a race, a people, or a community depending on the level of abstraction and point of view being put forward."[2] *Song of the South* expands upon Walker's critical aesthetic approach of challenging viewers with her Morrisonian "re-memory" of America's dark antebellum history in order to address the larger issue of the present state of race relations and racism in American today. With this new body of work, Walker incorporates performative and multisensory elements of sound, live action, and filmed images. The visual, emotive, and conceptual effects of these performative elements empower Walker's traditionally two-dimensional still image works. These changes result in a more nuanced and conceptually rich reflection on America's past and how it has shaped contemporary concerns and social justice issues surrounding race, gender, and sexuality. In this work Walker also incorporates her own personal and collective experiences as an African American woman with even greater intimacy than in her previous projects, resulting in the production of a richly layered and provocative work of art. Over the past few years, Walker's oeuvre has experienced what I call a "performative turn" noted by an increasing desire to more fully stage and embody her cut black paper silhouettes from which she first became known. This transitional moment, highlighted here, reflects an even greater attentiveness to the viewer's presence, an increasing use of filmic interventions, and the incorporation of the artist's own body as both a represented image and live performer. With these recent developments, Walker continues to exacerbate the stinging wounds of history while challenging us to address the trauma of the past as manifested in today's societal ills, proving that creative acts can play an important role in stimulating social awareness and transformative behavior.

Kara Walker has described her work as a form of "excavation," not in terms of a site of scientific rediscovery of a culture's physical objects, but rather as a site that "is psychological, emotional and physical."[3] Her work provokes viewers to excavate, contemplate, and evaluate deep-seated collective and individual perpetuations of racism, sexism, and homophobia. Through a layered multidimensional body of work, weaving together fiction, history, autobiography, and popular culture, Walker states: "what I'm interested in as far as art goes is how contemporary values and individual neurosis project themselves into the blank spaces between the fact of (for instance) slavery's influence on the American system, and the power of its influence over the American imagination."[4] Walker's art plays a vital yet challenging role in confronting a culture deeply plagued by racism and general xenophobia, a daily form of psychological trauma inflicted on its victims, directly or indirectly, be they young or old, through such experiences as overt verbal slurs, minority exclusion, or institutional and casual forms of racist oppression, all of which add up to a long, continual history of racial trauma. This essay considers the performative genealogy of Kara Walker's art and looks closely at its most recent manifestation, one which moves toward a greater sensory embodiment of trauma, in turn stirring a greater empathic realization of the extent to which slavery's historical legacy remains with us all today.

In October 1994, Kara Walker debuted *Gone, An Historical Romance of a Civil War as It Occurred between the Dusky Thighs of One Young Negress and Her Heart* (1994), at New York's Drawing Center, only months after she completed her MFA at the Rhode Island School of Design. Several landmark group and solo exhibitions soon followed, bringing national and international attention to Walker's trademark black silhouette imagery. She garnered even greater notoriety when she became the youngest person to win the prestigious MacArthur Foundation "genius" award in 1997, the same year she was included in the Whitney Biennial. In 2002 she served as the United States Representative to the São Paulo Biennial. Numerous catalogue essays and articles have been generated by Walker's art, ranging from strongly supportive to disdainfully critical.[5] Her work has even been the subject of several dissertations, and the recent publication of *Seeing the Unspeakable: The Art of Kara Walker* (2004) by Gwendolyn DuBois Shaw adds a much needed cultural contextualization to her art, particularly in relation to eighteenth- and nineteenth-century American history, as well as art history.[6] The range of written material on Walker clearly results from the provocative nature of her work, which includes themes of social power, race, gender, illicit sexuality, and violence, rooted in the antebellum world and continually manifested in today's contemporary American society. A gamut of historical and contemporary references weaves itself throughout Walker's oeuvre, from historic slave narratives to neo-slave narratives, minstrelsy, pornography, history painting, popular films, and Harlequin romance, as well as her own personal experiences.[7] From these various sources, Walker "acts out"—with characters and personas that take on slavery's sexual, psychological, and traumatic abuse, in an often shockingly yet productive manner. Walker confronts the pathological ramifications of a marginalized history upon which the foundation of privilege and prosperity for a majority of Americans has been built, which simultaneously plagues the political, economic, societal, and educational realities of others.

With the background and training as an art historian, I bring to my study of contemporary art an interdisciplinary approach to Walker's practice, drawing on an evolving engagement with transcultural aesthetic theories, feminism, critical race theory, queer theory, literary theory, and popular and cultural studies. I come to Walker's new work as an art historian looking at performance within the field of the visual. I have long been drawn to creative work that promotes a viewer or participant to consider their own racial, sexual, gendered, and/or class consciousness and I am equally interested in the concept of artistic fictions as a kind of evidence for confronting sociopolitical problems. The ability of Walker's art to reawaken and provoke historically dis-remembered racial and sexual trauma connects directly with the present, regardless of whether, as Gwendolyn Dubois Shaw notes, "these memories of trauma and feelings of guilt are lived or received." She continues, "They remind us that as postmoderns living in an increasingly diverse image world, we are all haunted by slavery."[8]

What at first may appear as familiar cliché images of plantation life, rendered in an artistic form long associated with familial traditions of recording loved ones, Walker's signature silhouette figures, hand-cut from black paper and attached to white walls, reveals upon closer examination scenes of sadistic violence and scatological indecency. The historically marginalized figures found in Walker's imagery, the "Mammie," the "Pickaninny," the "Nigger wench," and so on, have historically been rendered by the dominant culture in both fine and popular arts, as either passive "Uncle Toms" or sexually deviant "Jezebels" and "Black Bucks."[9] In Walker's hands, these stereotyped characters become liberated and haunt back. The moment of visual discernment between first seeing quaint silhouettes and then discovering a scene of violent subversion creates a perceptual play which is also conceptual in that it triggers reflection on how ways of viewing connect to ways of knowing.[10] Throughout her oeuvre, Walker seeks to visually articulate and make tangible the unspeakable trauma of generations, then and now, oppressed on the grounds of their skin color and/or gender. This desire to expose and give form to the psychological trauma inflicted by a racist and sexist society represents the nucleus of Walker's practice. From scenes first spread across museum walls—freeze frames of a dark passion play—to her most recent embrace of the moving image and live performance, Walker persistently seeks to explore new strategies for making provocative and powerful work that will stimulate reflection, humbleness, and the inspiration to achieve social justice.

Theatrical references have long informed Walker's practice. She once stated, "Art is not a truthful place. The location of a painting is a stage," and she often notes her love of history painting as a stage, filled with characters, as portraits, on that stage.[11] The inspiration for the piece *Insurrection! (Our Tools Were Rudimentary, Yet We Pressed On)* (2000), for example, an image of a slave revolt where the house slaves go after their master with utensils of everyday life, comes from the nineteenth-century surgical theater paintings of Thomas Eakins.[12] Walker then combined the history painting genre with the silhouette, a form also connected to memory, although one of sentimentality but a form also used to identify, illustrate, and describe. However, part of Walker's interest in the silhouette resides in its appeal as a form which lends itself to the *avoidance* of the subject, and the sense of "not being able to look at it directly."[13] Such formal and conceptual contradictions lie at the heart of Walker's practice, creating important tensions between form and content that foster rich interpretive possibilities.

Walker's images take on a duality of existence, living simultaneously in both the past, as a form of history painting, and the present, as an activist aesthetic seeking to engage in contemporary social and political debates. Her imagery calls to mind the way in which the iconography of the antebellum era, melded through popular culture, continues to shape America's racialized social and political consciousness. Walker's earliest piece, *Gone, An Historical Romance . . .* (1994), a reference to Margaret Mitchell's best-selling novel *Gone with the Wind* (1936) and its epic melodrama as filmed in 1939, reflects Walker's decade-long engagement with this issue. The movie, one of the most commercially successful films ever made, has, according to historian Tony Horwitz, "done more to keep the Civil War alive, and to mold its memory, than any history book or event since Appomattox."[14] In Tara McPherson's thought-provoking study, *Reconstructing Dixie: Race, Gender, and Nostalgia in the Imagined South*, the author reveals the complex and ongoing mythologizing of the film, which experienced countless television reruns in the Reagan-era 1980s and 1990s.[15] With her most recent film and performance work, *Song of the South* (2005), Walker again takes on popular entertainment's sugar coating of the past and romanticizing of America's dark psycho-dramatic history, this time inspired by Walt Disney's 1946 film of the same title.

During a 2005 interview with writer Scarlet Cheng on the making of her own *Song of the South*, Kara Walker recalled the image that sent her many years ago on her current path, a vintage postcard she saw in her early twenties of a young black women in a tattered frock, holding up a fan, with the caption "Some class, eh?" The image sent Walker reeling, because, as she put it, "there are so many potential voices in it. . . . It sent me back and forth, thinking how as an artist we react to images, how as a black woman with some conscience do I react to this image? I was trying to figure out what exactly my own voice was, what was not spoken about in my own work."[16] Walker acknowledges her fixation with the past but repeatedly notes its connection to the present, stating that her work "has to do with the need to or tendency to rehash and repeat and never quite let go of something you know you need to let go of. Just when you think you can let go, then New Orleans gets flooded, and thousands and thousands of black people suffer."[17] In discussing *Song of the South* (2005) with Walker, which opened only four days after Hurricane Katrina struck the Gulf Coast of the United States, Cheng noted the emotion in Walker's voice as she "compared the holding of hurricane evacuees, most of them black, in the Louisiana superdome to slave ships that brought their ancestors to this country."[18]

Born in 1969 in Stockton, California, Walker moved to Atlanta, Georgia, with her family at the age of thirteen. "My golden years were in Stockton," Walker stated dryly in a recent interview, adding, "Entering puberty and the South at the same time was sort of two traumas at once. I suddenly found myself in this place which was so much stranger than anything I could have dreamed up. I found a very definite separation. It was very black or white; there was no room for the in-betweeners, people with mixed backgrounds."[19] Growing up and living in a racist and sexist society informs Walker's work on multiple levels, particularly her adolescent years living in Atlanta, which included the time a Ku Klux Klan flyer appeared on her white boyfriend's car, which spelled out for him "all the evils of black women, describing what sort of peril he was in, and identifying stereotypes of disease and moral degradation," a moment Walker notes as an awakening.[20] After completing her BFA from the Atlanta College of Art in 1991, Walker headed to Rhode Island to pursue her MFA and, as she puts it, "to make work that would actually stimulate others, and not just myself."[21]

African Americans, from novelist to civil rights leaders, have long used the autobiographical form to examine ideological issues and to situate their personal preferences within the larger political context.[22] In *Bearing Witness: Selections from African American Autobiography in the Twentieth Century* (1991) Henry Louis Gates Jr. argues that the will to power for black Americans was the will to write; and the predominant mode that writing would assume was the shaping of the black self in words.[23] As one scholar put it, autobiography "fulfilled the need to define the individual 'black self' to a society that denied the existence of a black reality."[24] Walker's practice consistently evokes what can be considered the first African American autobiographical form, that of the slave narrative, along with its complicated history of having both a questionable authenticity while also being a critically important record of American slave history, life, and experiences. During the antebellum period the slave narrative became an integral part of the abolitionist campaigns beginning in the 1830s when many narratives were filtered through white abolitionist ghost writers or others who used the texts for evangelical purposes as conversion narratives.[25] Walker's art consistently reminds us of the fact that subjects such as sexual violence, often seen as taboo, were either edited or dismissed altogether from such narratives, which her work seeks to visually reinscribe, bringing to the surface these hidden, ignored, and denied crimes against humanity. Mindful of this complicated past of the slave narrative, Walker's increasingly performative developments have occurred alongside an increasing tendency to reveal more intimate aspects of her own psychological self. Walker draws on her own biography, as have many other African American female authors of the neo-slave narrative, from Toni Morrison to Octavia Butler, yet Walker's work also differs from the narrative forms that suggest a resolve or a moment of self-discovery.

With his *Narrative of the Life of Frederick Douglass, an American Slave, Written by Himself* (1845), the author and former slave aimed to make the personal political, by telling his story to assist in the political movement aimed at the abolition of slavery.[26] Walker draws on the heritage of the slave narrative genre, noted in her use of lengthy titling and subtitles, the incorporation of the word "narrative" and authenticating terms such as "self-taught," "by a Negress," or "by Myself." She also makes the personal political by drawing on her own autobiographical experiences as they connect to broader concerns, including the psychological pain inflicted on the victims of racism and sexism as well as the moral responsibility of others to alleviate and eliminate such pain. In the introduction to *Literary Trauma: Sadism, Memory and Sexual Violence in American Women's Fiction*, Deborah Horvitz focuses on a group of writers whom, she writes, "assume responsibility for 'witnessing' and testifying to traumatic events that are pervasively cultural and, at the same time, experienced and interpreted as personal."[27] This concept of testimony or "bearing witness" to that which is both personal and cultural in terms of trauma provides a useful perspective in considering Walker's own practice and its evolving development.

Walker's performative turn can be traced to her first light projection pieces made and exhibited in the spring of 2000 for her solo show at the Centre d'Art Contemporain in Geneva, titled *Why I Like White Boys. An Illustrated Novel by Kara E. Walker, Negress.*[28] The exhibit space was composed of several wall pieces incorporating Walker's signature black paper cutouts, but this time combined with mechanical overhead projection machines placed on the floor, which projected onto the walls swaths of color and figures cut from paper and plastic transparencies. The centerpiece of the exhibit, entitled *Insurrection! (Our Tools Were Rudimentary, Yet We Pressed On* (2000), covered three walls and included dark silhouetted figures projected alongside or over the paper versions pasted to the wall, as well as projected landscape elements of trees, clouds, and tall windows.[29] The imagery of this piece suggested the interior space of a plantation home, "the big house," located on the large center wall with nature forms spilling out to the squared-off walls on either side, creating a cyclorama of sorts, a recurring formal element in Walker's silhouetted wall piece installations. As with her previous wall pieces, Walker's silhouetted antebellum characters carried on in disturbing acts of mayhem, violence, and illicit sex over all three walls; however, with the inclusion of the projected light, the work elicits the viewer to participate as yet another character implicated in the scene before them.

In this work, the viewer's own shadow-double cast itself into the work as an ephemeral "ghost." Standing closest to the projectors would cast the viewer's body as a long and ominous shadow from floor to ceiling, or, when only a few feet from the wall, the shadow matched up to the scale of the pasted silhouettes. The viewer's shadow theatrically charged the gallery space, blending in a convincing formal manner with Walker's own orchestrated imagery. In choosing to use overhead projectors, Walker sought to activate the space and have the projectors serve as a kind of stand-in for the viewer, as observers, while also thinking of the overhead projectors as didactic tools, noting, "they're a schoolroom tool. So they're about conveying facts. The work I do is about projecting fictions into those facts."[30] Walking in front of *Insurrection!*, the viewer's shadow may overlap with either the victim or the abuser, creating psychologically jarring shifts that, depending on the viewer's own racial and/or gendered experiences, could lead to a moment of awkwardness, repulsion, introspective horror, or even

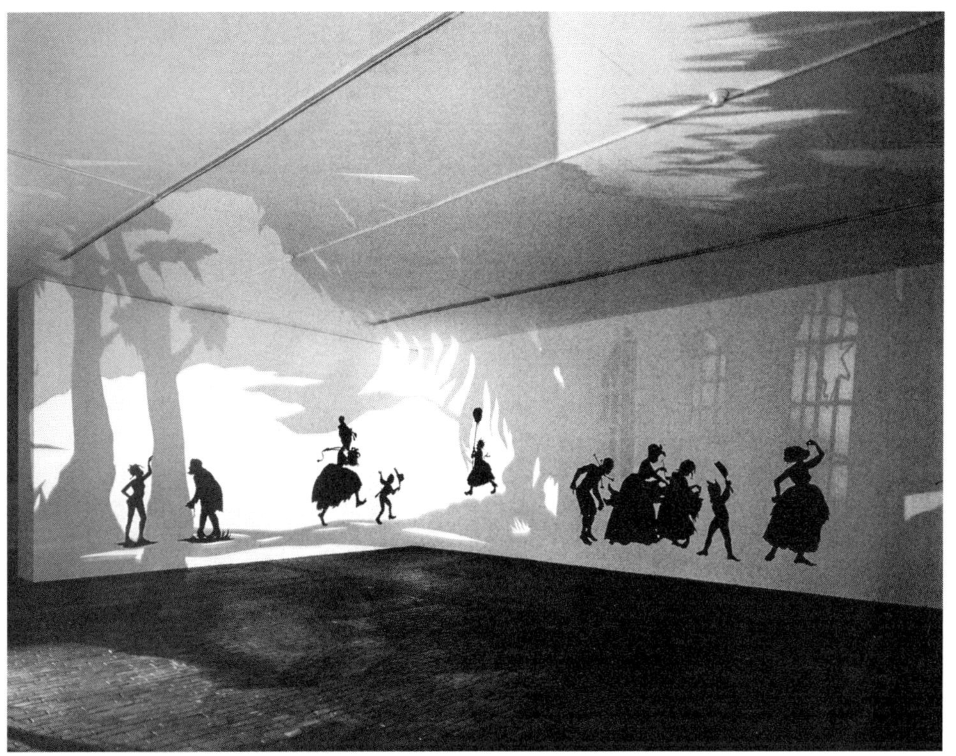

Kara Walker, *Insurrection! (Our Tools Were Rudimentary, Yet We Pressed On)*, 2000. Cut paper silhouettes and light projections, dimensions variable. Installation view: *Why I Like White Boys. An Illustrated Novel by Kara E. Walker, Negress*, Centre d'Art Contemporain, Geneva, Switzerland, 2000. Photo: Sarina Basta. Artwork © Kara Walker, courtesy of Sikkema Jenkins & Co., New York; Sprüth Magers, Berlin.

a traumatic flashback. With this light projection piece, Walker came closer than ever in creating a virtual space which co-opts the viewer to unwillingly act alongside the silhouetted cast.[31] The viewer's involuntary placement in the work marked a hallmark moment in Walker's formal and artistic development. This and additional projection pieces were the catalyst that would spur Walker's increasing desire to engage the physical presence of actual bodies, both her own body and that of the viewer/participant.[32]

In 2004, Kara Walker created *Fibbergibbit and Mumbo Jumbo: Kara E. Walker in Two Acts*, an installation and live performance piece with herself as the main character; a culmination of a long-term residency begun in 2001 at the Fabric Workshop in Philadelphia. The piece marked a dramatic turning point in Walker's creative process and formal development.[33] The room-filled installation presented an antebellum campsite located in a marsh, haunted by a "phantasmagoria of colored projections."[34] Willow trees and swamp grass cut from plywood and painted black encircled a burlap tent in the middle of the gallery. On one side hung a fabric backdrop upon which moving shadows of Walker's familiar antebellum characters appeared by rear projection. For the first time Walker incorporated a video that included several images of herself topless and backlit dancing the Charleston, reminiscent of Josephine Baker (an image that appears in previous work), and in a second video Walker wears a bonnet, hand extended, gesturing and begging for alms.[35]

The exhibit also included a one-night-only performance by Walker, held on March 26, 2005, in which she sat under a plywood tree for about an hour, and then without notice performed for eight minutes with James Hannaham, her collaborator and cousin, both barefoot and dressed in tattered frock dresses made by Walker herself during the residency. Approximately five hundred people were in attendance, some directly in the space of the performance and others watching a projected version in an adjacent gallery.[36] For Walker, the title "Fibbergibbit and Mumbo Jumbo" referred to "the 'marginalia at the edges of [her] practice,' representing a range of contradictions about the relationship between the self and the other in addressing such personal subjects."[37] The multiple video and shadow images of Walker in the installation allowed her to be "present" in the work at various levels, in a kind of conversation with herself that revealed more of herself than she has ever done in the past. The performance began with Hannaham, in the character of a woman, on his hands and knees inside the tent, loudly rummaging through pots and pans, while speaking and mumbling to himself a series of disjointed phrases, such as: "Wet his lips and stick him to the wall," "He don't know that he is black," "Aunt Jemima, Dianna Ross, that Mother Fucker," "I said who free?"[38] This lasted approximately two minutes, after which Walker stood up, sauntered toward Hannaham, and provoked him to come out of the tent, after which she asked him: "What's black and orange and beautiful to behold?" to which he replies, "A nigger on fire." Hannaham then moves behind a tree and listens on while Walker, for the remaining five minutes of the performance, reads from a written text, while holding a typically male pipe, an interesting complement to Hannaham in female drag. She informs the audience that the inspiration for the piece came from a conversation she overheard one night in a landscape "resembling this one" of two "Negroes," while she stood "knee deep in muck." She then comments on her various observations of that night, from the dialect she overheard of "soft southern obedience" and the "simple and soulful way" the two women "reiterate the complex mythology of the ancient Greeks . . . plain folk performing the mundane tasks of life, they out lick their so called 'Betters' those with years of the best schooling behind them have lost all touch with the fertile, tactile ground that enriches the souls of Black folk."[39] In both the installation and performance, Walker's moving images and spoken word relived and retold of a psychic "re-memory," moving between fantasy and reality, as she both played the role of someone else while also playing herself as observer and narrator. Reflecting on the piece, Walker stated, "It's me, standing in the middle of the landscape that exists in my mind."[40] Walker continued her monologue, as she "set the scene," noting the ideal vantage point, the sway of the women's hips, and how one woman bore the scars of multiple lashings and the expression of a wet nurse. As with her previous projection pieces, viewers again found themselves participating in the work, but now standing in the midst of a multi-dimensional mixed media installation, their bodies part of the artist's imaginative fictional space, listening or overhearing a scene as Walker herself claimed to have overheard.[41]

An interesting element included in the *Fibbergibbit and Mumbo Jumbo* installation was the thirty to thirty-five marionette crows made of black paper and hanging from the ceiling. The fact that the crows wore black top hats immediately called to mind the animated racist black crows that have appeared in such films as Walt Disney's *Dumbo* (1941). The racist origin of this character goes back to nineteenth-century fictional illustrations of a dancing Jim Crow wearing a black top hat.[42] As Walker first broached in *Gone*, she again references racist history as reproduced and perpetuated in popular forms, not only for adult consumption, but animated for the youngest of minds, an important theme she would take up the following year, which would again, and more overtly, reference Disney's work.

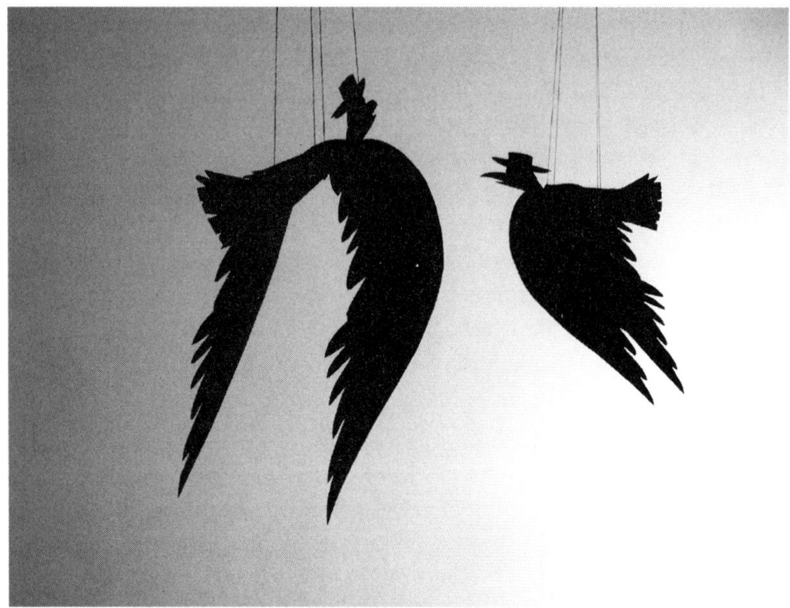

Kara Walker, in collaboration with the Fabric Workshop and Museum, Philadelphia, detail from *Fibbergibbit and Mumbo Jumbo: Kara E. Walker in Two Acts*, 2004. Dimensions variable. Painted wood, paper, thread, coffee-stained muslin, instant coffee–stained canvas, metal armatures, Mylar, colored gels, light bulbs, motorized turntables, foamcore, video projectors, flashlights, record player, burlap, and linen. Photo: Aaron Igler. Reproduced with permission of the Fabric Workshop and Museum (FMW), Philadelphia. Artwork © Kara Walker, courtesy of Sikkema Jenkins & Co., New York; Sprüth Magers, Berlin.

In 2001 Walker stated in an interview, "The idea of shadow and puppet theater has been on my mind for the longest time. It seems like the obvious solution somehow for some issues that I'd like to talk about formally, like how one interacts with the work and how the work acts on you."[43] This statement tellingly reveals Walker's evolving thought process in relation to her concern for her viewers and her own physical presence in the work. In her first solo exhibition in Los Angeles, in the fall of 2005, Walker brought these ideas to life with her own version of Walt Disney's *Song of the South*, at the Gallery at REDCAT located in the Frank Gehry–designed Walt Disney Concert Hall complex.[44] The subject and location of the exhibit created, as one critic wrote, "a nicely ironic symmetry."[45] Walker's multimedia installation offered a kind of backstory to Disney's Oscar-winning film of the same title first released on November 12, 1946, one of the first films made by Walt Disney that successfully combined live action and animation.[46] Disney based his now both loathed and celebrated film on the stories of "Uncle Remus," a warm and jovial former Black slave, created and written by Joel Chandler Harris, a white man who grew up poor near Atlanta, Georgia, during the Civil War.[47] Harris spent a lifetime compiling and publishing the tales he claimed to have heard as a child from former slaves and began publishing his stories of Uncle Remus, Br'er Fox, and Br'er Rabbit in the *Atlanta Constitution* in 1876.[48] Scholars have noted that Harris apparently did not perceive the full significance of the fables, which he garnered from the Black people of his day. "He failed to recognize, for example, that many of the tales were veiled protest against enslavement. . . . He overlooked the fact that the use of the word 'Brer' was a common denominator for *a brotherhood of spiritual and material goals and ideals.*"[49] When released, Disney advertised the film as "The happy, heartwarming picture of the Old South," a fictional work reflecting an historical amnesia re-created in other well-known classics like *Gone with the Wind*. The premiere of the film at the Fox Theater in Atlanta occurred only four months, almost to the day, after the brutal lynching of two black couples, George and Mae Murray Dorsey and Roger and Dorothy Malcolm, in Walton County, Georgia. The men had just returned home from active duty in World War II. Christopher Knight, in his very favorable review of Walker's exhibit, identified the chilling proximity of these two events in 1946 and stated that "Walker's unhappy, heart-wrenching picture" was one that "offers bittersweet context" to this dark moment in history.[50]

In developing the piece, Eugene Joo, director of the Gallery at REDCAT, encouraged Walker to produce something experimental as the artist set out to explore "the theatricality of space."[51] In the center of the large square gallery, Walker erected a full circle of approximately thirteen plywood, moss-covered trees, propped up by two by fours and painted black on the side facing inward toward the circle. A wooden arrow sign, hand-painted with the words "Folks is advised: Dis Aint fer Chillun," marked the entrance into the clearing of trees that read as clichéd visual signifiers of the Old South, reminiscent of animated films and cartoon imagery of the 1940s and 1950s. However, the starkness of the black trees carried an ominous and foreboding feeling, as opposed to something "happy and heartwarming."

The installation included the premiere of Walker's first film, a fifteen-minute looped 16-mm piece titled, *8 Possible Beginnings or: The Creation of African-America, a Moving Picture by the young, self-taught, Genius of the South K. E. Walker,*[52] executed in the manner of an old, grainy, silent movie, with scratched frames and flickering light that, according to Walker, resulted from "fortunate processing" as she chose to keep most of the flaws "because they looked really nice."[53] Shadow puppets, animated by Walker, appear in seven of the eight film sections divided by one short live action sequence in the middle. Title cards, printed text, and some voice sections narrate the film. Background music plays throughout most of the film, including slave labor folk songs and musical showtunes reminiscent of early Disney films. For the installation, the film continually looped from a rear-projection machine onto a large piece of white scrim stretched between two large trees at the opposite end of the clearing's entrance. On either side of this main projection screen, rear projection images looped on two additional but smaller white scrims stretched between trees. A single, lit, colonial-looking candle appeared on the one to the left and on the right. Male slave bodies, shackled and linked head to foot, appear continually dragged along the bottom of the screen.

The darkened gallery, lit only by the film, the two smaller side-projected images, and residual light coming from the building's entrance, created a space that moved from meditative and soothing to mysterious and foreboding. As there were no chairs, most viewers chose to sit on the cool-tiled gallery floor as they watched the film, creating an experience similar to children watching a performance, a brilliant juxtaposition to the dark and chilling adult subjects of the installation, inspired by a Disney film made for children. One of the most interesting conceptual plays of the space occurred from the feeling of being "behind the scenes," as one walks up to the exposed and unpainted wooden supports of the trees, to then enter the clearing to be surrounded by haunting southern trees, feeling as if one had walked into the scene and onto the studio set of *Gone with the Wind*. On the night of the second performance, the space gradually filled to capacity as people sat on the floor, shoulder to shoulder, for close to thirty minutes, watching the looped film while waiting for the performance to begin. This experience in itself made a disturbing yet powerful connection to the interior of the slave ships that appear in the first

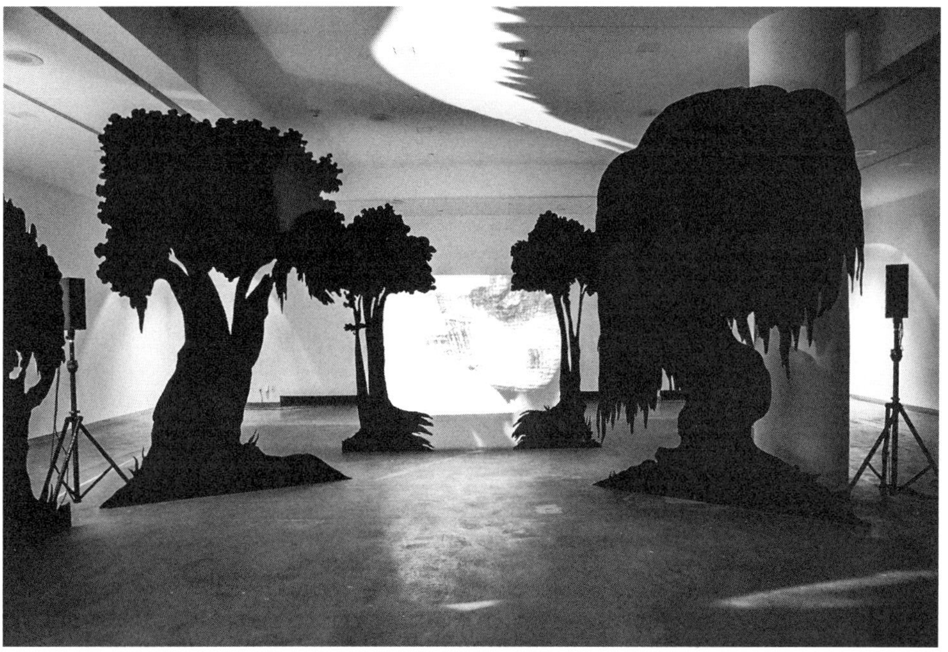

Kara Walker, *Song of the South*, 2005. REDCAT, Los Angeles, CA, 2005. Photo: Scott Groller. Artwork © Kara Walker, courtesy of Sikkema Jenkins & Co., New York; Sprüth Magers, Berlin.

sequence of Walker's film. These experiential and vivifying aspects of Walker's installation heightened one's empathic response, as viewer and participant, to a greater degree than Walker's projection pieces. The interfacing of sound and motion, along with the juxtaposition of two- and three-dimensional elements, created an engaging conceptual play between reality and fiction. These qualities vivified Walker's subject, creating a push and pull aesthetic that provoked a more visceral and material response. This presented an effective strategy, enhanced by the film and performance, for inspiring greater reflection on the psychological and physical trauma of chattel slavery, by enlivening what we already expect and have naturalized in our historical reception of Walker's two-dimensional work and titles.

In discussing the film, Walker stated that she "wanted to retell the story of coming into being . . . by using a few elements of the African American cosmology—middle passage, slavery."[54] Stemming from her previous work, the eight sections of the film created interesting dialectical shifts that moved between references to the historical past and lived present, but now done in a more conceptually rich and layered manner that prompted one to contemplate *how* the past is remembered and relived today. The film begins with a section titled "Along a Watery Road," which presents a slave ship at sea and a captain proclaiming, "Toss dem uppity Niggers!," followed by a sequence of floating bodies with their "new world" signifiers literally cut out of their flat, black-paper skins, including "African," "Authentic," "Negroes," "Fakers," and "Wannabees." These terms recall the broadsides that advertised the sale of slaves, while also referencing contemporary debates on "degrees" of blackness, passing, and miscegenation. "Motherland" then emerges from the sea, her African coiffed hair disguised as an island with a palm tree. She proceeds to eat the floating bodies shown in the film traveling through the paper silhouette of her long digestive tract until ingested and expelled as a mound of excrement on the shores of America.

In the second sequence of the film, the mound of excrement transforms into the character "King Cotton" now "reborn" as a robust black male slave working on a cotton field. The image of King Cotton, coming into being as he rises from the ground on one knee with his arms above his head, visually connects to a similar figure of a praying man that appeared in Walker's earlier wall piece, *The End of Uncle Tom and the Grand Allegorical Tableau of Eva in Heaven* (1995). Gwendolyn Dubois Shaw has identified this "praying man" as a "direct descendent of the kneeling slaves prevalent in antebellum abolitionist visual culture," specifically, Shaw notes, the kneeling slave in Josiah Wedgewood's pendant "Am I Not a Man and a Brother?"[55] But rather than chains, an umbilical cord binds the figure in Walker's *The End of Uncle Tom*, which Shaw sees as having palpable symbolic significance because "under slavery, birth was the beginning of a life of unending misery and oppression for its victims."[56] In Walker's film, King Cotton proceeds to walk through the field to the tune of a slave labor "pick'n cotton" song, while a series of still images appear behind him, including a nineteenth-century documentary photograph of slaves or sharecroppers picking cotton, followed by a historical drawing of slaves working at Eli Whitney's cotton gin machine.[57] Whitney's invention, which separated the cotton fiber from the seed, was so improved by the 1820s that cotton became "king," especially in the Mississippi Delta, Alabama, and Georgia.

Walker's King Cotton then meets up with a white male slave owner and the two begin to wrestle before engaging in oral and anal "shadow puppet" sex. At the end of the sex scene, the white master sexually implants his "cotton seed" into the anus of King Cotton. Impregnated, King Cotton's belly expands and grows with the Cotton Spirit child he will soon deliver in a later scene. In a drawn sketch by Walker included in the exhibition brochure, the slave master spits cotton seeds into King Cotton's mouth as the slave simultaneously gives birth to a stalk of cotton. Walker's drawn and animated images present a violently surreal human Whitney cotton gin, which highlights the history of human slave labor in this country and the equally unspoken history of bodily rape and molestation of slaves, both male and female, by their owners, often resulting in a kind of production line of "new labor" offspring. At the same time, Walker, in choosing not to show the more commonly referenced and historically recognized heterosexual rape of female slaves by their male slave owners, reminds the viewer of the often ignored or little documented homosexual rapes of slaves by their masters, a topic that scholars have only recently begun to further address and theorize, both historically and in relation to such subjects as homophobic rape fantasies.[58] The theme of reproduction also metaphorically connects to the manner in which generations pass down white supremacist mythical beliefs and racist behaviors, in turn giving birth to new generations that will likely repeat the ugly past.

This male-on-male sex scene, which shifted between appearing forced or consensual, (producing an uncomfortable satirical quality due to the convergence of puppets and sex), along with the fantastical impregnation of the male slave, raised numerous contemporary and historical debates surrounding sexuality and race in America.[59] Here Walker interjects the subject of sexuality alongside racially defined social and political histories and debates both broadly across the United States as well as within the African American community. Specifically, I am thinking here of the "down low" (self-described straight Black men who secretly have sex with men), just now being spoken about in recent books and magazine articles and described by some as a "new phenomena" with down low blogs and chat rooms.[60] Walker's inclusion of the intersection of race and sexuality, a topic increasingly receiving greater scholarly and theoretical attention, stirs one to contemplate both the historical legacies of slavery and African American sexuality along with related legal battles both present and past. The June 26, 2003, *Lawrence v. Texas* landmark Supreme Court decision comes to mind, which overturned the United States Supreme Court's 1986 *Bowers v. Hardwick* case, which upheld sodomy laws from privacy challenges. The 2003 case involved the consensual sex between a white male and a black male "caught" in a bedroom by Texas police. The decision declared sodomy laws, which fourteen states, Puerto Rico, and the military had until the 2003 *Lawrence v. Texas* ruling, an unconstitutional violation of liberty and privacy rights. Current heated debates on gay marriage and the topic of miscegenation in Walker's film also lead one to then recall the 1967 *Loving v. Virginia* decision in which the Supreme Court ruled in favor of a mixed race couple whose marriage had been judged illegal by Virginia law, which put an end to state prohibitions against inter-racial marriage. This ruling occurred only two years before Walker herself was born, whose own husband is white, a topic she perhaps references in the titling of her previously mentioned 2000 exhibit, *Why I Like White Boys. An Illustrated Novel by Kara E. Walker, Negress*. Walker's art brilliantly leads one to reflect on contemporary social issues regarding race and sexuality without making explicit reference to present time; rather, she chooses to ground her imagery in things not discussed from the past, from which she stirs a bubbling-up to the surface of such contemporary public and private debates.

An additional point to briefly consider here lies in the excremental creation of King Cotton in relation to the subject of shame as connected to queer and racial identity. Walker, as she has done in her previous work, confronts shame head-on, channeling the subject of debasement alongside romance, the grotesque, and pretensions to gentility, brought together as a motivating and political force. The combination of elements surrounding King Cotton in the film brings to mind Kathryn Bond Stockton's theorization of Georges Bataille's writings in relation to the subject of debasement and pleasure as connected to scatological and sexual desires. Stockton, one of the most recent thinkers on debasement, sex, and rape, offers a conceptually and theoretically rich discussion of this topic in her most recent publication, along with other scholars who have begun to offer important critiques on the topic of race and sexuality.[61] Walker's layered references to race, sexuality, and shame hit on several conceptual and deeply important theoretical subjects deserving of further study.

Following the impregnation of King Cotton, and also at the mid-point of the film, Walker interjects into her low-tech shadow-puppet imagery the only live action sequence in the film, which subtly spoofs Disney's widely popular breakthrough in animation and live action that took place in his own *Song of the South*. The short scene presents a black female (not Walker) filmed wearing a headscarf, cutting out the silhouette of a male figure seated in profile and appearing in a dark silhouette before her, in the foreground of the image. The caption reads, "We find Bess, a comely Negress taking her master's likeness." Here, Walker indirectly reinscribes herself (the silhouette artist) into the film while also suggesting that "to take her Master's likeness" might also relate to miscegenation and the rape of slaves. This interlude, according to Christopher Knight, "creates a role reversal, nicely complicating the paternalistic idealizing space of the Disney film."[62] The insertion of live action/real bodies brings the reality of the lived experience of African Americans, past and present, abruptly yet powerfully into the consciousness of the viewers who, up until this point in the film, find themselves submitting to the willing suspension of disbelief around puppets and animation. The live action interlude ends and the film turns back to the puppet animation, with King Cotton's "birthing scene," as the pregnant male slave lies back down on a kitchen table while crying out in text, "Massa Knock me up!" A fellow female slave and midwife delivers the newly born stalk of cotton, discarding King Cotton's miscegenated homosexual offspring by tossing it over her shoulder; it lands in a field of cotton where it transforms and grows into a Cotton Spirit. This scene hauntingly recalls the actual slave infanticides that occurred as a form of resistance throughout slavery and stirs recollection of the famous literary version of such an act in Toni Morrison's classic, *Beloved*, also based on an actual event.[63]

In scene six, entitled "A Darkey Hymn—'All I Want,'" a shadow-puppet silhouette of a young black girl slowly moves across the screen while being followed by the leering arms of a creepy white male figure who continually lurches toward her. In this only narrative voice section of the film, a young girl (Walker's daughter) presents a series of statements; some repeated or followed by the adult female voice of Walker herself. The numerous short phrases of self-loathing and fear (roughly twenty) included: "I wonder how long it will last . . . Don't talk about it . . . Everything is good . . . People scrutinize me . . . I wish I was white . . . Go with the flow . . . I guess he will hurt me . . . I wonder what it will feel like . . . ," and the last being "I guess this is what happened to Abby." In her sketch of this scene in the gallery brochure, Walker wrote "Black Self Hate"—"My Soul, my killer interior," which reaffirms the film's thematic engagement with the psychologically destructive force of traumatic racial hate and subsequent self-hatred and shame left in its wake.

In the final scene, the viewer's perspective shifts as the camera angle takes us to the back of the puppet stage, exposing Walker herself, the wizard behind the curtain. We see the arms and face of the artist as she holds up the shadow puppets representing Uncle Remus and Johnny, the seven-year-old white boy, who represent Walker's most direct reference to Disney's 1946 film and its two lead characters.[64] In Walker's film, Johnny pleads "please, please" to Uncle Remus to tell the tales of Br'er Fox and Br'er Rabbit. But the stories Uncle Remus tells do not resemble the humorous moral tales of animals in Disney's Briar Patch. Rather, Walker's twenty-first- century version of the "laughing place" as told by Uncle Remus includes the image of a giant cotton stalk—a fully grown "Cotton Spirit"—which now has risen from the ground and morphed into a tree with ropes hanging from its limbs. Uncle Remus gives in and placates the young boy by beginning "Long ago, fox and rabbit . . ."—at which point a silhouetted fox and rabbit appear and begin to pull on the ropes lifting up black-paper male bodies of "strange fruit," hanging lynched and lifeless in the tree. With this final scene, Walker's melancholic and powerful film comes to an end, to be rewound and retold again, and again, like the daily and cyclical acts of oppression and hate that impact so many of humanity's brothers and sisters.

For the opening and closing events for *Song of the South*, Walker came to Los Angeles and performed her own live shadow-puppet show in the Gallery at REDCAT.[65] For the closing performance, which I attended, the space was full to capacity with over eight hundred people tightly seated on the floor, or standing squeezed between the trees, a powerful allusion to the packed human cargo of slave ships as mentioned earlier. The loosely structured and slightly improvised performance took place on a small, backlit, white scrim screen set into one of the trees. In a series of approximately eight sets or scenes, Walker, through the character of her own "Kara" puppet, introduced and discussed the

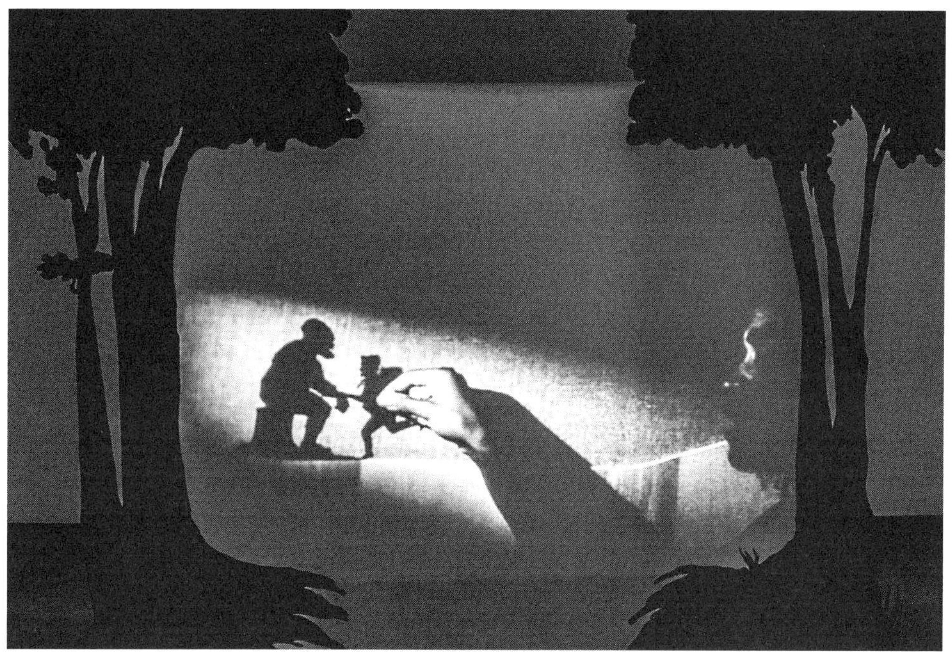

Kara Walker, still from *8 Possible Beginnings or: The Creation of African-America, a Moving Picture by Kara E. Walker*, 2005. Video (B&W with audio). 15:57 minutes. Installation view: *Song of the South*, REDCAT, Los Angeles, 2005. Photo: Scott Groller. Artwork © Kara Walker, courtesy of Sikkema Jenkins & Co., New York; Sprüth Magers, Berlin.

members of her filmic cast while also enacting their character voices. With no gesture or announcement, as she had done at the Fabric Workshop and Museum, Walker began the performance. The show opened with two of Walker's Cotton Spirit figures bouncing about in front of a silhouetted winding path. Walker and her assistant voiced the lines of the Cotton Spirits singing the "pick'n cotton" song heard in the film, followed by a quick chorus from the 1975 super soul musical "The Wiz"—"let's ease on down, ease on down the road," setting the stage for Walker's satiric performance down history's lane. The "Kara" cut puppet then greets the audience, a contemporary version of the artist herself, a silhouetted profile rendered with a chin-length bob of hair, similar to Walker's actual hair at the time, and wearing a pair of belted boot-cut jeans. This portrait departed from her usual doppelganger image as an antebellum "Negress" or "pickaninny" in tattered frocks.

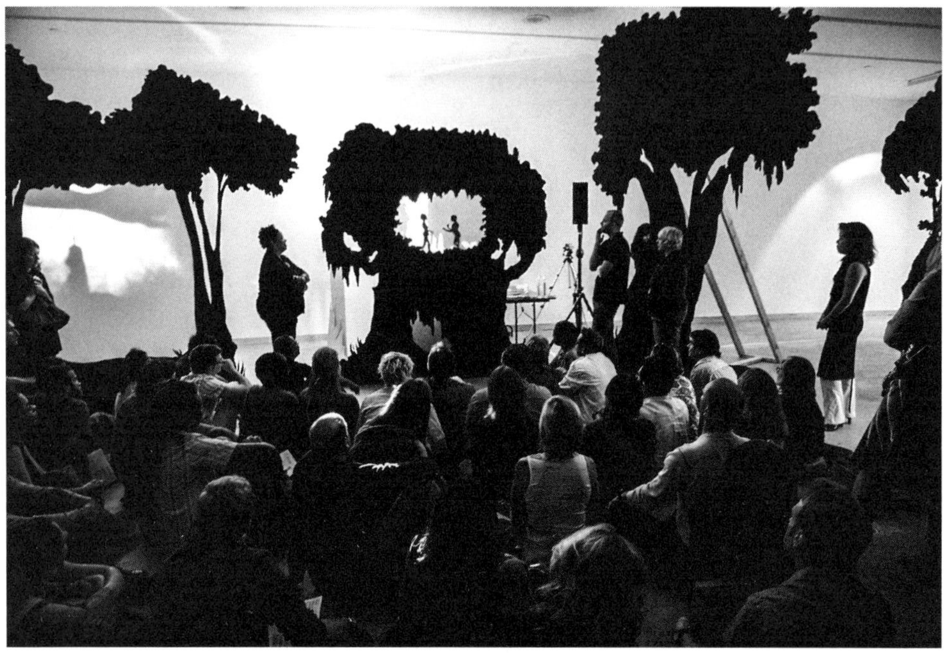

Kara Walker, *Song of the South*, 2005. Photograph of Walker's live shadow-puppet performance, September 3, 2005. REDCAT, Los Angeles, CA, 2005. Photo: Scott Groller. Artwork © Kara Walker, courtesy of Sikkema Jenkins & Co., New York; Sprüth Magers, Berlin.

Silhouetted in profile, Walker's puppet self-portrait appeared to be topless, with flat, puckered breasts that hauntingly recalled the historical images of female slaves as photographed by Joseph T. Zealy.[66] Walker's subtle contour-lined torso brought such images to mind, along with other examples of the exploitation of black female bodies, most notably the nineteenth-century case of twenty-year-old Saartjie (Sara) Baartman, the Khoikhoi black women taken from the Eastern Cape of South Africa and exhibited as a sideshow attraction in England and France as the "Hottentot Venus." Upon her death, without consent, Baartman's "vagina [was] cut out and put into a jar in Paris," as Walker described it in an interview.[67] Baartman's dissected brain, along with her genitals, were displayed, "in the name of science," at the Musée de l'Homme ("Museum of Man") in Paris where they could be seen until as recently as 1985.[68] The subject of female exploitation, rooted in the history of black female slaves, consistently informs Walker's artistic practice.

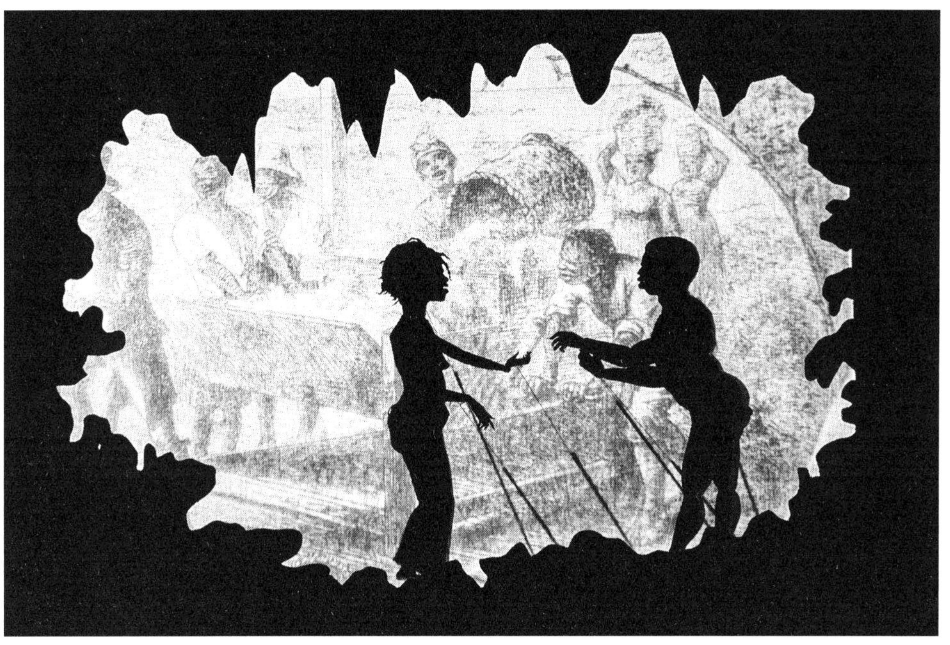

Kara Walker, *Song of the South*, 2005. Photograph of Walker's live shadow-puppet performance, September 3, 2005. REDCAT, Los Angeles, CA, 2005. Photo: Scott Groller. Artwork © Kara Walker, courtesy of Sikkema Jenkins & Co., New York; Sprüth Magers, Berlin.

For the next scene of the puppet performance, Walker introduced King Cotton, whom she describes as symbolic of black males historically viewed as less than human, "a long-standing American tradition," she says, "emblematic of recent racists' characters," who are often shaped around the idea of having an "animal nature" with their heightened "sexuality."[69] Walker states that this character can be viewed as a "fantasy of sorts," noting his ability to bear the "Cotton Spirit," a decision she made because, as Walker noted to the audience, "I'm tired of making the female bodies the ones being exploited." The Kara puppet then proceeded to flirtatiously dance with King Cotton until the two become sexually involved, to which Kara yells out, "I haven't done this in a while. . . . I'm in ecstasy, Mr. Cotton please don't go away!" Here again, Walker weaves humor and pain into a powerful message about exploitation and stereotypes of racialized male and female sexuality.

Walker then introduced the Mammy, or midwife, from the film, which Walker's puppet persona struggles to name, saying, "This is

Auntie? Mammie? Oprah?" followed by "well it doesn't really matter; she is an amalgamation of types, not really a person." This satiric statement by Walker strikes at the ongoing perpetuation of black women as types, pervasive still in popular culture, most recently by Black men performing and acting in drag.[70] Walker thus simultaneously critiques and reclaims the amalgamated stereotype, in a manner similar to Betye Saar's mixed media sculptural piece, *Liberation of Aunt Jemima* (1972). Addressing the Mammie and King Cotton, Walker stated, "Since you guys got good at singing and dancing in my movies, can you do a dance for us?" to which she then addressed the audience, encouraging the crowd to cheer the figures on to a performance. Walker chides, "Come on, do the cotton song" while several members in the audience called out similar requests. This was perhaps the most awkward and darkly satiric moment of the whole performance, as the audience, perhaps unknowingly for some, became agents in the long history of exploitive entertainment, beginning with slave masters shooting at the feet of their slaves to "make them dance." While some laughed, others fell awkwardly silent. Walker has spoken of this uncomfortable humor in her work, describing it as a type "that makes it difficult for [me] or a viewer to decide just how hard to laugh. That uneasiness is an important part of the work."[71] This uncomfortable humor, of deciding whether or when to laugh, is an aspect of Walker's work that highlights how what we laugh at often determines or is determined by our sense of self.[72] Using humor to aid in one's ability to share and listen to stories of psychological trauma and racism certainly has its own history as an art form, particularly in terms of African American comedy, from Richard Pryor and Whoopi Goldberg to Chris Rock and Dave Chappelle.

For the next section of the performance, Walker more directly inscribed her physical presence into the work (which I am told she did not do in the first performance) by coming directly in front of the stage and sitting on a stool closely placed before the seated audience. Walker then reenacted a scene similar to that of the last act of the film, the moment Uncle Remus tells the little white boy about the Briar Patch. Walker, sitting on the stool, placed the small paper figures of Uncle Remus and the boy on her knee, while her assistant directed a small flashlight on the shadow-puppet figures, creating a miniature ventriloquist performance. Walker, speaking in the voice of the little boy, pulls the characters into 2005, as the boy excitedly talks of how much he learned about "his heritage" and "how people came from the earth," from Walker's *Song of the South* at REDCAT, to which Uncle Remus, seeking to settle him down, says, "I'm not gonna take you to any show like that again." The formal presentation of Walker, sitting *in front* of the stage, brilliantly corresponded to the final section of the film, in which Walker appears animating the same shadow puppets from *behind* the stage. By directly inscribing her physical presence with the audience during this moment of the performance, Walker inspires what I would argue to be the most direct and empathic aspect of the work, and perhaps a sign of things to come.

Walker then returns to the back of the puppet stage and presents "Motherland," stating, "Once there was a flood, one like yesterday, folks always getting scared of floods." This double reference here to both biblical floods and the Great Mississippi Flood of 1927 so central to Blues tradition and the government's disgraceful response to Hurricane Katrina and its victims, reflects a brilliant and dark moment in the performance, salting a very recent and still open wound. Motherland then eats several characters, including the Kara puppet. Walker then brings the old white slave master to the stage, in his "gentleman" attire, who says, "I think I should have the last word" and then continues to make statements to justify his authority, telling the audience of his "vast knowledge of negroes," his "large collection of Black literature," and that his father "collected great black spirituals and black labor."

With the insertion of her own contemporary body, Walker more directly addresses the past through her present self, both as a two-dimensional representation as well as a more direct visceral presence through the theatricality of her actual body. This dual strategy of portraying herself facilitates Walker's ability to make the work generate a greater awareness as to the extent to which the contemporary legacy of slavery continues to impact the African American community. Consider, for example, Janet Jackson's "wardrobe malfunction" at the 2004 Superbowl. Writer and photographer Carla Williams, in her essay "Body Baggage," provides further historical perspective to this twenty-first-century media event:

> Black Women's breasts, their bodies, and their sexuality remain great taboo in American culture. We can deny it or exaggerate it, but god forbid we actually consider the history of their bodies

over which, starting with slavery, they have had little control, particularly in how they have been represented. In photography—this one-second peep show has instantly become a series of flipbook-like still photographs freely available for download—there are numerous precedents to help understand why a breast isn't just a breast when race is involved.[73]

Walker's live puppet performance showcased Walker for the first time using the image of her postmodern self to both channel and reference the historical enslavement of black female bodies as wet nurses, nannies, cooks, and mothers to offspring, often conceived by the rape of their masters, a silenced past that continues to feed into today's racist and sexist realities.

Walker's performance brings to mind what literary critic Henry Louis Gates calls "double-speak," a concept developed in his theory of "signifying" to describe African American literary texts that "talk to each other" as a kind of postmodern form of revision and critique.[74] Through metaphor, myth, and satire Walker's performance spoke to and referenced the film, the audience, and Disney's own production, speaking to and from the past and present simultaneously. Through this strategy, along with her powerfully dark and satiric humor, Walker layers into her art the power of the "uncanny moment." Mark Reinhardt, in writing about the role of the uncanny in Walker's work, cites Freud, stating:

> In "The Uncanny," he [Freud] argues that the unexpected overcoming of repression is both the necessary and the sufficient condition of having an uncanny experience: we find uncanny not that which is "new or alien," but, rather, "something which is familiar and old-established in the mind and which has become alienated from it only through the process of repression"—that is, "something repressed which recurs."[75]

Reinhardt goes on to note Freud's distinction that the "frightening" quality of the uncanny lies not in intrinsic properties of the persons, places, or things encountered, but in the fact that (citing Freud) "an emotional impulse, whatever its kind, is transformed, if it is repressed, into anxiety."[76] The performative turn of Walker's most recent work certainly takes the role of the uncanny to a new level, nuanced by a greater employment of satiric humor and the presence of her own postmodern identity. With these elements, along with her ongoing commitment to engage and confront her audience, Walker puts her own flesh into "Scenes of the South."

Walker notes that her images can leave her "shocked" as well, stating, "Confronting the viewer with the contradictory desires and interpretations that he or she cannot bear to acknowledge, my work reveals images that I too am shocked to encounter in the dark alleys of my imagination."[77] The ability of Walker's art to shock serves as an interventionist strategy that ruptures the membranes of silence and complacency in order to awaken one into action, and hopefully begin a process of positive change and long overdue healing. Walker's practice, and in particular her own transformative evolution toward performance, reminds us of the importance of close introspective self-analysis in dealing with trauma. A deep and honest sense of self by those who are privileged is equally important in enabling one to better understand and appreciate the suffering of those marginalized and oppressed because of their ethnicity, gender, or sexual orientation. A considerable difference exists between experiencing a traumatic event or racist moment directly versus knowing of it vicariously through a visual or textual conduit, such as a movie, book, or photograph. However, art can play an important role in creating empathic responses for victims of various forms of oppression, while offering victims a form for which their own traumatic psychological thoughts are difficult to articulate into words. Artistic forms then can aid in bringing people closer to "what if feels like," which might encourage them to remedy the problem on a personal or communal level.

Walker's art reminds us of the distance left to travel as Americans struggle to come to terms with our history of enslavement and a collective memory of distorted nostalgia. Writing on this point, Ann Cvetkovich states:

> Genocide, slavery, and many other traumas of "American" history (broadly conceived as a transnational one that exceeds the borders of the United States) are part of its founding and yet have too often been ignored or forgotten, especially as trauma. . . . The challenge is that these national traumas are buried more deeply in the past

than the Holocaust, the Vietnam War, and other geopolitical sites of trauma where there are living survivors, and thus they require different theoretical and memorial strategies.[78]

Walker's practice indeed proves itself as one possible visual and performative strategy for addressing the historic trauma of slavery buried under a selective historical "amnesia." Increasing numbers of female and multicultural creative practitioners seek to resist amnesias of oppression, a process that leading American poet Adrienne Rich wrote about in her 1983 essay "Resisting Amnesia: History and Personal Life," in which she argued for feminists to "become *consciously* historical" and to strive "for memory and connectedness against amnesia and nostalgia."[79] The art of Kara Walker, and her increasingly performative means, awakens us out of our slumber, pushes us out of our cynicism or resignation, and inspires one to continue the struggle to defeat all forms of oppression.

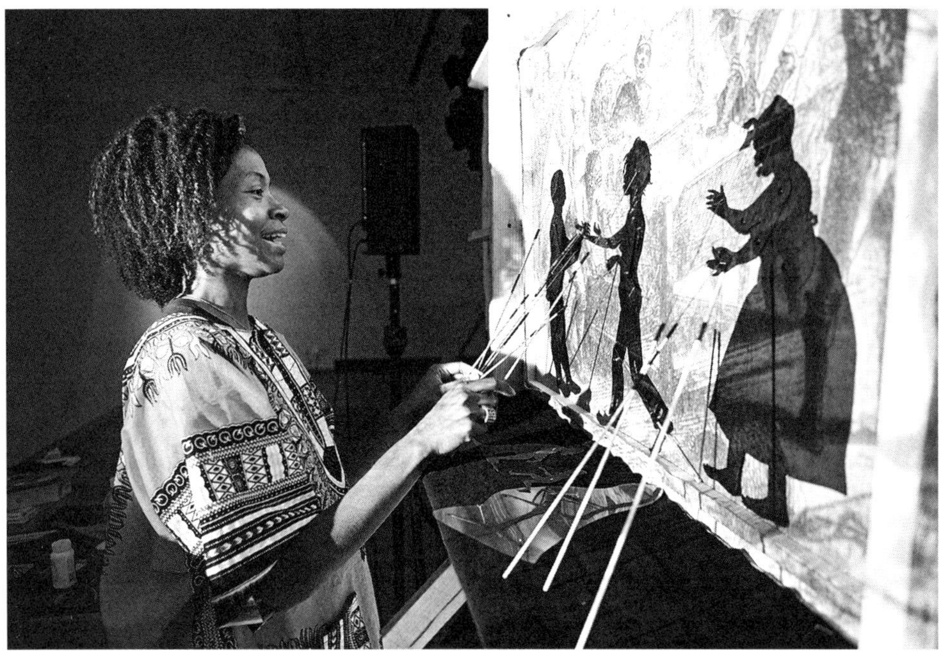

Kara Walker, *Song of the South*, 2005. Photograph of Walker's live shadow-puppet performance, September 3, 2005. REDCAT, Los Angeles, CA, 2005. Photo: Scott Groller. Artwork © Kara Walker, courtesy of Sikkema Jenkins & Co., New York; Sprüth Magers, Berlin.

Acknowledgments

I would like to take this opportunity to thank Joshua Chambers-Letson, anupama jain, and the anonymous readers for their critically insightful suggestions and thoughtful comments. Thank you also to Ellie Bronson and Teka Selmen of Sikkema Jenkins & Co., Dan Byers of the Fabric Workshop and Museum, Margaret Crane of REDCAT, and Jeanne Vaccaro, managing editor of *Women and Performance*, for their gracious support and helpful assistance.

Notes

1. One element of the installation, the 16-mm film, was later exhibited with Walker's dealer, Sikkema Jenkins & Co. in New York City from March 4 to April 1, 2006, as part of a gallery show that did not include the installation elements nor any performances.

2. Ron Eyerman, *Cultural Trauma: Slavery and the Formation of African American Identity* (Cambridge: Cambridge University Press, 2001), 1–2.

3. Kara Walker, interview with Silke Boerma, in *Kara Walker*, ed. Stephan Berg (Hannover: Verlag, Kunstverin Hannover, 2002), 165.

4. Walker, interview with Boerma, 169.

5. Many have written on the controversy surrounding Walker, as led by artists Betye Saar. For a detailed discussion of that controversy, see Gwendolyn Dubois Shaw, *Seeing the Unspeakable: The Art of Kara Walker* (Durham, NC: Duke University Press, 2004), chapter 4, "Censorship and Reception," 103–123.

6. Dubois Shaw, *Seeing the Unspeakable*.

7. Literary examples of the "neo-slave" narrative would include Octavia Butler's *Kindred* (1979), Charles Johnson's *Oxherding Tale* (1982), and Toni Morrison's *Beloved* (1987).

8. Dubois Shaw, *Seeing the Unspeakable*, 61.

9. Scholar Donald Bogle, who has written numerous books about representations of blacks in popular media, arranges the screen stereotypes into a simple taxonomy that he believes encompasses the range: the tom, the coon, the tragic mulatto, the mammy, and the brutal black buck. See Donald Bogle, *Toms, Coons, Mulattoes, Mammies, and Bucks: An Interpretive History of Blacks in American Films*, 4th ed. (Continuum Publishing, 2001).

10. Mark Reinhardt similarly notes this aspect of Walker's silhouettes in "The Art of Racial Profiling," in *Kara Walker: Narratives of a Negress* (Cambridge, MA: MIT Press, in cooperation with the Frances Young Tang Teaching Museum and Art Gallery at Skidmore College and Williams College Museum of Art, 2003), 113.

11. Kara Walker, in interview for the PBS series *ART: 21—Art in the 21st Century*. DVD released November 18, 2003. A broadcast series by National Public Television on contemporary visual art and artists in the United States today. A transcription of excerpts from Walker's interview can be found at http://www.pbs.org/art21/artists /walker/index.html.

12. Kara Walker, in *Art:21—Art in the Twenty-First Century* (New York: Harry N. Abrams, 2003), 69. Companion book published in conjunction with the video *Art:21 Art in the Twenty-First Century* (2003).

13. Walker, in *Art:21* (DVD).

14. Tony Horwitz, *Confederates in the Attic: Dispatches from the Unfinished Civil War*, 1st paperback ed. (New York: Vintage, 1998), 296. As cited by Reinhardt in "The Art of Racial Profiling," 111.

15. Tara McPherson, *Reconstructing Dixie: Race, Gender, and Nostalgia in the Imagined South* (Durham, NC: Duke University Press, 2003).

16. Kara Walker, quoted in Scarlet Cheng, "Out of Her Shadows," *Los Angeles Times*, October 19, 2005, E3.

17. Walker, quoted in Cheng, "Out of Her Shadows."

18. Walker, quoted in Cheng, "Out of Her Shadows."

19. Walker, quoted in Cheng, "Out of Her Shadows."

20. Kara Walker, "Pea, Ball, Bounce," an interview by James Hannaham, *Interview*, November 1998, 116.

21. Kara Walker, "Interview with Kara Walker," in *Kara Walker, upon My Many Masters—An Outline* (San Francisco Museum of Modern Art, 1997), n.p. This interview with Alexander Alberro was first published in the February 1996 issue of *Index*.

22. V. P. Franklin, *Living Our Stories, Telling Our Truths: Autobiography and the Making of the African-American Intellectual Tradition* (New York: Scribner, 1995), 11.

23. Henry Louis Gates Jr., *Bearing Witness: Selections from African American Autobiography in the Twentieth Century* (New York: Pantheon Books, 1991).

24. Franklin, *Living Our Stories, Telling Our Truths*, 12.

25. See introduction to Alan Govenar, *African American Frontiers: Slave Narratives and Oral Histories* (Santa Barbara, CA: ABC-CLIO, 2000), xxiv–xxx. Govenar notes that, overall, more than 6,000 antebellum slave narratives were published, which differ significantly in character from the 2,194 accounts of ex-slaves compiled in interviews by the Works Progress Administration (WPA) between 1936 and 1938 (xxxi).

26. Franklin, *Living Our Stories, Telling Our Truths*, 13.

27. Deborah Horvitz, *Literary Trauma: Sadism, Memory and Sexual Violence in American Women's Fiction* (Albany: State University of New York Press, 2000), 1.

28. In 1998, two years before she introduced projected light into her installations, Walker created *Safety Curtain*, for the 1998/1999 session at the Vienna State Opera House, Austria, which may have further stimulated Walker's growing interest in performance.

29. Other wall pieces also made for this 2000 installation in Geneva included *Salvation* (2000), *Mistress Demanded a Swift and Dramatic Empathic Reaction Which We Obliged Her* (2000), and *Emancipation on Tour* (2000).

30. Walker, in *ART:21* (DVD).

31. This point has also been noted by other writers, including Elizabeth Janus, in "As American as Apple Pie," *Parkett*, no. 59 (2000): 140.

32. Several more works using the projected light followed, including *Darkytown Rebellion* (2001) and *They Waz Nice White Folks While They Lasted (Says One Gal to Another)* (2001), both first installed in Walker's solo show at Brent Sikkema, New York.

Followed by *For the Benefit of All the Races of Mankind (Mos' Specially the Master One, Boss) An Exhibition of Artifacts, Remnants, and Effluvia EXCAVATED from the Black Heart of a Negress VII* (2002), first exhibited at the Kunstverein Hannover, Germany.

33. This work was on view in the fifth-floor gallery of the Fabric Workshop and Museum (FWM), March 26–August 14, 2004.

34. T. J. Demos, "Kara Walker—The Fabric Workshop and Museum," *Artforum* (Summer 2004): 251–252.

35. Descriptions of this work come from Demos, "Kara Walker."

36. I am most thankful for the assistance of Dan Byers, Assistant to the Directors at the Fabric Workshop and Museum for sharing with me his recollections of the performance and installation as well as providing video footage of the performance for my research.

37. Kara Walker, quoted in gallery notes, FWM (2004).

38. My transcription here and what follows comes from the recorded dialogue taken from a review copy of a recorded video of Walker's 2004 performance provided by the FWM.

39. Recorded dialogue taken from a review copy of a recorded video of Walker's 2004 performance provided by the FWM. Walker went on to say that "these two characters, unwittingly observed, whose likeness I have striven to capture, were women folk, may be important to some and of little import to others. For it is these down trodden new driven members of the darker of the fairer sex whose sentence long ignored will now have their say."

40. Gallery notes, FWM.

41. Gallery notes, FWM.

42. According to Ronald L. F. Davis, the term "Jim Crow" is believed to have originated around 1830 when a white minstrel show performer, Thomas "Daddy" Rice, blackened his face with charcoal paste or burnt cork and danced a ridiculous jig while singing the lyrics to the song, "Jump Jim Crow." Rice created this character after supposedly seeing (while traveling in the South) a crippled, elderly black man (or some say a young black boy) dancing and singing a song ending with these chorus words: "*Weel about and turn about and do jis so, Eb'ry time I weel about I jump Jim Crow.*" Some historians believe that a Mr. Crow owned the slave who inspired Rice's act—thus the reason for the name. See Ronald L. F. Davis, "Creating Jim Crow: In-Depth Essay," http://www .jimcrowhistory.org/history/creating2.htm.

43. Kara Walker, in "Thelma Golden/Kara Walker, a Dialogue," in *Kara Walker: Pictures from Another Time* (Ann Arbor: University of Michigan Press; New York: DAP, 2003). The interview took place in December 2001.

44. Walker's work was on view from September 3 to October 23, 2005. Ironically, while on view, Disney animation fans began an online buzz centered around rumors of a potential re-release of Disney's 1946 film *Song of the South*, to celebrate its sixtieth anniversary. Whether or not Walker knew of this when she began her version of *Song of the South* is uncertain. But this may not be relevant, since by 2004, Kara Walker had already made reference to Disney and racist imagery with her inclusion of the black crows in *Fibbergibbit and Mumbo*.

45. Christopher Knight, *Los Angeles Times*, CalanderLive.com, September 12, 2005, http://www.calendarlive.com/galleriesandmuseums/knight/cl-et-walker12sep12,0 ,2977060.story.

46. *Song of the South* had subsequent re-releases in 1956, 1972/1973, 1980, and the last in 1986. Disney has up until now refused to re-release the film on VHS or DVD owing in large part to the film's glossed over-idealization of "happy plantation life" in the post–Civil War American South. Several websites have suggested that the film will be re-released on DVD in the fall of 2006 to celebrate its sixtieth anniversary. Amazon.com was accepting advance orders at the date of June 25, 2006. [Editor's note: The edited version has not been re-released as of August 6, 2021.]

47. An extremely popular and expansive website dedicated to "Celebrating and preserving this Walt Disney Classic" is run and owned by Christian Willis, who boldly states on the opening page that "Generations have grown up on Uncle Remus' tales of Br'er Rabbit and this site exists to make sure this movie is never forgotten." See www.songofthesouth.net (accessed November 14, 2005).

48. Harris's first collection of folk poems and proverbs was published in 1881 as *Uncle Remus: His Songs and Sayings*, followed by additional published collections, including *Uncle Remus and Br'er Rabbit* (1905).

49. Henry Spalding, *Encyclopedia of Black Folklore and Humor* (New York: Jonathan David Publishers, 1972, 1990), 7.

50. Critic Christopher Knight noted that after watching Walker's version of *Song of the South*, he looked up the history of lynching in America, which led him to learn of the horrific July 1946 lynching, and noted that it was "the last of more than 3,000 mob lynchings of African Americans in the United States." He also stated, "The barbarous assault ignited a national outcry, prompting President Truman to begin a push for civil-rights changes that ultimately desegregated the military. J. Edgar Hoover's FBI investigated the crime, but nobody was indicted, nobody was arrested, and nobody was ever punished. Recently a state senator from Georgia pleaded with prosecutors to take the decades-old case to a grand jury." See Christopher Knight, "A South Disney Didn't Dream Of," *Los Angeles Times*, September 12, 2005, E1.

51. See Cheng, "Out of Her Shadows."

52. [Editor's note: This was the title given for the REDCAT show in 2005; the film is now referenced as *8 Possible Beginnings or: The Creation of African-America, a Moving Picture by Kara E. Walker*.]

53. Walker, in Cheng, "Out of Her Shadows."

54. Walker, in Cheng, "Out of Her Shadows."

55. Dubois Shaw, *Seeing the Unspeakable*, 58–59.

56. Dubois Shaw, *Seeing the Unspeakable*, 60.

57. Slave labor songs were primarily about the two dominating forms of slave labor in the nineteenth century, picking cotton and laboring on the railroads, which became two of the most important themes for blues musicians. "From these slaves came the children who grew up to become the great early blues singers and musicians (see 'Panama Limited' by Bukka White)." See Max Haymes "Background to the Blues," http://www.earlyblues.com/background_to_the_blues.htm.

58. For more on this topic, see William F. Pinar, *The Gender of Racial Politics and Violence in America: Lynching, Prison Rape, & the Crisis of Masculinity* (New York: Peter Lang Publishing, 2001), and Daniel Kim, *Writing Manhood in Black and Yellow: Ralph Ellison, Frank Chin, and the Literary Politics of Identity* (Stanford, CA: Stanford University Press, 2005).

59. One such debate that came to mind was the controversy that arose over the heterosexual "puppet sex scene" in the 2004 film *Team America: World Police* (2004) directed and produced by Tray Parker, co-creator of *South Park*, in which the heterosexual, yet androgynous (no sexual parts) plastic nudity of two white characters got more attention than the larger political satires of the film. More explicit sections were taken out for the R-rated release in order to avoid NC-17 ratings. Walker's puppet sex, however, takes on greater political implications in simultaneously confronting the subject of miscegenation, rape, and sexuality.

60. See J. L. King and Karen Hunter, *On the Down Low: A Journey into the Lives of "Straight" Black Men Who Sleep with Men* (New York: Broadway Books, 2004). *Essence* published an essay on this topic in the August 2004 issue by Taigi Smith entitled "Deadly Deception." In April 2004, *The Oprah Winfrey Show* aired an episode on "men living the down low," inspired in large part by King's book, who himself came out to his wife as a down-lower, and in October 2006, Oprah aired the female version of the DL in a show titled "Wives Who Confess They Are Gay."

61. For more on this topic, see Kathryn Bond Stockton, *Beautiful Bottom, Beautiful Shame: When "Black" Meets "Queer"* (Durham, NC: Duke University Press, 2006). Stockton's discussion of the critical genealogy of shame in her introduction includes a very interesting section on Bataille (pp. 8–22). See also Roderick A. Ferguson's "queer of color critique" of such abjection in *Aberrations in Black: Toward a Queer of Color Critique* (Minneapolis: University of Minnesota Press, 2004); Daniel Y. Kim's literary historization of Black Nationalist imaginaries of sodomy and faggotry as inherently white in *Writing Manhood in Black and Yellow: Ralph Ellison, Frank Chin, and the Literary Politics of Identity*; and *Black Queer Studies: A Critical Anthology*, by E. Patrick Johnson and Mae G. Henderson, eds. (Durham, NC: Duke University Press, 2005).

62. Knight, "A South Disney Didn't Dream Of."

63. Referring here to the well-known public story of one such case, that of Margaret Garner, who in 1856 upon being captured with her family while trying to escape from a Kentucky plantation killed her three-year-old daughter and attempted to kill her three sons. This real-life event inspired the scene in Toni Morrison's *Beloved*, when Sethe kills her own favorite daughter.

64. For the character of Uncle Remus, inspired by the Harris's published folktales, Disney cast James Basket, an African American, as the first actor in the film, playing the role of Uncle Remus, for which Basket would win his own Oscar, the first to be won by an African American.

65. For the opening Walker performed solo, and for the closing performance on October 23, 2005, she worked with the aid of her assistant, Paula Wilson.

66. In 1850 Harvard scientist Louis Agassiz commissioned Zealy to photograph slaves for his published book on racial hierarchies, *Types of Mankind* (1854), which included "scientific" photographs of female slaves, their clothing unceremoniously pulled down to their waist, their bare breasts exposed as they were cataloged by the camera as pictorial "evidence" of their inferiority and "specimens" of labor. Gwendolyn Dubois Shaw also discusses Agassiz's photographs in relation to Walker's work in *Speaking the Unspeakable*, 44.

67. Kara Walker, interview with Boerma, 165.

68. In May 2003, prompted by the 1994 request of then South African President Nelson Mandela, France finally returned Baartman's remains to the land of her birth. Janell

Hobson looks at the historical display of Bartman's body in relation to contemporary issues surrounding issues of black women, beauty, and the media in *Venus in the Dark: Blackness and Beauty in Popular Culture* (New York: Routledge, 2005).

69. Phrases and words given by Walker in her October 2005 performance at RED-CAT, which I attended.

70. I am thinking here of recent films made by Martin Lawrence such as *Big Momma's House* and Tyler Perry's series of *Chitl'n Circuit* plays and the movie *Madea's Family Reunion* (2006), in which male actors play large women in fat suits.

71. Walker, "Interview with Kara Walker," in *Kara Walker, upon my Many Masters.*

72. Mark Reinhardt, in "The Art of Racial Profiling" (p. 114), notes a similar point in which he also sites Sander L. Gilman, *Difference and Pathology: Stereotypes of Sexuality, Race and Madness* (Ithaca, NY: Cornell University Press, 1985), 176.

73. Carla Williams, "Body Baggage," originally published in *New York Newsday* on February 8, 2004, and circulated on the web through various black community and scholarly networks. The piece can also be accessed through her website at http://www .carlagirl.net/writing/bodybaggage.html.

74. Henry Louis Gates Jr., *The Signifying Monkey: A Theory of African-American Literary Criticism* (New York: Oxford University Press, 1988).

75. Reinhardt, "The Art of Racial Profiling," 116. Reinhardt cites Sigmund Freud, "The Uncanny," in *The Standard Edition of the Complete Works of Sigmund Freud*, ed. James Strachey et al., vol 17 (London: Hogarth Press and the Institute of Psychoanalysis, 1981), 241.

76. Freud, "The Uncanny," 241.

77. Kara Walker, "The Debate Continues, Kara Walker's Response," *International Review of African American Art*, 15, no. 2 (1998): 48–49.

78. Ann Cvetkovich, *An Archive of Feelings: Trauma, Sexuality, and Lesbian Public Cultures* (Durham, NC: Duke University Press, 2003), 6.

79. Adrienne Rich, "Resisting Amnesia: History and Personal Life," in *Blood, Bread and Poetry: Selected Prose, 1979–1985* (New York: Norton, 1986), 145. Quote cited by Nancy K. Peterson in *Against Amnesia* (Philadelphia: University of Pennsylvania Press, 2001), 6.

Subtleties of Resistance: Sweetness and Violence in Kara Walker's *A Subtlety*

Tavia Nyong'o

The Photograph is violent: not because it shows violent things, but because on each occasion it fills the sight by force, and because in it nothing can be refused or transformed (that we can sometimes call it mild does not contradict its violence: many say that sugar is mild, but to me sugar is violent, and I call it so).

—Roland Barthes, *Camera Lucida* (1980)

The 2014 site-specific installation *A Subtlety, or the Marvelous Sugar Baby,* billed as the first major public art project by the well-known African American contemporary artist Kara Walker, provides a useful case study of *afrofabulation,* or the shocking irruption of the black past within the ostensibly "postracial" present. Erected in the postindustrial neighborhood of Williamsburg, Brooklyn—in one of the few remaining waterfront spaces left unclaimed by the encroaching glass and steel condo towers of the power elite—*A Subtlety* took shape as an act of temporary monumentalism, an "homage," according to the full title of the work posted at its entrance, "to the unpaid and overworked artisans who have refined our sweet tastes from the cane fields to the kitchens of the New World." Before entering Walker's installation we should pause over this homage, recalling, as the artist herself has, how it belongs to a long line of black feminist counter-proposals to amnesiac acts of American monumentalism. In particular, *A Subtlety* recalls the efforts of black clubwomen who organized in protest against a 1923 proposal to erect a statue in the nation's capital to the "memory of the faithful colored mammies of the South."[1] In mocking fulfilment of that failed proposal, Walker's installation shockingly precipitated all the sordid history that the screen memory of the "faithful" mammy represses. But can such conscious travesty fully succeed of divesting itself from the violent histories it channels? Or does "complicity" itself become a medium within which the contemporary black artist now works?

It is not just the fraught genealogy of monumentalism that Walker's *A Subtlety* should call our attention to, after all, but the political economy of public art in our neoliberal, globalized present. By now we are familiar with the deployment of "creative capital" rhetoric in the gentrification of urban centers like New York, London, Berlin, Cape Town. If the unbuilt mammy monument in Washington, DC, represents one historical moment in the cultural logic of imperial nation-building, surely the participatory dynamics popularizing a project like *A Subtlety* represent another, more recent one. Today, artists are not only viewed as urban trailblazers for predatory real-estate interests, but their art publics and lifeworlds constitute a kind of durational performance, shifting the atmospherics of a given postindustrial locale from dreary to lively, from boring or dangerous to exciting, and, most often, from dark to light. The very success of *A Subtlety* is a symptom of the gentrification process it is powerless to thwart. The question is whether a self-awareness of this complicity can lead elsewhere than pure cynicism. By materializing the violent histories of sugar refining, displaying in real time racial capitalism's destruction of the black body, can *A Subtlety* slow down the racial whitening and lightening process of gentrification, rendering it, molasses-like, tacky and viscous?

These questions turn us toward the inter-animation of form and content in an artwork that, from its very title and location, advertised its fraught relations to the materials used to construct it. The giant sugar sculpture, which drew long weekend lines for two increasingly hot summer months, paid an ironical tribute to the historical structure that temporarily housed it, a former sugar refinery about to fall victim to the very forces of capitalist creative destruction that at one point made it the single largest supplier of sugar to the American diet.[2] Walker's ephemeral installation juxtaposed the cavernous, industrial, aging bulk of the iconic building with the subtle traces of black lives and labor that were—like the other "millions of indispensable actors in the dramas of the circum-Atlantic world" that Joseph Roach writes of in *Cities of the Dead*—"forgotten but not gone."[3] Forgotten but not gone well describes the horrific past and present of Caribbean sugar production: the sight of black bodies bruised and broken on the wheel of sugarcane harvesting and processing. Forgotten but not gone also describes the violent extraction of sweetness and profit from black bodies working in tropical plantations, a mode of production that is anything but over and gone. The combined and uneven development of global capitalism was rarely more clearly on view than here, in a public art project that worked simultaneously as reputation laundering for the Fanjul brothers, corporate barons whose blood money (extracted from cane fields in the Dominican Republic where Haitian migrants labor in postslavery conditions) bankrolled the exhibit.[4] The piece cannot begin to make sense without accounting for the manner in which Fanjul Corp., owners of Domino Sugar, stand to profit from the deindustrialization of their former factory, and the reimagining of its extended footprint as a further extension of the creative capital. As a kind of parting gift from their liquidated workers to the visiting crowds and prospective tenants of future condominiums, Domino Sugar supplied the forty tons of sugar used for this potent work of social sculpture. But what sort of bitter pill does this spoonful of sugar help us swallow? How does an artist work with materials so literally as well as metaphorically complicit with the savage destruction of black life, life the artwork itself seeks to memorialize and transfigure?

Part of the answer must lie with the transformed status of the public sphere under neoliberalism, thinking of neoliberalism here primarily as the ruthless privatization of everything. If Walker's silhouette installations comprise interventions, as Darby English has argued, within the venerable genre of landscape painting, then *A Subtlety* comprises her leap into the any-space-whatever of hypercapitalism.[5] This fact was announced by the invitation to take digital photos of the installation, to be tagged and shared on social media using the hashtag #karawalkerdomino. The invitation to shoot and circulate images of Walker's installation, quickly dubbed the "Mammy Sphinx," invites both comparison and contrast with a prior summer sensation in New York City: Random International's 2013 *Rain Room* at MoMA in which water fell from the ceiling, magically without ever falling on the attendees. A

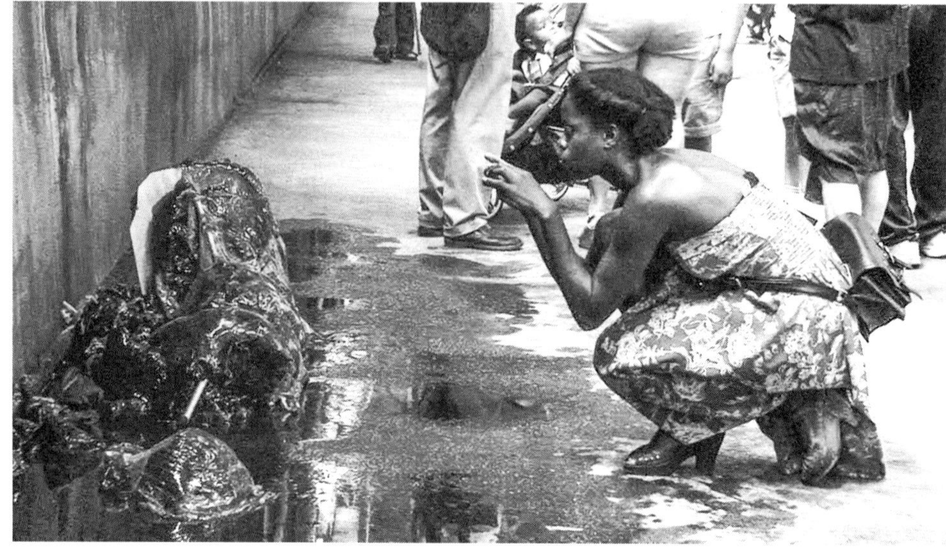

Kara Walker, still from *An Audience/Rhapsody*, 2014. Digital video with sound, 27:18 minutes/6:38 minutes. Artwork © Kara Walker, courtesy of Sikkema Jenkins & Co., New York; Sprüth Magers, Berlin.

similar participatory prophylaxis was at work in Williamsburg where viewers were enjoined to look and pose but not touch or taste (the sugar was laced with rat poison to ward off pests), even as the heat and perspiration of their bodies, combined with the gathering miasma of summer, acted by imperceptible degrees on the giant sculpture and, even more decisively, on the fragile molasses "sugar babies" that dotted the perimeter of their giant "mammy." If the public sphere was born, as Terry Eagleton suggests, in a discursive struggle against the absolutist state, the atomization and reaggregation of individual affective response to a public work of art that characterizes our neoliberal present must represent a kind of absolute victory of capital over both state and citizen.[6]

The violences digitally recirculated in images taken at the exhibit also condensed on the artwork itself. As the weeks went on, the sphinx shed layers of her sugary skin, and the sugar babies bent, bled red-black blood, and then broke, losing lollipops and limbs that were dutifully gathered each night and placed into the baskets that those babies left standing humbly proffered to the public the next weekend. Starting empty, the baskets thus gradually filled with the sticky, sickly detritus of their siblings' disintegration—reversing the usual disappearing act of racial capitalism—and literalizing a metaphor of "refinement" accomplished through violence, maiming, and death. As the eyes of these sculptures sweated undead molasses tears, one could find refracted a shocking image of a black childhood rendered unthinkable to an anti-black world, except when it appears coated in delectable chocolate, maple syrup, cane sugar, or licorice.

But one need not even have approached one such sculpture, or considered how one's presence, aggregated with those of many thousands of others, was accelerating its decay, to grasp what Roland Barthes, in my epigraph, locates as the violence that inheres to the image even or especially in its permanence. "Relational aesthetics" may no longer be quite the de rigueur curatorial watchword of the day, but it has been routinized, popularized, democratized, and banalized. A participatory "common sense" pervaded the promotion of *A Subtlety* as a "destination" experience one can and should document and upload to the digital cloud with the hashtag #karawalkerdomino.[7] And we should pause over the telling syntax of that hashtag, which runs together the artist's signature with the corporate brand in a manner that uncannily repeats the commodifiability of black bodies. The relational capitalism of social media enacts subtleties of complicity and resistance as viewers rub elbows, snap photos, step over sugar-stained floors, in and out of each other's way, ask questions or give the cold shoulder, and, in general, make an atmosphere, make a scene, enliven the place with the kind of free contribution of our time, passions, and interests that communicative capitalism, Jodi Dean has argued, can then amass as hierarchical corporate profit and power.[8] Within the frame of the digital photo, in particular the smartphone "selfie," there is little room to make any gesture of resistance that is not immediately assimilated to the profit structure of the corporations that produce and circulate #karawalker-domino. All publicity is good publicity when it is the massification of individual acts of complicity and resistance disseminating and rebranding Domino Sugar as a patron of the social arts, as a contributor to the well-being of the city, rather than as peddlers of poison and merchants of postindustrial malaise and tropical neo-slavery.

The ingenuity of *A Subtlety*, and of afrofabulation more generally, is what of this process it already knows, anticipates, stages, and unsettles. To trace this counter-power within visuality, one must sketch a diagram of the forms of power in the contemporary revanchist city at play in the single site of the Domino Sugar factory, and unfold all the shadowy genealogies that its use for contemporary capitalist speculation cannot tell. The conversion of Williamsburg from industrial waterfront to bourgeois playground is not simply a classic revanchist tale of class warfare, as many anti-gentrification activists might assert. It tells that tale of course, but tells it through a commodity that passes through every link in the commodity chain binding social media to slavery, Chelsea art galleries to the Caribbean, and the historical rupture inaugurating the trans-Atlantic trade with the black social life Paul Gilroy has famously described as a "counter-culture of modernity."[9] If *A Subtlety* was reducible to its materials, locations, investments, and publicity, it could not have encoded this alternative and fugitive legacy that it also, almost against expectations, animated. The enduring significance of this installation, I argue, will lie in the subtleties of both complicity and resistance that it manifested.

II

If sweetness is linked to power, as the historical anthropologist Sidney Mintz has shown in his classic study of the role of sugar in modern history, then the violences of refinement are part of the afterlives of slavery.[10] In "postracial" America (which Greg Tate acidly calls "whipping postracial America") slavery is often treated as an inexplicable crime of the distant past, with no discernible connection to the way Americans conduct their contemporary lives as liberal and democratic citizens. This "racial innocence" is itself a product, one of the priciest, of the violent process of refinement.[11] Walker's sphinx is anything but subtle in its riposte to racial innocence, but it is equally unforgiving to liberal guilt. At a time when anti-black racism, whether structural or interpersonal, is increasingly treated as a thing of the past, a time when "playing the race card" is denounced as excessive, hysterical, and exaggerated, what more brilliant response could there be than to whip up a wondrous confection out of a shit-ton of sugar, give it a big booty and an inscrutable smile, and plop it down just across the water from Manhattan? *A Subtlety*, commentators have noted, confabulates two distinct stereotypes of black women: as nurturing mammies, on the one hand, and as hypersexualized jezebels, on the other. Walker's work is already well known for how it stokes anal-oral erotic fantasies of a plenitudinous dark flesh available to suck on, eat from, tear to pieces, and be consumed by. Here that vision is rendered with reference to the medieval craft tradition of sugar sculptures called "subtleties," which descend to the present from genteel European aristocrats, who were themselves emulating Arabic civilization.[12] In the "kitchens of the New World," enslaved cooks were, indeed, treasured by the master race who owned, raped, beat, and loved them, loving especially the subtle creations that sooty kitchenhands delivered to polished tables. What Christina Sharpe has called a "monstrous intimacy" tethers postslavery subjects to the unfinished, unredeemed narratives of the many who involuntarily labored to reproduce their unfreedom.[13] The scandalous picture of slavery Walker projects onto museum walls and, now, into privatized public space is itself another screen memory, one in which the violences of refinement, the civilizing process, performs its own vanishing act. The horrors of slavery are screened off by the enigmatic, obscene, pseudo-Afrocentric sphinx, leaving the possibility of black sociality in or around this "public space" a dangerous possibility. The piece, while frequently framed in relation to a white or nonblack audience, presumed to be conveniently ignorant of the violent histories it carries; it would be inoperative, I maintain, without the responses and actions of a black counter-public whose reading of the piece, while never unified, is revealing in its very expansive plurality.

Walker is far from the first Afro-diasporic artist to reckon with sugar as an aesthetic material. Bone-deep knowledge of this process of industrial production, won at the cost of life and limb, has been carried into the aesthetics of sugar, cane, and its waste products across African American and especially Caribbean art. *A Subtlety* belongs to a tradition not the least for its materials, but for its exploration of the dynamic through which refined whiteness is never the permanent state New World society imagined it could be, but an unstable state of creolity always threatened by its ongoing metamorphosis into something else, darker and messier. In the *casta* paintings of early modern Mexico, creole artists depicted the imagined consequence of miscegenation on white, red, and black New World populations. In this tradition, racial whitening culminated in a social type named *tente en el aire*, "hold yourself in mid-air," with the trace of blackness visible only "in the blood." But the subsequent generation gave birth to the *torna atrás*, the "return backward," which we can read as a sort of eternal recurrence of blackness after the intergenerational attempt at violent refinement and racial upward mobility had been tried and failed.[14]

The comic outcome of the *casta* painting tradition—told over many story panels—is telegraphed in a single image by Walker's juxtaposition of an emphatically white mammy and her molasses-dark babies. The deadly quality of racial refinement is held at a different distance from the heart by the anonymous woman of color who wrote on the wall outside the exhibit: "I died for sugar back then . . . and sugar is killing me NOW!!" This response reorients the piece, and it is crucial that it appeared as a result of the collective action taken by the black feminist activists who developed the #WeAreHere hashtag and accompanying Tumblr page (http://weareherekwe.tumblr.com/), a platform unaffiliated with either Walker or Creative Time (the nonprofit arts organization that sponsored the exhibit), which created a counter-archive of responses—both at the installation itself and online.[15] The intramural black sense of sugar as a *pharmakon*, as the food that is poison, as the sweetness that will kill us, was reflected in the refusal to either directly protest the exhibit or simply accept the neoliberal terms upon which the public was invited to experience it. Of the many visual and textual responses to the piece occasioned by the #WeAreHere hashtag, and other activists' convergences and teach-ins like it, "I died for sugar back then . . . and sugar is killing me NOW!!" stands out to me now as the kind of realization that brings the war home, that metabolizes history as a social process in the present.

III

The counter-publicity and collective participation incited by *A Subtlety* thus came quickly to exceed the intentions or aims of the artist, whose particular genius, in this case, was to unleash a contingent process beyond her individual control, but one that she would inevitably, as its author, be held in taut relation. The masochistic relation of the artist to her work has been commented on by prior critics and, indeed, by Walker herself. Carrying the weight of that awful history is hard enough, but what about the complicity of the artwork's staging in the recirculation of dehumanizing images of black women? The first wave of discontent with the piece came in wake of the discovery of a genre of digital images in which individual visitors made fun of and/or eroticized the exposed genitalia of the sugar sculpture. In the any-space-whatever of the "selfie" photograph, with its reverse and slightly fish-eye lens enlarging the face against the backdrop of its surrounding, the immense and threatening scale of Walker's confection could be reduced to a size where her breasts, buttocks, and vulva could be virtually touched, pinched, licked, and poked. Outraged commentators seized upon such images as evidence of the shamelessness of an anti-black, anti-feminist "public" that Walker had empowered. That these images circulated on Internet sites where images of actual black women are routinely exoticized and eroticized, degraded and debased, only added fuel to this fire. The photos of Walker's sphinx circulated within an ecology of racialized shame that thrives on the unequal distribution of our susceptibility to it. Neoliberalism seeks to further shut down the resources with which black feminist counter-publics could emerge, both by positing the experience of art as individual, subjective, and beyond critique, and by absorbing critique itself into its endless drive for commodifiable "content" to circulate.

One aspect of the "subtleties of resistance" that emerged in response to the uncritical popular reception of Walker's installation, therefore, was the necessity of staging an immanent critique of racial capitalism in order to gain a critical foothold. Refusing the double bind of either protesting the exhibit or passively accepting the terms of individualized participation, black feminist activists and some of their allies instead organized equally ephemeral counter-publics constituted around the radical concept of valuing black lives. Organizing through an alternative hashtag, #WeAreHere, and through a series of on-site convergences and interventions culminating in a July 5 counter-national independence day celebration, these activists sought to shift the mood around the piece from an inward-directed depression, guilt, or shame to outward-facing outrage, interest, and conviviality. Different from, but no less important than, an ideological critique of Walker, Creative Time, or Domino Sugar, this affective counter-public stirred up by #WeAreHere indexed a long, fugitive circum-Atlantic history of "thiefing sugar," to adopt Omise'eke Natasha Tinsley's emotive name for an erotics of female same-sexuality fabulated out of the violent ungenderings of the Middle Passage.[16] That is to say, the conviviality that momentarily flashed up and around the installation, a quasi-anonymous convergence of the murmuring multitude that faded away as quickly as it appeared, did not seek to organize around the myth of an integral humanist subject injured by coarse sexuality or crass commercialization. Rather, it looked to a counter-tradition reflected in the writings of black feminist theorists like Hazel Carby, Hortense Spillers, and Sylvia Wynter, one that is fiercely skeptical of the gradualist and meliorist promises of humanitarian reform, and that instead seeks to performatively enact a future in the present, a collective afrofabulation of what a world transvalued out of anti-blackness might look, sound, or feel like. Afrofabulation is thus a social practice or, better, a practice of the social individual. To approach it we must dispense with our customary fixations on the individual versus the collective, the artist versus their public. Fabulation is not, as Henri Bergson feared, a form of collective hallucination. It is the creative reenchantment of the present as seen by the illumination the imminent future (like a rapidly gentrifying site) can throw upon the past (the whole history of slavery and sugar production). Fabulation is recursive rather than causal, inventive rather than explanatory. It is metamorphic and plastic and, as such, (im)properly begs the question of what lies outside or beyond it; what, if any, its ethical limits may be.

IV

I close this essay on Kara Walker's fabulation of black history with a return to the historical and metaphorical sugar refinery for one last little sweet souvenir. In her writing on Walker, the psychoanalytic critic Joan Copjec has argued that Walker displays an ethics of sublimation that accords with a Lacanian construal of feminine jouissance as "the lack of lack." While Copjec reads Walker's famous wall silhouettes, her argument aligns well with Walker's latest project. Copjec praises Walker demolishing the myth of history as a "mother," in whose womb or bosom we can be held, and therefore for offering us an ethical path out of historicism. Her artwork, in Copjec's analysis, becomes an out-work, one that cannot be contextualized by any museum or wall text. History is not its container, but that which it contains. Copjec asks, through Walker, what it means to think of "history not as a mother" but as "an internal object that lives the subject as the double of another."[17] This "internal object" is not, however, an authentic self, but a fold or, even better, a systolic valve through which blood is pumped, in which sugars are broken down, energy is consumed, and the illusion of "refined" foods is expeditiously dissolved and discharged as urine and fecal matter. Imagine there is no "woman," Copjec suggests, and it seems Walker's new sphinx echoes this dare. There was no sweet secret inside the sphinx, just Styrofoam. It was only coated with sugar, and both the sugar and the Styrofoam have already been disassembled and carried away. The fantasy of plenitude or enigmatic wisdom is what Plato called an *agalma*, a glittering mirage of inner wisdom that, if one seeks it, will only split off the self from the identity it pursues. Separating thought from the symbolic order, as Walker's artwork does, can unleash a furious and, as we've seen, volatile ferment of imaginary and affective aggression. Perhaps the artist is even complicit in these aggressions. But how could she not be complicit, for they were always already there, as evidenced by the viscosity of race through which sugar and gentrification are linked. Arun Saldanha describes the sociology of race as a kind of performative stickiness: race is experienced as the difference between the bodies one slips past and the bodies one clumps with, the bodies one finds tasty and the bodies one summarily declares distasteful.[18] Racism is the guiltiest of pleasures; how then to sublimate it into an aesthetic or ethic?

The gentrification of the sugar refinery may represent, in Saldanha's terms, a phase shift within the lifetime of a particular site, like a gray iron heating up to red, or water reaching its boiling point. Gentrification forcibly and violently alters the viscosity of race in order to upwardly redistribute life chances and livability to the light and the white. But this violent process regularly precipitates sublimations, things that fall out of solution, objects that resist, and subjects that meet up, make contact, break bread, and find a way home or at least a way out of the social factory, which by the end of the day has shuttered its gates, turned out the lights, unplugged its cords, and now stands, illuminated by moonlight, looking as empty as it really is.

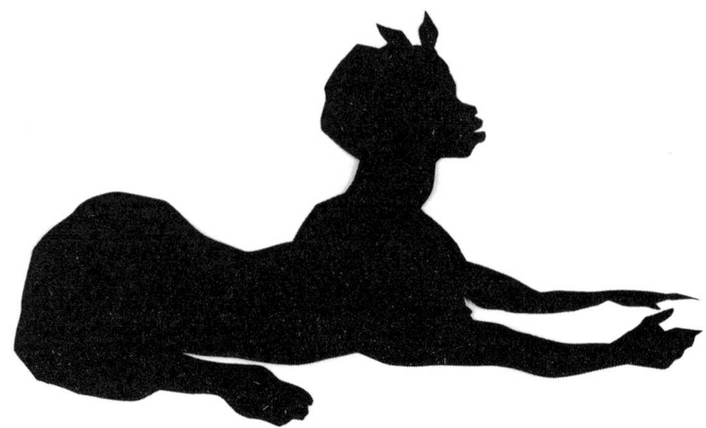

Kara Walker, *Untitled*, 2014. Cut paper on archival board, 7.5 × 12.5 inches, on 16 × 20 inches. Artwork © Kara Walker, courtesy of Sikkema Jenkins & Co., New York; Sprüth Magers, Berlin.

Notes

1. Joan Marie Johnson, "'Ye Gave Them a Stone': African American Women's Clubs, the Frederick Douglass Home, and the Black Mammy Monument," *Journal of Women's History* 17, no. 1 (2005): 62.

2. Leigh Raiford and Robin J. Hayes, "Remembering the Workers of the Domino Sugar Factory," *The Atlantic*, July 3, 2014, http://theatlantic.com/business /archive/2014/07/remembering-the-workers-of-the-domino-sugar-factory/373930/.

3. Joseph Roach, *Cities of the Dead: Circum-Atlantic Performance* (New York: Columbia University Press, 1996), 31.

4. On accumulation through dispossession, see David Harvey, "The 'New' Imperialism: Accumulation by Dispossession," in *Socialist Register 2004: The New Imperial Challenge*, ed. Leo Panitch and Colin Keys (London: Merlin, 2003), 63–87. For a critique of Walker's acceptance of support from Domino Sugar, see Carol Diehl, "Dirty Sugar: Kara Walker's Dubious Alliance with Domino," Carol Diehl's Art Vent, June 16, 2014, http://artvent.blogspot.com/2014/06/dirty-sugar-kara-walkers-dubious.html.

5. Darby English, "A New Context for Reconstruction: Some Crises of Landscape in Kara Walker's Silhouette Installations," in *How to See a Work of Art in Total Darkness* (Cambridge, MA: MIT Press, 2007), 71–135.

6. Terry Eagleton, *The Function of Criticism: From the Spectator to Post-Structuralism* (London: Verso, 1984), 9.

7. On the "relational aesthetics" debate, see Nicolas Bourriaud, *Relational Aesthetics*, trans. Simon Pleasance and Fronza Woods, with Mathieu Copeland (Dijon: Les Presses du réel, 2002); Claire Bishop, "Antagonism and Relational Aesthetics," *October*, no. 110 (2004): 51–79; Shannon Jackson, *Social Works: Performing Art, Supporting Publics* (New York: Routledge, 2011), 45–59.

8. Jodi Dean, *Democracy and Other Neoliberal Fantasies: Communicative Capitalism and Left Politics* (Durham, NC: Duke University Press, 2009).

9. Paul Gilroy, *The Black Atlantic: Modernity and Double Consciousness* (Cambridge, MA: Harvard University Press, 1993), 1–40.

10. Sidney W. Mintz, *Sweetness and Power: The Place of Sugar in Modern History* (New York: Penguin, 1986).

11. Robin Bernstein, *Racial Innocence: Performing American Childhood and Race from Slavery to Civil Rights* (New York: New York University Press, 2011).

12. "By the sixteenth century, the habit of using sugar as decoration, spreading through continental Europe from North Africa and particularly Egypt, began to percolate down from the nobility. . . . It was possible to sculpture an object out of this sweet, preservable 'clay' on any scale and in nearly any form, and to bake or harden it. Such displays, called 'subtleties,' served to mark intervals between banquet 'courses.'" Mintz, *Sweetness and Power*, 87–88.

13. Christina Elizabeth Sharpe, *Monstrous Intimacies: Making Post-Slavery Subjects* (Durham, NC: Duke University Press, 2010).

14. For multiple examples of these types, and a definitive study of the system of wondrous classification of the natural world within which they were nestled, see Ilona Katzew, *Casta Painting: Images of Race in Eighteenth-Century Mexico* (New Haven, CT: Yale University Press, 2004).

15. The organizers of We Are Here are Ariana Allensworth, Salome Asega, Taja Cheek, Sable Elyse Smith, and Nadia Williams.

16. Omise'eke Natasha Tinsley, *Thiefing Sugar: Eroticism between Women in Caribbean Literature* (Durham, NC: Duke University Press, 2010).

17. Joan Copjec, *Imagine There's No Woman: Ethics and Sublimation* (Cambridge, MA: MIT Press, 2002), 103.

18. Arun Saldanha, *Psychedelic White: Goa Trance and the Viscosity of Race* (Minneapolis: University of Minnesota Press, 2007).

"Stories of Mortal Terror": Kara Walker's *Six Miles from Springfield* and *Lucy of Pulaski (2009)*

Vanina Géré

Six Miles from Springfield on the Franklin Road and *Lucy of Pulaski* are two films first presented by Kara Walker as a video installation roughly twenty-five minutes in length at the Art Gallery of Ontario in 2009, under the overall title *National Archives Microfilm Publication M999 Roll 34: Bureau of Refugees, Freedmen and Abandoned Lands: Six Miles from Springfield on the Franklin Road and Lucy of Pulaski.* In *Six Miles*, Walker tells the story of a Black family, the Willises, violently attacked by white supremacists at night. At the beginning of the film, we see the members of the film going on about their daily chores. Night comes; white men break into the Willises' house, drag the family out. The father is shot in the head; the house is burned down; the daughter, Amanda, is raped by the attackers in the woods. In *Lucy of Pulaski*, we are told about Lucy Reynolds, a young Black woman presented as the "cause" of a fatal quarrel between Calvin Lamberth, a white man, and Calvin Carter, a Black man. We see Reynolds and Lamberth having sex, and Carter threatening to chastise Reynolds for her relationship with Lamberth. Reynolds tells Lamberth about it; he plots an attack on Carter as retaliation. Carter and his friends, warned about the white men's plans, prepare to defend themselves; a violent confrontation ensues, resulting in a riot and the death and wounding of several Black men.

Each story is based on records Walker found on the U.S. National Archives and Records Administration website.[1] These records belong to an archive of official administrative documents—reports, depositions, registers, and other documents—that were produced by the Freedmen's

Bureau at the beginning of the Reconstruction era (1865–1877)[2] in several former slave states. Also known as the "Bureau of Refugees, Freedmen and Abandoned Lands," the Bureau, in Walker's own statement for the eponymous exhibition at Sikkema Jenkins gallery (2007), "provided assistance to tens of thousands of former slaves making the transition from slavery to freedom."[3] With headquarters and personnel in all former slave states, the administration issued their own records and reports, producing an impressive archive.[4] While some of the records in the digitized archive document marriages or education, many are records of violent white supremacist crimes, attesting to what African American Studies scholar and writer Saidiya V. Hartman terms "the reign of terror that accompanied the advent of freedom."[5] The full title of Walker's films is a combination of various webpage entries and fragments of texts the artist borrowed from the online records.[6] For the title of the first film, Walker quoted from the deposition of Amanda Willis, as she stated the location of her family's house. For the title of the second film, Walker chose the name of Lucy Reynolds—presented as "a colored strumpet," in the wording of the official record—making her the unfortunate heroine of the story.[7]

Walker encountered the Freedman's Bureau archive in 2007, and she mined it for several years afterward. Until then, her sources ranged from various texts of fiction to nineteenth-century silhouettes, history paintings, and countless images borrowed from American and Western visual culture.[8] However, to my knowledge, she had never used the stories of real people before. How, and to what extent, I wondered, had the nonfictional nature of this source of inspiration influenced her artistic response to it?[9] Previously, Walker's art had proffered a response to the myths and fictions of the so-called antebellum South, as a personal counter-narrative filled with explicit images of all kinds of violent acts, suggesting how representations of slavery had irredeemably contaminated its memory. In the mid-1990s, her leap into the imaginary had been a departure from the approach of visual artists who had turned to the history of slavery through documentation, such as Renée Green, Glenn Ligon, Lorna Simpson, or Fred Wilson.[10] How, then, would Walker navigate actual, official history, and how would she go about telling actual "stories of mortal terror"?[11] If she had depicted the sexual exploitation, murder, and riots in an often grotesque, sometimes ambiguous manner,[12] putting the violence back into the "palatable" representations of U.S. chattel slavery of the nineteenth century,[13] how would she translate into images the official depositions of long-gone victims of violence? If she had told her own truth by appropriating the imagery of the antebellum South, how would she tell the truths of (dead) others? Would ethics play a part in her artistic process, and how would that be translated into the artwork? And, as Hartman phrased her dilemma regarding telling the stories of two Black girls who died during the Middle Passage: "Why subject the dead to new dangers and to a second order of violence?"[14]

Based on an in-depth analysis of *Six Miles* and *Lucy of Pulaski* and interviews with Walker and her collaborators, musician Jason Moran and filmmaker Laurie Butler, this essay analyzes the artistic choices made to adapt the means of representation to their subject. Although not a piece of "archival art" as defined by Hal Foster in "An Archival Impulse,"[15] the film diptych evinces a critical, reflexive position to the official archive they reclaim. Narrative structure and the relation between music and the moving image in the film play an important part in telling the stories of the dead. The explicit re-presentation of the artist's own body (and those of her assistants) in the films stresses their proximity to their sources (the transcripts from the Freedmen's Bureau archive) while paradoxically allowing for aesthetic distancing. A tension between narrative and performance, appropriation and distance, the past and the present, and the archive and the fictional characterizes the 2009 films. Disrupting the suspension of disbelief, Walker proposes an artwork that can be better understood through the prism of Bertolt Brecht's notion of epic drama, offering a singular materialist take on the puppet-shadow theater. The significance of gesture in *Six Miles* and *Lucy of Pulaski* focuses the viewer's attention on the coincidence of the artist and her collaborators' psychic and physical engagement with an awareness of the remoteness of the past. The films, particularly *Six Miles*, negotiate the task of working from stories of terror and dispossession, choosing imagination and image-making over the refusal to produce scenes of historical violence. As such, the films evince the "productive tension" Hartman sees as unavoidable "in narrating the lives of the subaltern, the dispossessed, and the enslaved."[16]

Walker and the Bureau of Refugees: Archive Art?

Six Miles and *Lucy of Pulaski* are part of what I would call the "Bureau of Refugees" series, a body of work Walker created between 2007 and 2009 using the archival records from the Freedmen's Bureau.[17] In her 2007 Sikkema Jenkins exhibition, Walker showed a series of small, framed cut-paper silhouettes, entitled *Bureau of Refugees*.[18] In the exhibition statement, Walker explained that she had come across the Freedmen's Bureau webpage randomly, after entering key phrases related to racist violence and lynching into her Internet search engine as she was struggling with her own reflections on painting and "postmodernism."[19] Two years later, in a two-person exhibition with Mark Bradford, also at Sikkema Jenkins, Walker presented other works explicitly linked to the Bureau archive *and* to her own previous work from it: a series of twenty small- to mid-format paintings with text entitled *Every Painting Is a Dead Nigger Waiting to Be Born* (2009), along with the film diptych.

The way Walker herself presented the results of her online research in the 2007 exhibition catalogue may suggest the relation between the work and the archive as nothing but a fortuitous encounter. Fortuitous, and fortunate, determined by a congruence of the following external circumstances. At that historical moment, not only was online searching an established mass phenomenon,[20] but the mass digitization of all sorts of archives was well under way.[21] The Freedmen's Bureau archive had been microfilmed in the 1970s; beginning in 2001, the microfilms were published as part of a five-year project pushed forth by Representative Juanita Millender McDonald, a sponsor of the Freedmen's Bureau Records Preservation Act (2000). And it was in 2007 that a pilot project for the digitization of U.S. National Archives was launched in partnership with private digitization companies. Walker's happening upon the Freedmen's Bureau archive was the result of the convergence between the economic and technological revolutions of access and treatment of information, on the one hand, and a strong, progressive public policy, on the other. Yet, that Walker should have found the Freedmen's Bureau archives by entering phrases related to white violence and terror into her search engine is a micro-event that undermines the transparency ideology at the heart of such an endeavor as making a mass of historical documents "accessible," as the search results accidentally revealed the instability of the online archive as a coherent discourse on freedom. Subject to the vagaries of the indexing preferences of search engine algorithms and the Internet user's navigation history, the contents of the archive Walker found gave evidence not of emancipation as historical progress, but rather of the pervasion of white terror. Walker did not explicitly articulate this contradiction in any statement, nor did she adopt the serendipitous nature of her encounter with the archive into an artistic protocol or research method that would open up a never-ending flow from one body of archive to another. The only way the 2009 films point to the archive as a source in their mode of presentation is through the textual collage of their titles: *National Archives Microfilm Publication M999 Roll 34: Bureau of Refugees, Freedmen and Abandoned Lands: Six Miles from Springfield on the Franklin Road and Lucy of Pulaski*. Finally, Walker did not set the official record against an alternative corpus of archives of her own. For all these reasons, Walker's work on the Freedmen's Bureau cannot be considered as "archive art" as defined by Foster. Rather, and despite the arbitrary nature of her original search, Walker's 2009 films attest to a strong, critical engagement with the archive beyond a mere source of inspiration[22] that can better be situated within the practice established by Hartman, as a "reclaiming" of an archival corpus thrice violent (as a record of acts of white terror, told from the dominant perspective, in the dominants' symbolic forms and language), as a reading "against the grain in order to write a different account of the past, while real-izing . . . the impossibility of fully reconstituting the experience"[23] of the emancipated Blacks. With and against the archive, Walker's work remains faithful to the text of the records, while bringing into view the mind-numbing amount of white violence the Freedmen's Bureau archive documents, but whose effects it cannot convey. Artistically, how does the relation to the archive translate into the films?

Narrative Clarity

Like her previous three films (*Testimony: Narrative of a Negress Burdened by Good Intentions* [2004]; *8 Possible Beginnings or: The Making of African America* [2005]; *. . . calling to me from the angry surface of some grey and threatening sea. I Was Transported* [2006]), *Six Miles from Springfield* and *Lucy of Pulaski* combine shadow-theater performance and film. By 2008, Walker had come into full mastery of what one might call the shadow-puppet film. Yet unexpectedly, the narrative structure in the 2009 films returned to the linear format of her first film. Indeed, the stories develop from beginning to end without any interlude, and it suc-cinctly borrows from classic devices of character presentation. And the

2009 films possess a straightforward tonality, thanks to Jason Moran's music and the absence of any forms of the grotesque in the figuration of the bodies and settings. These characteristics enable the artwork to be as faithful as possible to the archival records—unadorned, so to speak.[24]

At the beginning of *Six Miles*, the camera zooms in on the four main puppet characters: "Mother," "Father," "Son" (Thomas Willis according to the official record), and "Mandy" (Amanda Willis). This presentation might remind one of fairy-tale archetypes, but it also adheres to Amanda Willis's point of view (which Walker chose to adopt rather than her brother's), as Willis referred to her parents as "mother" and "father" in her deposition.[25] Unusually for Walker's work, the characters are given a form of psychological depth.[26] In *Six Miles*, for instance, a close-up on Father's face, followed by a sequence in which he hacks down one of his attackers, enables the viewer to read Father's thoughts—and to perceive his desire to hit back. Almost half the film is dedicated to staging the Willises' daily life. The family members go about their day, taking care of their chores: chopping wood, plucking a chicken, doing laundry, and other activities.

The transition between the description of the family's day and the outbreak of violence is accompanied by the piano soundtrack, which in the first half, alternates between a contemplative mood, with the monotonous melody suggesting routine, and something more foreboding, in which the left hand plays a simple *basso continuo* while the right hand hits dissonant, high-pitched notes. As a sunset sequence unravels, the pace of the bass quickens into 32nd and 64th notes while the right hand starts hitting high-pitched notes more and more insistently. The atmosphere becomes more and more tense. Such a method of setting tension is also used in *Lucy of Pulaski*, when the violent outbreak of the climactic scene—the riot—is foreshadowed by the accelerated rhythm of the music before returning once again to the main musical theme in the final scene, when the camera films the cardboard-puppets that signal as the corpses of the rioters, adorned with red cutouts to represents pools of blood.

"With the addition of music, suddenly we had a new film":[27] Jazz Music and the Abstraction of Pain

The music of the film diptych was composed by jazz musician Jason Moran, a longtime friend of Walker's, also known for his collaborations

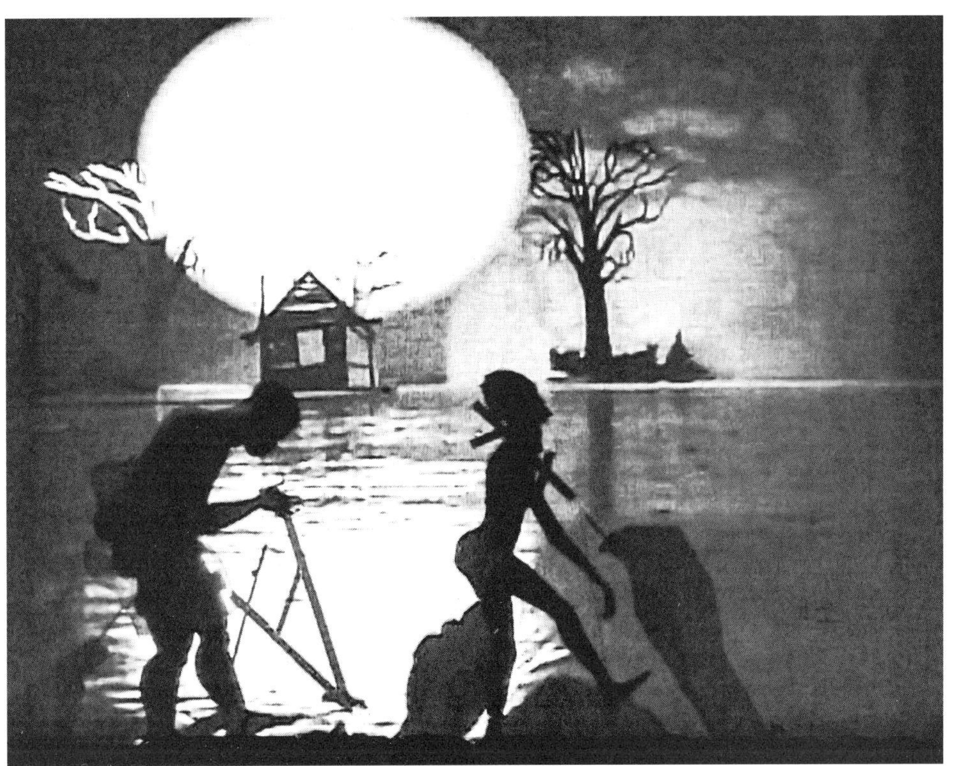

Kara Walker, still from *National Archives Microfilm Publication M999 Roll 34: Bureau of Refugees, Freedmen and Abandoned Lands: Six Miles from Springfield on the Franklin Road*, 2009. Video. 13:22 minutes, sound. Artwork © Kara Walker, courtesy of Sikkema Jenkins & Co., New York; Sprüth Magers, Berlin.

with visual artists such as Glenn Ligon and Joan Jonas. The soundtrack might remind the viewer of how silent films would often be accompanied by a piano or an orchestra. Moran composed the tracks after watching the films in the very late stages of the editing process, following instructions given by Walker, playing half a dozen improvisations from the theme of one of his earlier pieces, "The Field," from the album *Same Mother* (2005). Progressively, Moran established a relationship between the moving image and the music until he, in dialogue with Walker, settled on the final soundtrack. The music thus strengthened the tonality set by the visual artist.[28] For Walker, associating a musician such as Moran with her work was a new step in terms of artistic collaboration.[29]

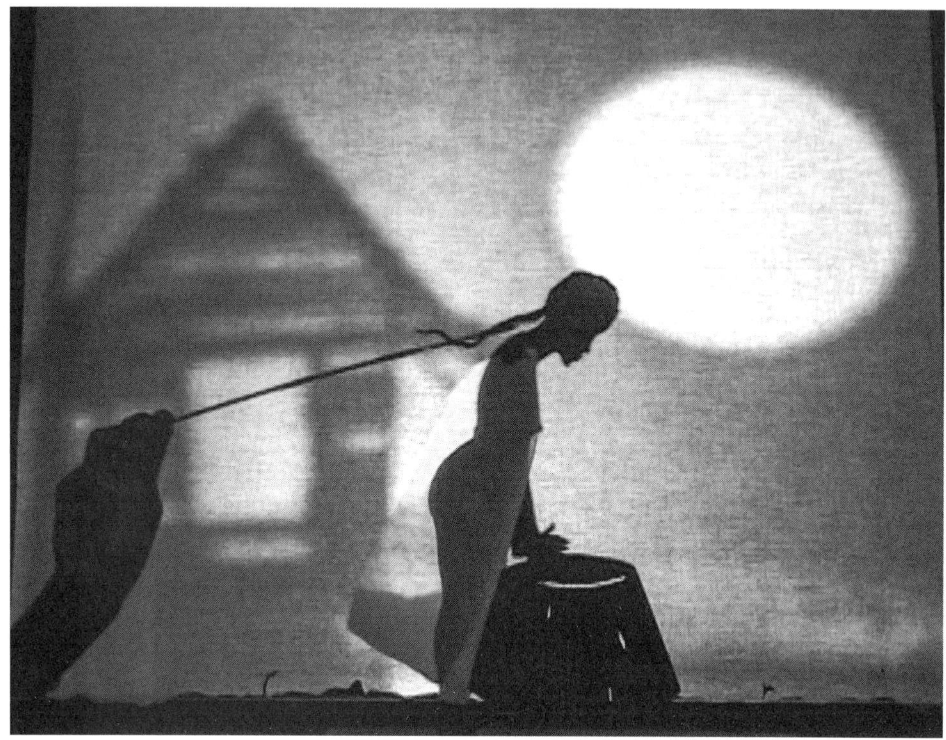

Kara Walker, still from *National Archives Microfilm Publication M999 Roll 34: Bureau of Refugees, Freedmen and Abandoned Lands: Six Miles from Springfield on the Franklin Road*, 2009. Video. 13:22 minutes, sound. Artwork © Kara Walker, courtesy of Sikkema Jenkins & Co., New York; Sprüth Magers, Berlin.

Moran strove to create a music that would match the stakes set by the moving images: he wanted to create a musical context that would communicate the horror of the stories of actual persons.

I watched the films for the first time, and thought, "Oh, wow! This is going to be very different from everything else I've done." Just because setting music to a race riot or setting music to a girl being raped, you know, it's not standard. But it is part of the abstraction that happens in jazz all the time. You know, these kinds of things that musicians will be thinking about while they're playing, but no one would ever know. So it would be like it's the first time it's put out in public view. . . . [These people], they existed . . . this is no

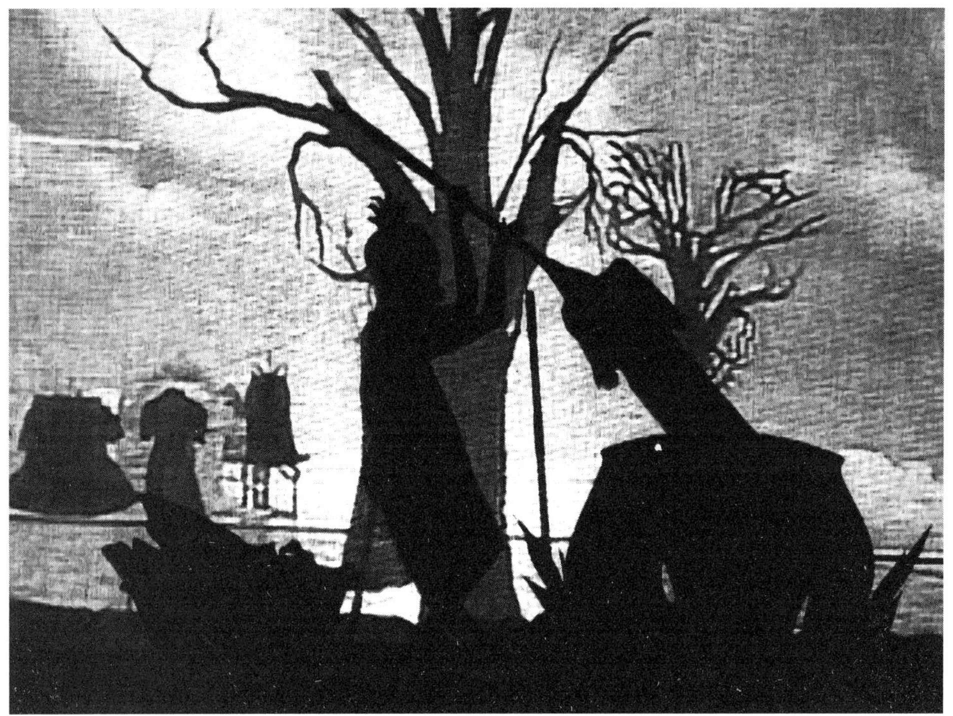

Kara Walker, still from *National Archives Microfilm Publication M999 Roll 34: Bureau of Refugees, Freedmen and Abandoned Lands: Six Miles from Springfield on the Franklin Road*, 2009. Video. 13:22 minutes, sound. Artwork © Kara Walker, courtesy of Sikkema Jenkins & Co., New York; Sprüth Magers, Berlin.

fabrication anymore, this is an actual event. I mean, when you look at [Walker's] picture of a little child with an inflated balloon-like penis floating in the air [in *Gone*], you know that's out of sight, out of the ordinary. But these are ordinary stories, that happened to real people.[30]

The collaboration with Walker brought to the surface the political undertones of instrumental jazz music for Moran—undertones encoding histories of dispossession and racial violence that have often been lost on unaware or unknowing (white) audiences. Although Moran was not involved in the creative process of *Six Miles* and *Lucy of Pulaski* from the start,[31] his participation in the overall process was determinant to its completion.[32]

A Departure from Previous Films? A "Brechtian" Shadow-Puppet Theater

Six Miles and *Lucy of Pulaski* show greater complexity in terms of film-making than Walker's previous films. "Obsolete" cinematographic technologies, such as back projection, are used to provide the setting: daytime skies for *Six Miles* and starry ones for *Lucy of Pulaski*, both shot outdoors. A large theater projector with an array of differently colored gelatin films is sometimes used to light up a scene as it is being shot, either following the main character or translating the moment as taking place either during day or night. Mixing devices from the cinema and the stage set up a dynamic relationship between distance and proximity in the films. In *Six Miles*, the set of the shadow-puppet theater that represents the Willis house in front of which the cutout puppets come and go is complemented by a complex projection apparatus that enables Walker to layer the image and play on the movement back and forth between depth of field and the flatness of shadow-puppet theater, thereby opening unexpected visual spaces. In the riot scene at the end of *Lucy of Pulaski*, the puppeteers' gestures, recorded live, are complemented by the projection of a previous recording of the scene, which allows for the apparition of many more silhouettes than those held up by the puppeteers. A fantastical impression of bodies multiplying is conveyed, suggesting the monstrous invasion of the image by the bodies of the white rioters, which end up pervading the field of the camera. Compared with Walker's previous films (shot statically for the most part), the use of various cinematographic techniques allows for a livelier, more fluid narration.

Yet despite the clear, linear narrative that unravels before the viewers' eyes, *Six Miles* and *Lucy of Pulaski* evince a high degree of aesthetic distancing, even greater than that apparent in *8 Possible Beginnings or: The Making of African America*, where the presence of the artist as puppeteer was already occasionally manifest.[33] The films consistently resort to Brecht's alienation effect, and perhaps more than any other work by Walker, they manage to pull us in emotionally and create the space for emotional distance—thereby allowing for our awareness of the tenuous balance between the two. Telling the stories of crimes committed against real persons, Walker seems to have momentarily set her strategies of seduction aside by representing the processes of filmmaking alongside the representation of violence.

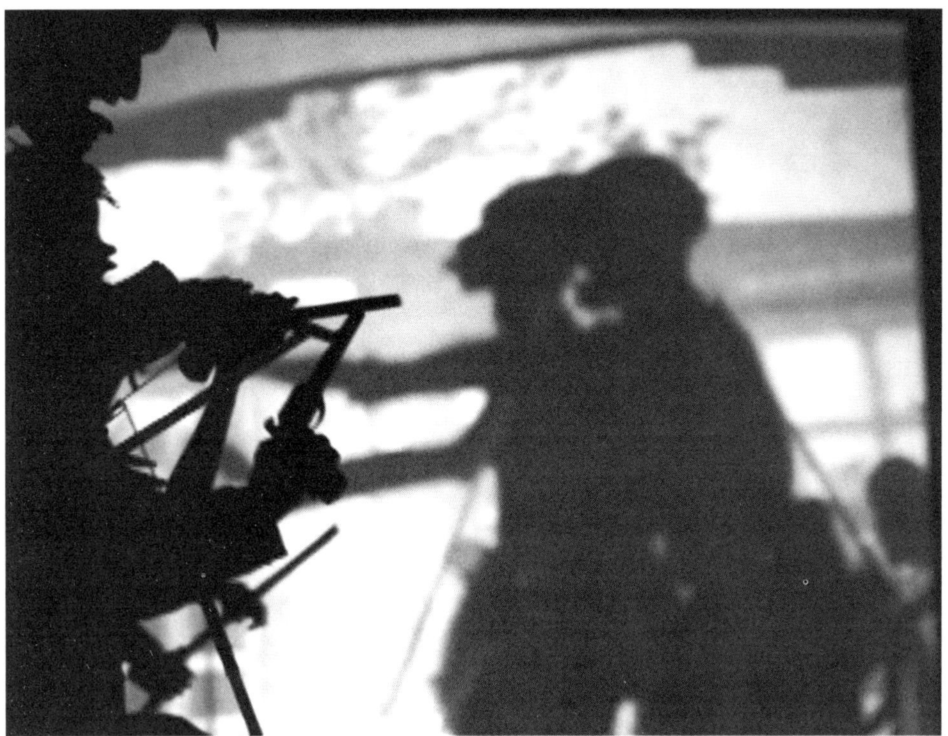

Kara Walker, still from *National Archives Microfilm Publication M999 Roll 34: Bureau of Refugees, Freedmen and Abandoned Lands: Lucy of Pulaski*, 2009. Video. 12:08 minutes, sound. Artwork © Kara Walker, courtesy of Sikkema Jenkins & Co., New York; Sprüth Magers, Berlin.

Six Miles and *Lucy of Pulaski* can be linked to Brecht's epic drama through Walker's choice to undercut dramatic tension (thus disrupting dramatic illusion) in several ways. The first sequence of *Six Miles* shows a shot of the attack at night. This prolepsis in the narrative, announcing one of the climaxes of the film, prevents the buildup of dramatic tension that would secure the viewer's full emotional adhesion to the unraveling of events. Undercutting dramatic tension, as Brecht argued, enables the artist to reestablish critical distance, inviting the viewer to adopt a reflexive position. What is more, the first sequence of the film shows the backstage of the puppet theater. While a film like *8 Possible Beginnings* gives the viewer a glimpse of the puppeteer's hands or of the artist's face now and then, the very opening of *Six Miles* directly focuses

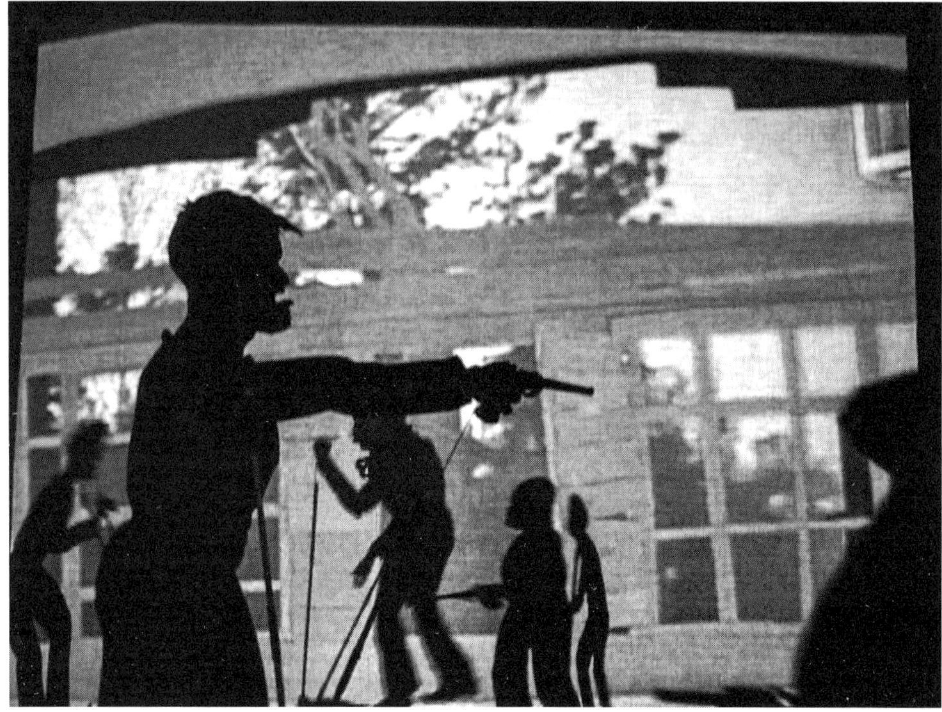

Kara Walker, still from *National Archives Microfilm Publication M999 Roll 34: Bureau of Refugees, Freedmen and Abandoned Lands: Lucy of Pulaski*, 2009. Video. 12:08 minutes, sound. Artwork © Kara Walker, courtesy of Sikkema Jenkins & Co., New York; Sprüth Magers, Berlin.

our attention on the artist and the film team at work. Further along in the film, the camera shifts its focus from the screen of the puppet theater—the stage—to the artist and her assistants behind it.

Six Miles also undermines dramatic illusion in the sense that it rejects the viewer's suspension of disbelief: we are not asked to accept the unraveling events presented before us as momentarily real as we usually would during a play or a film. Walker's choice of the puppet theater becomes all the more relevant given the fact that the puppeteer does not embody the character but handles a puppet standing for it. Indeed, Walker doubles down on the distancing potential of the medium, often showing the puppets as crafted material objects rather than as representations of shadows, notably in some of the most wrenching scenes. For instance, when Son takes Mandy in his arms after the

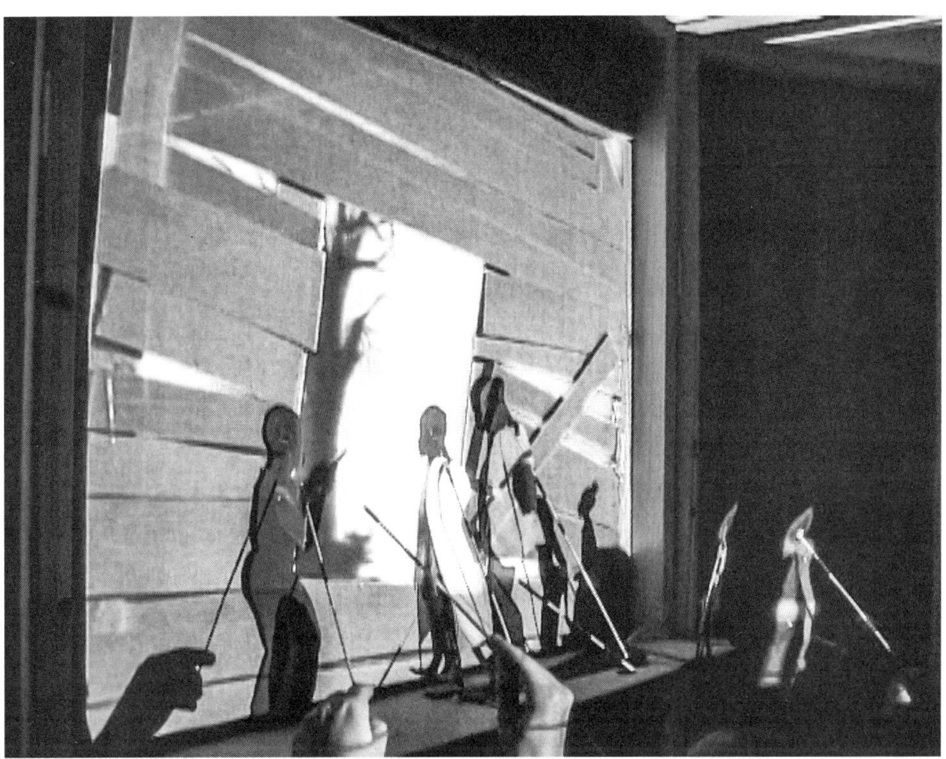

Kara Walker, still from *National Archives Microfilm Publication M999 Roll 34: Bureau of Refugees, Freedmen and Abandoned Lands: Six Miles from Springfield on the Franklin Road*, 2009. Video. 13:22 minutes, sound. Artwork © Kara Walker, courtesy of Sikkema Jenkins & Co., New York; Sprüth Magers, Berlin.

death of Father, we are shown the backs of the puppets, with the nails as articulations, etc. After that shot, the camera zooms out on the figure of Father, showing us the red gelatin film that signals his blood. The puppet no longer appears on the stage but rather lies down on the art-ist's studio table, on which a few backdrop elements have been set—the Willis house, a giant tree (a metonymy for the woods), and the path connecting the two. At this point, we are shown not only the backstage but the very fabrication site of the film set, distilling the artwork to its props and material conditions of production.[34] In *Lucy of Pulaski*, similar shots of the backs of puppets lying face down on the table can be seen, with subtitles giving the names of the riot victims (sometimes

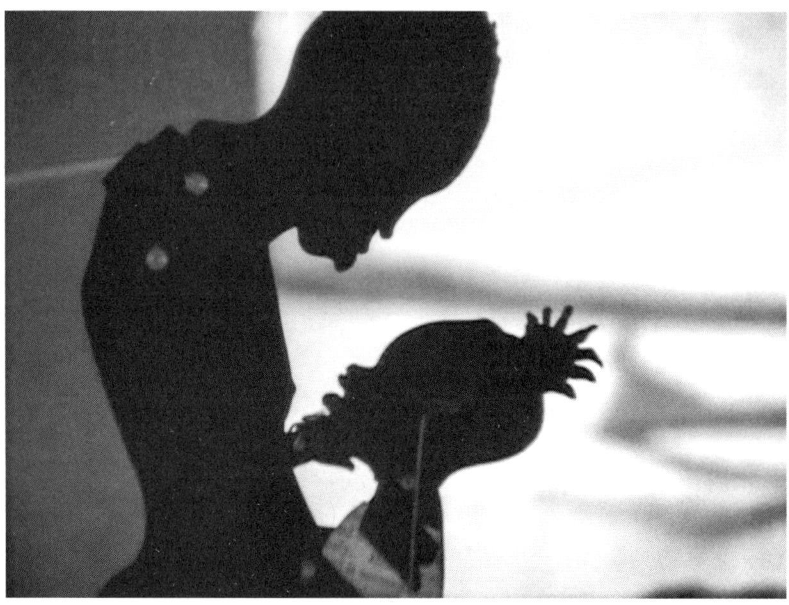

Kara Walker, still from *National Archives Microfilm Publication M999 Roll 34: Bureau of Refugees, Freedmen and Abandoned Lands: Six Miles from Springfield on the Franklin Road*, 2009. Video. 13:22 minutes, sound. Artwork © Kara Walker, courtesy of Sikkema Jenkins & Co., New York; Sprüth Magers, Berlin.

also referred to as "anonymous," after the text of the archive). By stressing the materiality of the puppets during the most trying scenes of the films, Walker subverts the usual function of the shadow-puppet theater, which reduces the three-dimensional world to a two-dimensional realm, connecting spectators to another realm of existence—the world of shadows, that is, the departed.

Indeed, showing the puppets as objects reduces the viewer's ability to be transported into another dimension and to relate to the characters the puppets stand for. Moreover, the economical means used to create the artifacts, mere cardboard and nails, can lead to movements that escape artistic control, as when the jerking motions of manipulated puppets suggest the last convulsions of dying men at the end of *Lucy of Pulaski*.[35] The films create a dizzying movement between stage and backstage—between representation, its making, and back to representation again. Integrating the accidents of production into the final work reinforces its attachment to a material, rather than spiritual,

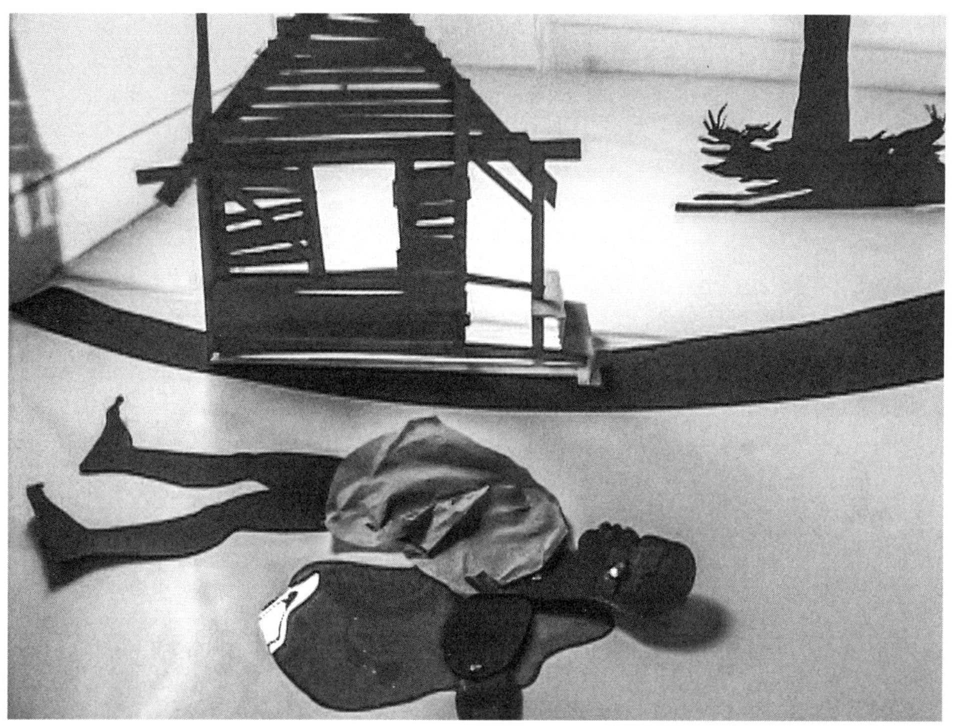

Kara Walker, still from *National Archives Microfilm Publication M999 Roll 34: Bureau of Refugees, Freedmen and Abandoned Lands: Six Miles from Springfield on the Franklin Road,* 2009. Video. 13:22 minutes, sound. Artwork © Kara Walker, courtesy of Sikkema Jenkins & Co., New York; Sprüth Magers, Berlin.

realm. Walker's disruption of dramatic illusion through shadow theater, a medium traditionally linked to death, also undermines the possibility of communicating the effects of violence. This can be related to Saidiya Hartman's insistence, in her account of her methodological approach to the archive in *Scenes of Subjection,* on the necessity to be aware of the impossibility of fully recovering the experiences of the enslaved and the emancipated. Hartman summons such awareness again in "Venus in Two Acts," in which she examines how one might reckon with "the precarious lives which are visible only in the moment of their disappearance."[36]

Amanda Willis is indeed only visible in the moment, not of her material disappearance, but of her dehumanization through violation.

She entered the archive and the possibility of historical memory only as a victim of violence, while her word is mediated by the dominant form and power apparatus that is the legal deposition. Similarly, the Black men mentioned by the "affidavit" on which *Lucy of Pulaski* is based only gain access to a form of historic existence "in the moment of their disappearance"; and Lucy Reynolds, as we have seen, is described as little more than a sexual object (the immediate "cause" of the "riot") in the archive. In "Venus in Two Acts," Hartman rejects the possibility of the miraculous recovery through art of the lost lives of enslaved Black women—of waking the dead through writing. Walker's materialist approach similarly does not attempt to produce the miracle of raising dead in order to communicate with the living (if only to vanish later). The artist uses a medium that connects the living to the dead while hinting at the necessary failure of such an endeavor at the same time. And Walker is no medium: the dead girl's voice is not heard through the artist's body. Indeed, no voices can be heard in *Six Miles* nor *Lucy of Pulaski*—which is not necessarily the case in all of Walker's films.[37]

Six Miles is silent in two ways: one never hears the characters speak, shout, or cry (this is also true for *Lucy of Pulaski*), and there are no text panels for dialogue (not the case for *Lucy*).[38] The absence of the human voice is particularly significant in *Six Miles* because the film addresses a theme already raised by Walker in *8 Possible Beginnings*: the rape of a child, in a scene in which the human voice played an important role. In *8 Possible Beginnings*, at chapter 6, entitled "A Darkey Hymn: 'All I Want,'" the viewer sees the puppet of a Black slave girl crying. A white man, identified as master or overseer, is walking behind her; from the puppet's stylized gesture, he might be either pushing her or caressing her. Throughout this ominous sequence, what we actually see is the man and the child walking through the stage of the shadow theater. As the viewer listens to the soundtrack—a recording of the voices of Walker and her daughter, Octavia, declaiming the same text in turns—it dawns on her that the adult male protagonist is about to rape or molest the character of the little girl. In *8 Possible Beginnings*, a work solely of the artist's invention, rape is neither plainly shown nor told about: it is alluded to via the puppets' movements (the girl wiping her face, which we can read as crying, and the man's pushing/stroking, which we can read as his intentions) and the spoken monologue (rape is mentioned through the periphrasis "what happened to Abby"). In

Six Miles, however, rape is represented explicitly. I would argue that Walker's artistic decision to *picture*—to depict via images—the act of sexual violence committed by white supremacists against Willis may be a function of her desire to be faithful to the facts as Willis recounted them. If *Six Miles* is silent, it is because the facts—and Willis—speak for themselves.[39]

In *Six Miles*, the rape of Amanda Willis (what is referred to as a "forcible connection" in the official record) is performed by the puppeteers and explicitly shown on screen. The viewer can see a man grabbing Amanda, taking her into the woods, forcing himself on her; close-ups on their crotches, then on Amanda's face, follow. Why did Walker choose to go further in the presentation of sexual violence in the 2009 film, especially as these events happened to an actual person rather than a character of fiction? One possible answer may lie in the fact that the 2009 films, which bear no satirical function, aim at presenting history.

"Saving Horror from Invisibility": The Paradoxical Coincidence of Engagement and Distance

At this stage, I would like to draw on Georges Didi-Huberman's analysis of the myth of Perseus and Medusa, as part of his defense of the right to represent historical horror in general, and the Shoah in particular.[40] According to Didi-Huberman, images help us in *imagining* what happened, a necessary condition to "save a piece of knowledge"[41] from historical horror, as a way to avoid it lapsing into indifference *and* counter its terrifying, paralyzing effect.[42] Didi-Huberman borrows the idea of the image as shield and weapon from film historian Siegfried Kracauer. According to this notion, the image is used to confront violence that cannot be looked at directly, lest it petrify the viewer and circumvent the work of knowledge. In Didi-Huberman's account, the shield of the ancient myth of Medusa—in which Perseus manages to make his way to the monster by looking at her reflection into his shield—is the image. Looking at the image, a scrap of knowledge from the experiences of others as one's fellows can be obtained, and dehumanized victims of violence can be recognized as one's fellow human beings.[43] Annihilated human beings will not come back, but a fragment of the memory of what they endured can be saved.[44]

> Perseus confronts the Gorgon in spite of it all, and this *in spite of it all*—the de facto possibility, despite a legitimate impossibility—is called *image*: the shield and the reflection are not only protections but weapons, ruse, technical means for beheading the monster. The initial impotent fatalism ("one cannot look at the Medusa") is replaced by the *ethical response* ("well, I will confront the Medusa all the same, by looking at her *differently*").[45]

Didi-Huberman was referring to documentary photographs; however, he does not exclude artworks from his overall argument on the function of images. No images of the "outrages" committed against Blacks are to be found in the Freedmen's Bureau archive online.[46] Walker created her own images after the text; she created her own shield, so to speak.

In the case of *Six Miles*, then, the "shield" is the "formal mechanisms of the image[s] produced"[47]—implying the material means of representation, artistic process, and choices, as well as the artistic gesture of translating the archive record into moving images. I would contend that Walker's approach to the rape of Amanda Willis bears a similar sense of ethical responsibility to Willis's memory and story to Didi-Huberman's. Indeed, *Six Miles* "saves, at least, a historical Real threatened by indifference."[48] The formal mechanisms of the image might enable the transmission of Willis's story, in spite of it all, while refraining from speaking for her. Walker does not substitute her own voice (in the literal and metaphorical sense) for Willis's, nor does she add text of her own to Willis's deposition. Kara Walker does not speak in Amanda Willis's name. Hence the crucial part of the jazz soundtrack: one can hear only the *abstractions* of traumatic events that will remain *unknown* forever. Music signals the impossibility to communicate trauma, yet it acts as the vehicle of emotion at the same time. Here, music takes on a mourning quality—a lament beyond language in the face of horror: pain and suffering cannot be grasped in full, but may be conjured through music.

That a work of art that pictures the horror of historic reality should incessantly remind the viewer of aesthetic distance is not exclusive of looking into Medusa's eyes. On the contrary, Walker's artistic endeavor implies a form of confrontation with the artwork's subject via the physical engagement of the artist and her assistants. Disrupting the suspension of disbelief and asserting the artist's control of the formal mechanisms of the image produced, the sequences showing Walker and her assistants at work also stress the performative aspect of the piece as an essential component of the final work, which is not the recording of the performance of a shadow-puppet show but an actual film. That Walker should portray herself (and her assistants) as the artist creates a *mise en abyme* that openly reveals the films as artifacts. The presence of the artist in the films signals her own accountability as image-producer and acknowledges the artist's "responsibility" with the formal mechanism of the image produced. This, according to Didi-Huberman, is a necessary condition to make horror "a source of knowledge," once it has been "reflected, renewed, and reconstructed as an image."[49] Which is exactly what *Six Miles* does.

As a medium, shadow-puppet theater is based on the handheld manipulation of puppet characters who take on a life of their own as protagonists for the viewer, yet that also serve, as objects, as an extension of the performers' bodies. As opposed to an actor, the puppeteer does not embody the character (which is kept at a distance, albeit a short one). Yet the puppeteer is physically engaged in the puppet's action, which she can also watch as she is performing. During the rape scene, Walker's hands appear, stressing the engagement of the body at the moment when the scene of trauma is enacted. Here it must be noted that Walker decided that the shoot would start with this scene. Unlike the rest of the shoot, which apparently took place in a relatively jovial atmosphere, the rape scene proved as trying for the puppeteers as for the camerawoman.[50] The sequence was filmed with a handheld camera, rather than a fixed camera as in Walker's other films.[51] Shot by Laurie Butler, the scene established maximum proximity between the action and the viewer, as the camerawoman was close enough to the action so that the puppeteers could actually see themselves in the screen of the camera. This proximity had a significant emotional effect on the camerawoman and the puppeteers. They not only saw the puppets they were manipulating but also saw themselves performing a rape scene: they could see their own implication in the enactment of the archival record. Through a unique combination of performance and filming style, Walker made it impossible for the art workers to remain emotionally distant during the making of the artwork, while making it possible to look at it, to reflect on it. A shield polished as a mirror, indeed.

Such maximum engagement—the felt necessity of getting everybody's "feet wet,"[52] of bringing the artists' bodies as close to the action as possible, of building up a trying, difficult relationship between the artists' tools, their own bodies, and the performance of the scene also took place in the creative process of creating the soundtrack for *Six Miles*. Embracing John Cage's use of the prepared piano, Moran put several objects on the piano strings, producing a more percussive sound, to translate the chaos of the riot scenes and the rape scene. Also, a prepared piano is more difficult to play:

> As a player, it's a different kind of physicality to make those sounds, too. For the riot, I needed to make it seem like there are sixty people running around, and consider the time when people are running in the dirt, or running on planks of wood . . . you just need to be as raucous as possible. . . . So preparing the piano to make that sound like things are thumping, or plotting, stomping—I was just trying to broaden that landscape, because I think at a certain moment, I was just playing a note on the piano, just playing the middle C. I think it resonated enough to match what was happening on the screen. I mean I really needed to feel the tension; and for the girl being raped, I needed to be pressing down on the string, with a bell, and hitting the note of the piano to make this kind of cry happen. . . . So it becomes a lot more physical as a relationship to the video.[53]

The confrontation with the text of the archive does not have a cathartic or exorcistic effect (a function of traditional shadow theater). On the contrary, such a confrontation has psychic consequences. Yet in spite of it all, Walker and her collaborators succeeded in making the artwork, allowing viewers to be touched by a fragment of Amanda Willis's story.

By presenting viewers with the history of Willis (and Lucy Reynolds), Walker shows viewers what those white supremacist men did to her. *This*, Walker's film states, is what they did to her. Walker asks us to acknowledge Willis as a fellow human being: a step in the direction of restoring the humanity they denied her. And in choosing Amanda Willis's story over her brother's, in making Lucy Reynolds the heroine of *Lucy of Pulaski*, Walker's work, as a Black feminist proposition, intuitively undermines what Hartman, in *Scenes of Subjection*, pinpoints as the "implicit masculinism of the new Black citizenship during the Reconstruction era."[54]

Reclaiming the full humanity of the victims, Walker's film thus belongs to an ethical approach to history and image-making. It does not restore the fragile nascent interracial social links whose building was at the heart of the Reconstruction, and which the white supremacists precisely aimed at (and succeeded in) destroying through acts of terror such as those committed against Amanda Willis and other Black persons, shattering the possibility of interracial class solidarity in the South. But capturing us into the historical past for a short moment, the film takes a powerful step in the present to create new social links: provided the viewer should choose to watch it rather than walk away, the film makes the viewer incorporate those images into their memory—as, to quote Didi-Huberman, the animated images "seize us before they flee," "touch us for a while, though they vanish in an instant."[55] Cultivating a common conscience, the film takes part in building a common history that is willing to look at the racist-sexist violence at its heart and that reckons with the humanity of others. Hence the significance of imagination in the film: "imagining," as in translating Willis's story into images, so that we may be presented with what happened to her; but also "imagination," as in Hartman's essay, that "labors" at painting "as full a picture" of the departed as possible.[56] In *Six Miles*, this means depicting Willis's daily life before the attack in order to provide a frame to help the viewer conceive of the Willises' existence beyond their sole apparition as "disappearance" and their administrative status as victims of violence. Those imagined sequences enable Walker to picture the family as ordinary people,[57] as agents, rather than objects. Last, I would argue that this also inscribes them within the resistance of love—and love as resistance—in the face of terror: when we can briefly see Son take Mandy into his arms, to comfort her. (Thomas Willis, as the historical record suggests, testified with his sister.) Although extremely brief, this occurrence of loving connection is rare enough in Walker's work to be noted.[58] In the present, this love must translate into solidarity: rather than just being seized by images of historic terror, let us grasp "the ongoing state of emergency in which black lives remains in peril"[59]—perhaps even provide care, and resistance.

Conclusion: A Work of Herstory

Six Miles and *Lucy of Pulaski* can be considered successful adaptations of artists' practices (and of the medium of the shadow theater embraced in an original, materialist manner) to the object of a necessarily fragmentary, difficult, self-reflective—but not altogether impossible—representation. With *Six Miles* and *Lucy of Pulaski*, adaptation meant testing one's medium, making it physically trying, and taking risks—putting one's own body and psyche at stake and at the very center of the formal means of representation, for example. In this way, aesthetic distance means the opposite of detachment: it means looking at horror as closely as possible through the shield of the formal mechanisms of the image produced. And the decision to look at horror, overcoming one's fear, is what constitutes the higher act of courage—the imagining *"courage to know."*[60] The artistic process, in other words, is the site of courage. Aesthetic distance enables one to look at Medusa, simultaneously reflecting the triple remove of the archive: first, as historically distant; second, as fragmentary, incomplete, and violent (as recording lives at the moment of their disappearance or violation); third, as ontologically remote—the nature of trauma foreclosing the possibility of fully knowing it. Yet a piece of knowledge can be obtained, through an ethical artwork that asks viewers to acknowledge the memory of what happened to one's fellow human being, calling them to look at racist-sexist violence in the present.

By taking a few lines from a historical record and turning them into one of her most powerful works of art, Walker went beyond working from the archive: presenting history, making a work of history (or rather, herstory)—rather than just out of history—she did activate the archive in Michel Foucault's idea of the archive-as-practice, as "the system that governs the appearance of statements as unique events," as that which determines that "all these things said do not accumulate endlessly in an amorphous mass . . . but shine, as it were, like stars, some that seem close to us shining brightly from afar off."[61] Amanda Willis will never come back from the dead; but her story, told by Walker, shines brightly on—even if from afar.

Notes

1. The U.S. National Archives and Records Administration, https://www.archives.gov/.

2. The Reconstruction Era (1865–1877) refers to the post–Civil War period that saw an effort to integrate former Black slaves politically as citizens, focusing on enfranchisement and education as well as fighting poverty and rebuilding the economy of the former slave states, occupied by the federal troops. The Reconstruction was notably

plagued by constant violence against Blacks and the birth of the Ku Klux Klan and other white-supremacist violent organizations; it ended in 1877, with the removal of troops from the southern states.

3. Kara Walker, *Bureau of Refugees, Freedmen, and Abandoned Lands* (Milan: Charta Editions, 2007), 3.

4. The Freedmen's Bureau Online: Records of the Bureau of Refugees, Freedmen and Abandoned Lands, https://freedmensbureau.com/freedmens-bureau.

5. Saidiya V. Hartman, *Scenes of Subjection: Terror, Slavery and Self-Making in Nineteenth-Century America* (New York: Oxford University Press, 1997), 13. The criminal records from the Bureau are, overwhelmingly, white supremacist attacks against Black persons, and are evidence of the emergence of the Ku Klux Klan.

6. Publication "M999" contains the "Records of the Assistant Commissioner for the State of Tennessee, Bureau of Refugees, Freedmen, and Abandoned Lands, 1865–1869." Within this category, the records are then filed under a specific state (here, Tennessee), and then, within the records for the state of Tennessee, as "Records Relating to Outrages" (e.g., violent crimes), and finally as "Affidavits Related to Outrages in Tennessee," https://freedmensbureau.com/tennessee/affidavits/index.htm.

7. *Six Miles from Springfield on the Franklin Road* is based on the record entitled "Henry and Amanda Willis," while *Lucy of Pulaski* is based on two sources: first, four statements by a J. T. Fisher, a John (X) Carter, a George (X) Carter, and an anonymous depositor, labeled on the Freedmen's Bureau website as "Affidavits Relating to Outrages Mar. 1866–August 1868." Second, the story is also recorded in an elaborated report from a Michael Walsh to a General Carlin, after an investigation of the riot in the town of Pulaski. Walker based *Lucy of Pulaski* on that report, which mentions a Lucy Reynolds as one of the immediate causes leading to the attack of Calvin Carter by Calvin Lamberth, resulting in the death of at least two Black men, the wounding of four (no white men injured). As the report goes on, Walsh clearly states the imbalance of power and preparation between the Black men and the white men, inferring the "readiness" of the white men to attack as evidence of the existence of an "organization" "called the Ku Klux Klan, having for its end the expulsion of loyal men whites and blacks from the counties of Giles & Maury and thus terrorizing similar to that which was general in this county about the breaking out of the rebellion." Walsh concludes by calling for the "prompt suppression" of the Klan. Michael Walsh, letter to Major General W. J. P. Carlin, January 11, 1868, Nashville, Tennessee, the Freedmen's Bureau Online, Records of the Assistant Commissioner for the State of Tennessee, Bureau of Refugees, Freedmen, and Abandoned Lands, 1865–1869, National Archive Microfilm Publication M999, Roll 34, "Reports of Outrages, Riots and Murders, Jan. 15, 1866–Aug. 12, 1868," https://www.freedmensbureau.com/tennessee/outrages/orangerhodes.htm.

8. The most famous works Walker has borrowed from are Margaret Mitchell's *Gone with the Wind* (1926), Harriet Beecher's Stowe's *Uncle Tom Cabin* (1859), and Thomas Dixon's *The Clansman* (1951). As for her visual sources, they include Eastman Johnson's *Negro Life at the South* (1859), Constantin Brancusi's *Endless Column* (1918), and the cyclorama painting *The Battle of Atlanta* (1886) at the Atlanta History Center. Walker's sources have been amply discussed in major publications on her work. See Gwendolyn DuBois Shaw's *Seeing the Unspeakable: The Art of Kara Walker* (Durham, NC: Duke University Press, 2004); Darby English, "A New Context for Reconstruction: Some Crises of Landscape in Kara Walker's Silhouette Installation," in *How to See a Work of*

Art in Total Darkness (Cambridge, MA: MIT Press, 2007), 28–71; Philippe Vergne, "The Black Saint Is the Sinner Lady," in *Kara Walker: My Complement, My Enemy, My Oppressor, My Love,* by Philippe Vergne, Sander L. Gilman, Thomas McEvilley, Robert Storr, Kevin Young, and Yasmil Raymond (Minneapolis, MN: Walker Art Center, 2007), 7–26; Yasmil Raymond, "Maladies of Power," in *Kara Walker: My Complement, My Enemy, My Oppressor, My Love,* by Vergne et al., 347–370.

9. This, combined with the quiet, restrained quality of the framed cutout series Walker presented in 2007 as the "Bureau of Refugees," small in scale and much less expressive than the rest of her work so far.

10. In his groundbreaking book, Huey Copeland presents the work of these four artists specifically in their relation to slavery. Huey Copeland, *Bound to Appear: Art, Slavery and the Site of Blackness in Multicultural America* (Chicago: University of Chicago Press, 2013).

11. "[W]hy I chose the *Bureau of Refugees* specifically as a starting point was just about how stories of mortal terror are transcribed in sort of legal situations and for legal purposes." Walker, interview with the author, September 17, 2009.

12. For instance, in *The End of Uncle Tom and the Grand Allegorical Tableau of Eva in Heaven* (1995), in *Slavery! Slavery!* (1997), and in *Darkytown Rebellion* (2001).

13. Vergne, "The Black Saint Is the Sinner Lady," 17.

14. Saidiya Hartman, "Venus in Two Acts," *Small Axe* 26 (June 2008): 1–14.

15. Hal Foster, "An Archival Impulse," *OCTOBER* 110 (Fall 2004): 3–22.

16. Hartman, "Venus in Two Acts," 12.

17. The time span of the creation and exhibition made from the Bureau of Refugees archive (roughly, 2007–2009) overlapped with Walker's itinerant retrospective at the Walker Art Center, the Musée d'Art Moderne de la Ville de Paris, the Whitney Museum, and the Hammer Museum (2007–2008), probably explaining why the works Walker presented at her gallery in 2007 and 2009—and the fact that they were archive-based—went below the radar of critical attention.

18. Every framed cutout was titled in reference to a specific "outrage" (i.e., violent attack) committed by whites against Blacks; the titles appropriated extracts of the Freedmen's Bureau's records, sometimes verbatim, sometimes more freely; sometimes extensively, sometimes succinctly; sometimes retelling the facts, sometimes just mentioning the date or place of the events. (Compare the two following titles: "Bureau of Refugees: May 29 Richard Dick's wife beaten with a club by her employer, Richard remonstrated—in the night was taken from his house and beaten with a buggy trace nearly to death by his employer and 2 others," as opposed to "Bureau of Refugees: Between Danville + Somerville.")

The exhibition also included small, frail paper cutout silhouette sculptures; large collages of newspaper clips and cutout silhouettes; and a series of fifty-two texts traced with Sumi ink on paper, arranged as a wall installation, entitled *Search for Ideas Supporting the Black Man as a work of Modern Art/Contemporary Painting. A Death Without End: an appreciation of the Creative Spirit of Lynch Mobs.*

19. Walker, *Bureau of Refugees,* 3.

20. For persons privileged enough to have daily access to a stable Internet connection and a computer. In 2003, Google registered over 3 million requests per day.

21. In 2007, a pilot project had been launched by U.S. National Archives and digitization businesses, as a partnership to make the archives more widely available and easier to access than in their original format or as microfilms. The National Archive had partnered with Google and with a digitization company then named Footnote, rebranded as Fold3, a business specializing in military archives. See https://www.fold3.com/about.

22. Walker worked on the Freedmen Bureau's records for the best part of three years, ordering microfiche from the National Archives and comparing the different accounts of the same event. She also created work that ironically addressed the Bureau of Refugees Series (in a series of quick text paintings entitled *Every Painting Is a Dead Nigger Waiting to Be Born* (2009), like a self-derisive jab at the longer project.

23. Hartman, *Scenes of Subjection*, 10.

24. Indeed, in her previous films, Walker resorted to irony and gallows humor (*Testimony, 8 Possible Beginnings*). Her characters are presented as grotesque (with caricature-like profiles in *Testimony* or, closer to the original sense of the grotesque, as monstrous, sexualized hybrids in *8 Possible Beginnings*, where the character of "King Cotton" forms out of a pile of excreted dead African men and gives birth to a cotton plant that will grow into a giant lynching tree with eyes; in *Miss Pippi*, the heroine's crinoline is also a tree). The narrative is interrupted twice with unrelated stories or "interludes" embedded into the main narrative in *8 Possible Beginnings* and *Miss Pippi*. None of this is the case in *Six Miles* and *Lucy*.

25. Walker, interview with the author.

26. Except in text pieces such as *Letter from a Black Girl* (1998) or chapter 6 of *8 Possible Beginnings*, which will be analyzed further along in this essay, most of Walker's characters are, indeed, flat—both literally and psychologically.

27. Laurie Butler, interview with the author, March 7, 2010.

28. Moran explained that Walker did not specify her intentions regarding *Six Miles* and that the impressionistic aspect of the music for that film appeared relatively self-evident to him. The final soundtrack is the result of a complex editing process. Moran, online interview with the author, October 28, 2011.

29. Prior to *Six Miles* and *Lucy of Pulaski*, Walker had already worked in a collective manner on a video such as *. . . I Was Transported* (2006), for instance. Walker sought technical assistance for that work from a filmmaker. However, she made her very first film, *Testimony* (2004), herself. Butler, interview with the author.

30. Moran, interview with the author.

31. According to Moran, Walker reached out to him about two weeks before the first presentation of the film at the Ontario Museum of Fine Arts in November 2008; the conception shooting and editing of the film took place from July to October 2008. Moran, interview with the author.

32. When the film diptych was first exhibited at the Ontario Museum of Fine Arts, it was presented as a video installation, similarly to the opening of *8 Possible Beginnings* at REDCAT in Los Angeles in 2005, and to *. . . I Was Transported*. The latter is the only film by Walker that has consistently been shown as a video installation, while most other films have been shown as such in subsequent exhibitions.

33. In *8 Possible Beginnings*, one can sometimes catch a glimpse of Walker's hands manipulating the cutout puppets or changing the backdrop. Now and again, the viewer

can see Walker's lips move, mouthing out dialogues as she records herself as story-teller, a puppet mistress cooking up a macabre farce. One cannot stress the distinction between the artist and her artistic persona enough, though: here, Walker stages her practice as play in an explicit manner—and stages herself as the very agent, as opposed to the puppet, of the creative process.

34. Walker shot some sequences alone in her studio, and others with her assistants. Butler, interview with the author.

35. Walker is notably interested in the shadow theater as a medium that allows for a certain type of interaction between the performer and her puppets. She explains how accidents in the movements of the puppets sometimes gave an unexpected direction to the work. For instance, one of the characters in *Lucy of Pulaski* was humorously nicknamed "self-defense expert" as an inside joke in the studio, because of the way the puppet's arms moved, reminding one of the kung fu movements in Blaxploitation films, for instance. Walker, interview with the author.

36. Hartman, "Venus in Two Acts," 11.

37. In *8 Possible Beginnings* and *Miss Pippi's Blue Tale*, Walker's voice can be heard distinctly.

38. Which is not the case for *Lucy of Pulaski*, in which interjections are sometimes introduced: "Carter!" calls out one of the characters at the beginning of the attack.

39. "On or about the 23rd day of October 1866 I saw three men at mother's house and after putting all of us out of the house and our clothes one of the men got me by the arm and told me to follow him, he brought me down into the woods and had forcible connection with me." Amanda Willis, transcription by Michl [*sic*] Walsh, November 26, 1866, signed "Amanda (X) Willis," "Affidavits Relating to Outrages Mar. 1866–August 1868," http://freedmensbureau.com/tennesse/affidavits/willis.htm.

40. Didi-Huberman, *Images in Spite of It All, Four Photographs from Auschwitz*, trans. Shane B. Lillis (Chicago: University of Chicago Press), part II, chapter 1, "Fact-Image or Fetish Image," 51–88.

41. Didi-Huberman, *Images in Spite of It All*, 176.

42. Didi-Huberman, *Images in Spite of It All*, part II.

43. Didi-Huberman, *Images in Spite of It All*, 161.

44. Didi-Huberman, *Images in Spite of It All*, 62.

45. Didi-Huberman, *Images in Spite of It All*, 179.

46. I would like to add that Walker did create artwork as a response to a *photographic* archive of terror—the James Allen archive of lynching photographs, which was presented as an itinerant exhibition in the United States in 2000–2002 and abroad (at the *Rencontres photographiques d'Arles*, Arles, France, in 2009). Walker produced collages incorporating cutout reproductions of the photographs, as in *Somebody Call an Ambivalence* (2007), which I have analyzed in detail. Vanina Géré, *Les mauvais sentiments: l'art de Kara Walker* (Dijon: Les Presses du réel, 2019), 204–210.

47. Didi-Huberman, *Images in Spite of It All*, 178.

48. Didi-Huberman, *Images in Spite of It All*, 180.

49. Didi-Huberman, *Images in Spite of It All*, 73.

50. "The first scene we did was the rape scene, the very first week of shooting. That was a little intense. That first scene was pretty simple, there was the tree and the staging

of the different characters coming upon this girl, and I'm shooting it, I'm shooting it handheld, and it's quite close . . . the players still see what I see when they're playing . . . when you're shooting something handheld, the emotional impact of it is bigger . . . you're right there. . . . It was a very wise choice of [Kara's] to play the scene first, instead of putting it off, so everybody got their feet wet. We couldn't do it for more than three days, we were all beginning to go nuts." Butler, interview with the author.

51. Butler explained that Walker had worked by herself with *Testimony*, but that she had started being assisted with film work with *8 Possible Beginnings*. Butler, interview with the author, March 7, 2010.

52. Butler, interview with the author, March 7, 2010.

53. Moran, interview with the author, October 8, 2011.

54. Hartman, *Scenes of Subjection*, 154.

55. Didi-Huberman, *Images in Spite of It All*, 170.

56. Hartman, "Venus in Two Acts," 11.

57. According to Walker, the first part of the film was "an attempt to . . . not really normalize it, like, "'it's just a day, and it's a day, and it's boring, and nothing's really happening, you know, we're just people, and these things happen.'" Walker, interview with the author.

58. Another such occurrence can be found in another piece based on the Freedmen's Bureau archive: Bureau of Refugees—Threatened to kill her and her sister if they did not leave the county (2007). In this image, one can see two cutout black silhouettes representing Black women holding each other in each other's arms, with a white-supremacist mob as a deep blue cutout backdrop. This image, in my view one of the most beautiful by Walker, imagines a love that existed in spite of it all among two Black women, two sisters.

59. Hartman, "Venus in Two Acts," 13.

60. Didi-Huberman, *Images in Spite of It All*, 178.

61. Michel Foucault, *The Archeology of Knowledge*, trans. Alan Sheridan (New York: Pantheon Books, 1972), 96.

Kara Walker: What Do We Want History to Do to Us?

Zadie Smith

What you leave behind is not what is engraved in stone monuments, but what is woven into the lives of others.

—Pericles, from Thucydides's *History of the Peloponnesian War*

Two women are bound at the waist, tied to each other. One is a slim, white woman, in antebellum underskirt and corset. A Scarlett O'Hara type. She is having the air squeezed out of her by a larger, naked, black woman, who wears a kerchief around her head. To an American audience, I imagine, this black woman could easily read as "Mammy." To a viewer from the wider diaspora—to a Black Briton, say—she is perhaps less likely to invoke the stereotypical placidity of "Mammy," hewing closer to the fury of her mythological opposite, the legendary Nanny of the Maroons: escaped slave, leader of peoples. Her hand is held up forcefully, indicating the direction in which she is determined to go, but the rope between her and the white woman is pulled taut: both struggle under its constriction. And in this drama of opposing forces, through this brutal dialectic, aspects of each woman's anatomy are grotesquely eroticized by her adversary: buttocks for the black woman, breasts for her white counterpart. Which begs the question: Who tied this constricting rope? A third party? And, if the struggle continues, will the white woman be eventually extinguished? Will the black woman be free? That is, if the white woman is on the verge of extinguishment at all. Maybe she's on the verge of something else entirely: definition. That's why we cinch waists, isn't it? To achieve definition?

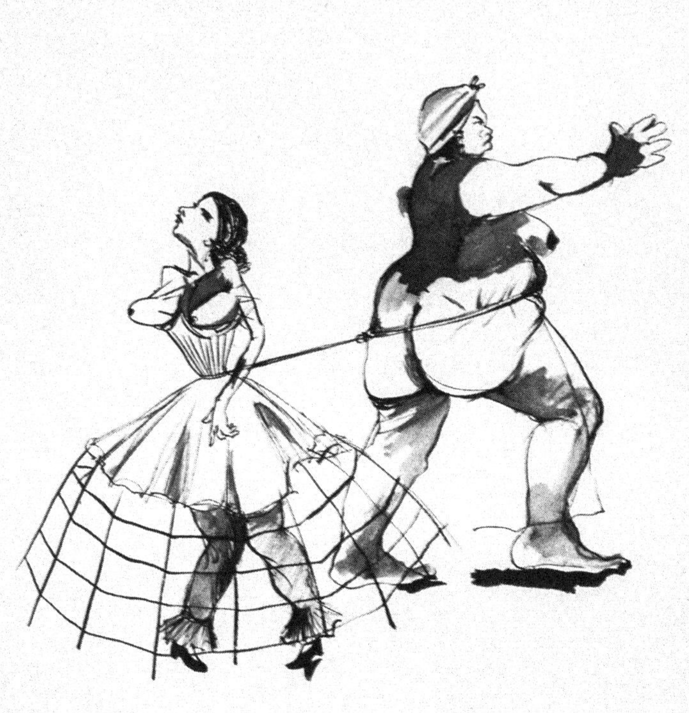

Kara Walker, *Untitled (What I Want History to Do to Me)*, 1995. Ink on paper. 17.75 × 12 inches (45.1 × 30.5 cm) each. Artwork © Kara Walker, courtesy of Sikkema Jenkins & Co., New York; Sprüth Magers, Berlin.

The two women are traced in Kara Walker's familiar, cartoonish line, which seems to combine in a single gesture the comic brevity of Charles M. Schulz, the polemical pamphleteering of William Hogarth, and the oneiric revelations of Francisco Goya and Otto Dix. The drawing was made, according to Walker, "somewhere in 94ish . . . when I was 24ish," which is to say at the very beginning of her career, when her drawings were still largely unknown, and few people knew or could guess at the busy chalk portraits that lurked on the other side of the newly famous—and soon-to-be notorious—paper cutouts. The sentence underneath the image reads: "what I want history to do to me." Its meaning is unsettling and unsettled, existing in a gray zone between artist's statement, perverse confession, and ambivalent desire. The sentence pulls in two directions, giving no slack, tense like the rope. And just as the eye finds no comfortable place to rest in the image—passing from figure to figure seeking resolution, desiring a satisfying end to a story so strikingly begun—so the sentence is partial and in unresolved motion, referring upward to the image which only then refers us back down to the words below, in endless, discomfiting cycle.

What might I want history to do to me? I might want history to reduce my historical antagonist—and increase me. I might ask it to urgently remind me why I'm moving forward, away from history. Or speak to me always of our intimate relation, of the ties that bind—and indelibly link—my history and me. I could want history to tell me that my future is tied to my past, whether I want it to be or not. Or ask it to promise me that my future will be *revenge* upon my past. Or warn me that the past is not erased by this revenge. Or suggest to me that brutal oppression implicates the oppressors, who are in turn brutalized by their own acts of oppression. Or argue that an oppressor can believe herself to be an oppressor only within a system in which she herself has been oppressed. I might want history to show me that slaves and masters are bound at the hip. That they internalize each other. That we hate what we most desire. That we desire what we most hate. That we create oppositions—black white male female fat thin beautiful ugly virgin whore—in order to provide definition to ourselves by contrast. I might want history to convince me that although some identities are chosen, many others are forced. Or that no identities are chosen. Or that all identities are chosen. That I feed history. That history feeds me. That we starve each other. All of these things. None of them. All of them in an unholy mix of the true and the false . . .

What I want history to do to me predates Kara Walker's forays into public art by many years,[1] yet in it we can find the problematic with which all public art—all monuments, all visual interventions into our public space—must ultimately wrestle. What do we want our public art to *do*? The official answer is, usually, "memorialize." We want our monuments to remember what has passed: our glories, our sufferings. Yet if you grow up, as Walker did, in the shadow of Stone Mountain, Georgia's monumental tribute to the "heroes of the confederacy"—carved into the sheer rock and looming over the majority black population—you will have many questions. Monument to whom? To what? To whose history? To which memories? Public art claiming to represent our collective memory is just as often a work of historical erasure and political manipulation. It is just as often the violent inscription of myth over truth, a form of "over-writing"—one story overlaid and thus obscuring another—modeled in three dimensions. In the United States, we speak of this. Discussions of power and erasure as they relate to monuments are by now well under way. The astonishing historical absence of public markers of the slave trade, for example—of landing sites and auction blocks, of lynchings and massacres—is a matter of frequent public discussion, debate and (partial) correction, albeit four hundred years after the first enslaved peoples landed on American shores. In the United Kingdom, meanwhile, we have to speak not simply of erasure but of something closer to perfect oblivion. It is no exaggeration to say that the only thing I ever learned about slavery during my British education was that "we" ended it. Even more extraordinary to me now is how many second-generation Caribbean kids grew up, in the 1970s and 1980s, with the bizarre notion that our families were somehow native to "the islands," had always been there, even as we pored over the history of "American slavery."[2]

The schools were silent; the streets deceptive. The streets were full of monuments to the glorious, imperial, wealthy past, and no explanation whatsoever of the roots and sources of that empire-building wealth. The English side of my own family lived in Brighton, but when we visited I had no clue that those gorgeous Georgian parades, glistening white, had slave sugar as their foundation. Between official memory and the subjective experience of millions, then, there was a chasm. Take, for example, the Victoria Memorial, that marble white magnificence in front of Buckingham Palace, with which Walker's latest piece of public art installation, *Fons Americanus*, a huge fountain installed in the Turbine Hall at Tate Modern, is evidently in discussion. As with so many British monuments, what appears to be an act of public storytelling is as least as much about silence as narrative. The self-conceived values of empire are confidently displayed, in the forms of classical figures embodying *Peace*, *Progress*, *Manufacture*, and *Agriculture* (represented by a woman in peasant dress with a sickle and a sheaf of corn; more to the point would be a black woman holding a sugar cane with a kerchief round her head). Cherubs abound, and mermaids and mermen and a hippogriff—symbolizing the nation's nautical domination—but there is of course no representation of the peoples thus subdued by this famed maritime strength, and no tourist standing before this memorial would have any idea that a portion of the money used to build it was in fact raised by West African tribes, who sent goods to be sold, the proceeds of which went to the memorial's fund. (The people of New Zealand, who also contributed to the fund, are acknowledged in an inscription upon the base.) How did these West African goods get to London? On the ships of Alfred Lewis Jones—the subject of a few monuments himself—eminent Victorian ship-owner and businessman, remembered, in England, as the "Uncrowned King of West Africa," for his myriad business interests on those shores. In the Congo, meanwhile, he made his mark as Liverpool's consular representative of King Leopold II of Belgium, and therefore as an apologist and enabler of one of the most brutal colonial enterprises in history, the infamous regime that established the common practice of limb removal by machete. (An abject fact I never fail to call to mind whenever I see Kara Walker's cutouts of black hands, severed from their bodies, bouncing around a white wall, or falling out of a traditional *mousgoum* hut, like a return of the repressed . . .)

Anyway, into this strange national historical amnesia enters Kara Walker. What lessons can she have taken from her American public art experiences? In the process of making her truly monumental *A Subtlety, or the Marvelous Sugar Baby* (2014), at the Domino Sugar factory in Brooklyn, New York, she began, as she often does, with free association, mining both her own mind and our collective consciousness for the many sweet and sour resonances of sugar: "Starting with sugar and molasses, and molasses as a byproduct of the sugar processing." And then asking herself: "What other byproducts are there?" Walker's historical

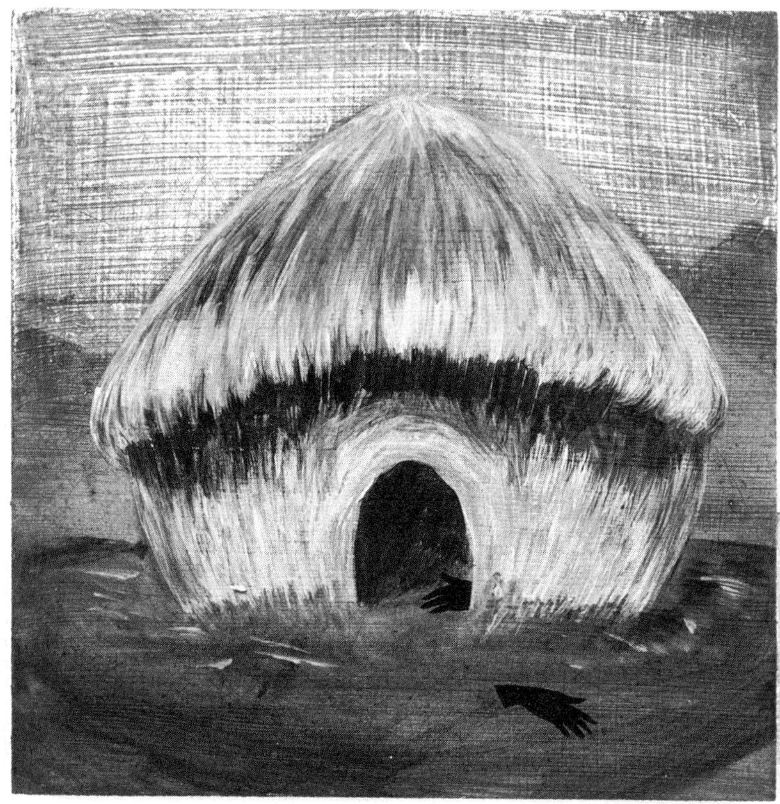

Kara Walker, *American Primitives: Untitled from American Primitives,* 2001. Paint, collage on board. 6 works: 6 × 6 inches (15.2 × 15.2 cm) each. Artwork © Kara Walker, courtesy of Sikkema Jenkins & Co., New York; Sprüth Magers, Berlin.

researches are never superficial, and her art practice has always included an almost equal amount of reading and writing, from which the visuals emerge. Researching sugar, she found herself once again neck-deep in blood and horror. Slave labor, colonization, land seizure, extractive capitalism, the exploitation of women and children, and then, later, the global cultivation of sugar addiction, a public health catastrophe that can be said to affect most profoundly the black and the poor. "And I got to the end and I was like *Ruins! Ruins!* But I couldn't just produce ruins."

What is the correct response to a ruinous history? What, if anything, is the artist's "duty" here? Should ruins always and everywhere

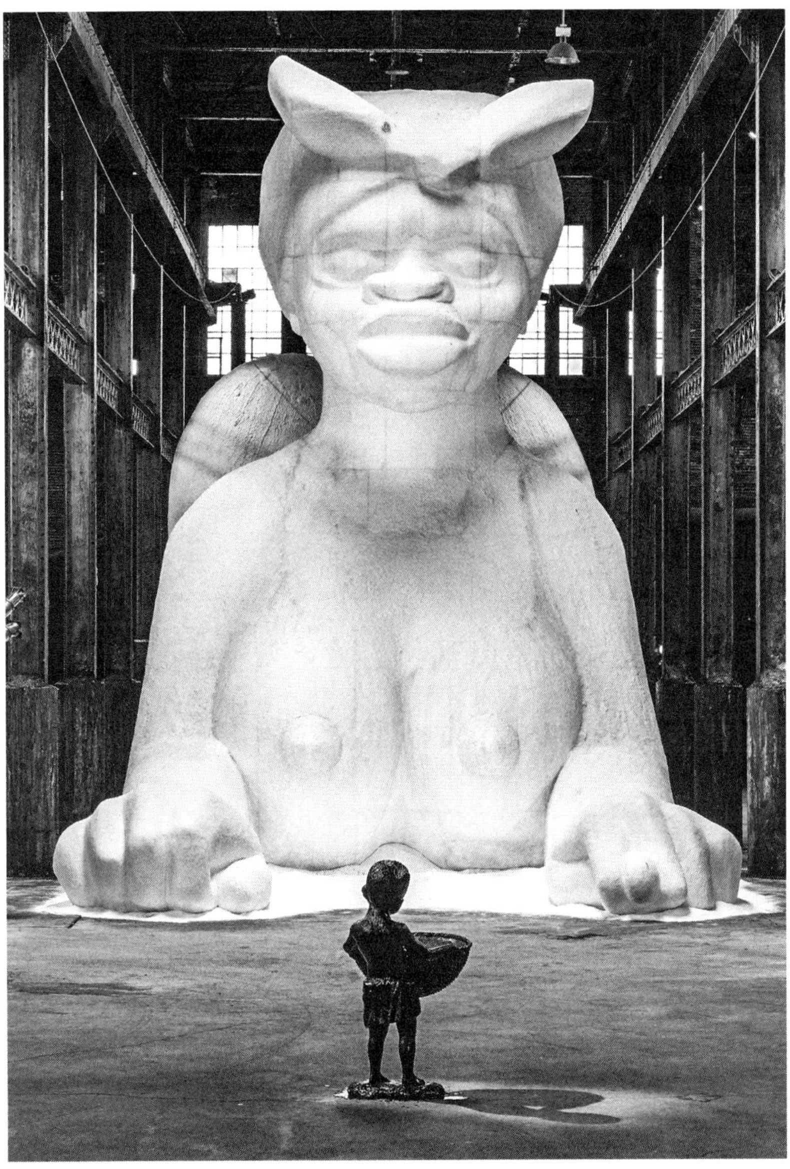

Kara Walker, *A Subtlety, or the Marvelous Sugar Baby, an Homage to the unpaid and overworked Artisans who have refined our Sweet tastes from the cane fields to the Kitchens of the New World on the Occasion of the demolition of the Domino Sugar Refining Plant*, 2014. Polystyrene foam, sugar. Approx. 35.5 × 26 × 75.5 feet (10.8 × 7.9 × 23 m). Installation view: Domino Sugar Refinery, a project of Creative Time, Brooklyn, NY, 2014. Photo: Jason Wyche. Artwork © Kara Walker, courtesy of Sikkema Jenkins & Co., New York; Sprüth Magers, Berlin.

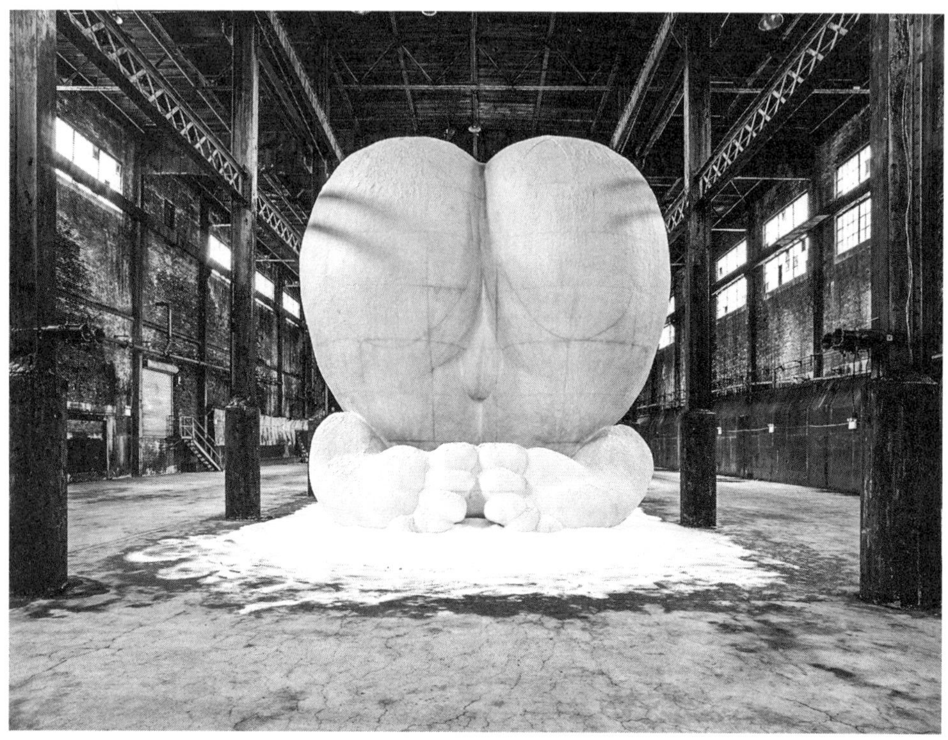

Kara Walker, *A Subtlety, or the Marvelous Sugar Baby, an Homage to the unpaid and overworked Artisans who have refined our Sweet tastes from the cane fields to the Kitchens of the New World on the Occasion of the demolition of the Domino Sugar Refining Plant*, 2014. Polystyrene foam, sugar. Approx. 35.5 × 26 × 75.5 feet (10.8 × 7.9 × 23 m). Installation view: Domino Sugar Refinery, a project of Creative Time, Brooklyn, NY, 2014. Photo: Jason Wyche. Artwork © Kara Walker, courtesy of Sikkema Jenkins & Co., New York; Sprüth Magers, Berlin.

be "reclaimed"? Should ruins be consciously rebuilt into something "positive"? If not the re-presentation of ruins, then what? Walker: "Up until that point I had been thinking of finger-wagging doom-laden things about the history of slavery and sugar and America. It didn't take into account what people wanted to look at. When I came up with the idea and made it, it reminded me of wanting to do the cut-outs, that sense of giving people something they wanted to look at, working with their attention span in a way."[3]

Walker's particular mode of engaging with our attention spans— her visual and conceptual provocations—have often caused furor, first from the generation above her, now not infrequently from the generation below. For when it comes to the ruins of history, Walker neither simply re-presents nor reclaims. Instead she eroticizes, aestheticizes, fetishizes, and dramatizes—with the consequence that she is accused of an unnecessary or inappropriate cultivation of the grotesque, of a prurient interest: "salaciousness." As if Walker's manner of aestheticizing ruin, *so that our attention may be kept upon it*, was a unique scandal in the history of art (or, at least, as if no black woman artist had a right to take up the tools Walker assumes as her inheritance and her right).

But this mode of relating to the ruins of the past is hardly without precedent. Approaching Walker's *Sugar Baby*, that summer in Brooklyn, first one passed a series of melting child figures, dripping molasses, holding in their arms or on their backs the kind of baskets field laborers use. They looked like those heartbreaking child "blackamoors" you spot in the corners of eighteenth-century paintings, carrying sweet delights for the pleasure of Milady. (Though to me they were the very picture of the Liberian child laborers I once saw tapping hot gum out of the trees, intended for the American tire market.) But there was an older echo, too: in their arrangement, pathing the way to the main event—to the Sugar Baby herself—they recalled the Stations of the Cross, one of the most familiar sequences in western art, the culmination of which is the crucified Christ. Like Walker's Sugar Baby, he is usually oversized, at the back of a long room, and we approach him, as we approached her, as a figure of worship, a subject of pity, of mournful contemplation, of sadomasochistic erotic interest, not to mention as the embodiment of an infamous historical crime.[4] All over Europe, in church after church, we encounter the same fascinating admixture of the sexual, the sadistic, and the sacred. The real scandal in the Domino factory, perhaps, was the identity of the object thus occupying our attention: not white and male but black and female.

If we had to choose an ur-Walker image—the one that comes to mind when we think of the artist—it would be *Slavery! Slavery!* (1997), shown in her blockbuster gallery show *My Complement, My Enemy, My Oppressor, My Love* in 2007–2008. The images themselves—violent, scatological, sexual, hateful, loving—exist in unholy mix, like the show's title. They are given no hierarchy, moral or otherwise. All elements are presented simultaneously.

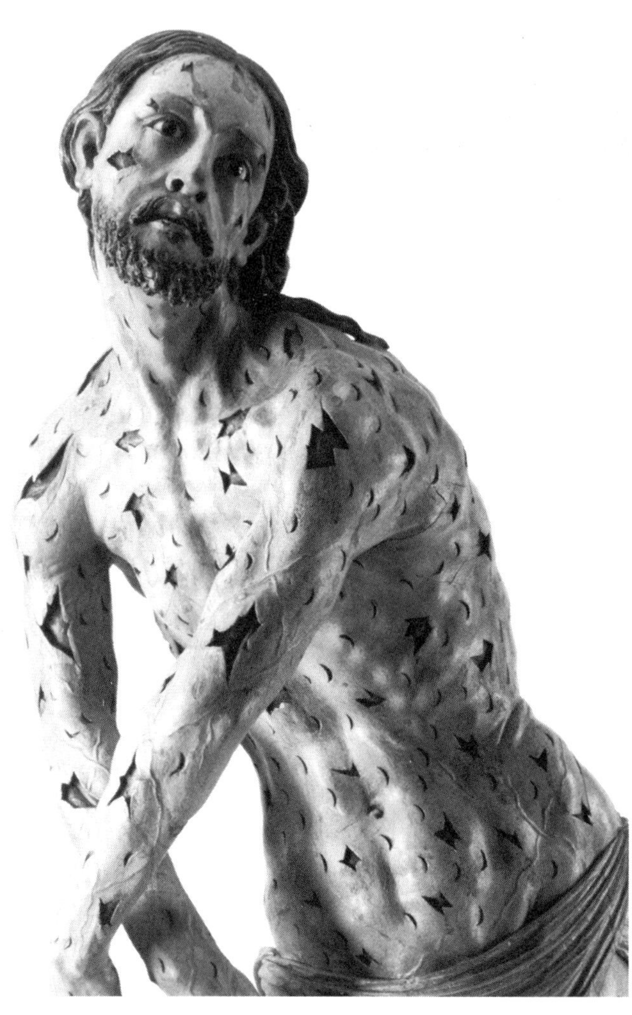

Anonymous, detail from *Christ at the Column*, 1697. Photo: Hendrik Zwietasch. Landesmuseum Württemberg, Stuttgart.

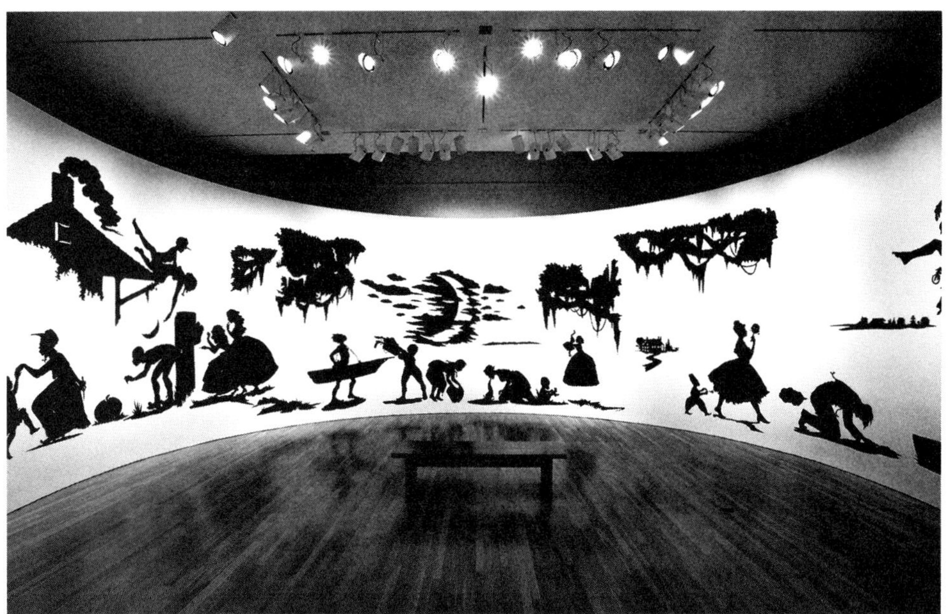

Kara Walker, *Slavery! Slavery! Presenting a GRAND and LIFELIKE Panoramic Journey into Picturesque Southern Slavery or "Life at 'Ol' Virginny's Hole" (sketches from Plantation Life)." See the Peculiar Institution as never before! All cut from black paper by the able hand of Kara Elizabeth Walker, an Emancipated Negress and leader in her Cause*, 1997. Cut paper and adhesive on wall. 132 × 1020 inches (335.3 × 2591 cm). Installation view: *Kara Walker: My Complement, My Enemy, My Oppressor, My Love*, Hammer Museum, Los Angeles, CA, 2008. Photo: Joshua White. Artwork © Kara Walker, courtesy of Sikkema Jenkins & Co., New York; Sprüth Magers, Berlin.

It was this early work that famously prompted the older artist Betye Saar to label the young Walker "a black artist who obviously hates being black," whose work was for the "amusement and the investment of the white art establishment."[5] Two statements that represent a terrific double bind—a rope thrown around one black woman to constrict another—and amount to an all-too-familiar injunction, directed at minority artists perennially and in all mediums. Your success, runs the argument, can only mean you are "playing up to" or "displaying our dirty laundry in front of" the majority audience. (The implication being: What else could account for it? Itself a sly depredation.) Under this logic you are either unconsciously giving "them" what they want (self-hatred) or you are *consciously* doing so (self-and-community betrayal). That the black artist might be following their own nose—pursuing their own preoccupations and obsessions—is here given no credence. The white viewer, in these debates, is really the only thing on a black artist's mind. More recently, the injunction has taken on a new flavor: now work is condemned for being insufficiently empowering, stuck in a regressive negative, neglecting to provide, for a black audience, some necessary form of "self-care," which care is considered especially vital now, during this desperate political moment. But uplift is not the only role of black art. It is possible to both admire the witty and righteous reclaiming of caricatures—like that of Saar's own "Aunt Jemima"—as well as the more recent, idealized, "positive" black stereotypes of queenly black women created by Simone Leigh, and still urgently desire to stand enclosed in a Walker diorama (which, in my experience, includes very few "amused" viewers, white or otherwise).

Walker operates on the premise that when you make history truly visible, both your own and that of your people or nation, there exists a challenge to show all of it, the unholy mix, the conscious knowledge and the subconscious reaction, the traumatic history and the trauma it has created, the unprocessed and the unprocessable. If you manage this, it will be, by definition *de trop*. But then again, too much for whom? The very idea that *Slavery! Slavery!* is an exaggerated or extreme or unnecessarily salacious image is to me strange, given the history through which it self-consciously tumbles.

Consider, for example, the case of one Thomas Thistlewood. Thistlewood was from Lincolnshire. He died in 1786, forty-seven years before Britain's Slavery Abolition Act was passed in 1833. There are no monuments to him in England, but he is notorious, among Jamaicans, for his 14,000-page diary, documenting his time as a plantation owner on our island. A lower-middle-class man, he was an autodidact, and the recto pages of his diary are filled with a meticulous account of his enlightened interest in medicine, horticulture, religion, political theory, and much else. The other half—the verso pages—record the 3,852 acts of sex he had with his slaves, and the regular vicious punishments he doled out to them, baroque in their sadism and perversion. Once, after a particular slave had run away and been caught, Thistlewood gave the man "a mod[erate] whipping, pickled him well, made Hector shit in his mouth, immediately put in gag whilst his mouth was full & made him wear it 4 or 5 hours." Apparently pleased with this novel punishment, he repeated it on many others. Often he flogged slaves and then

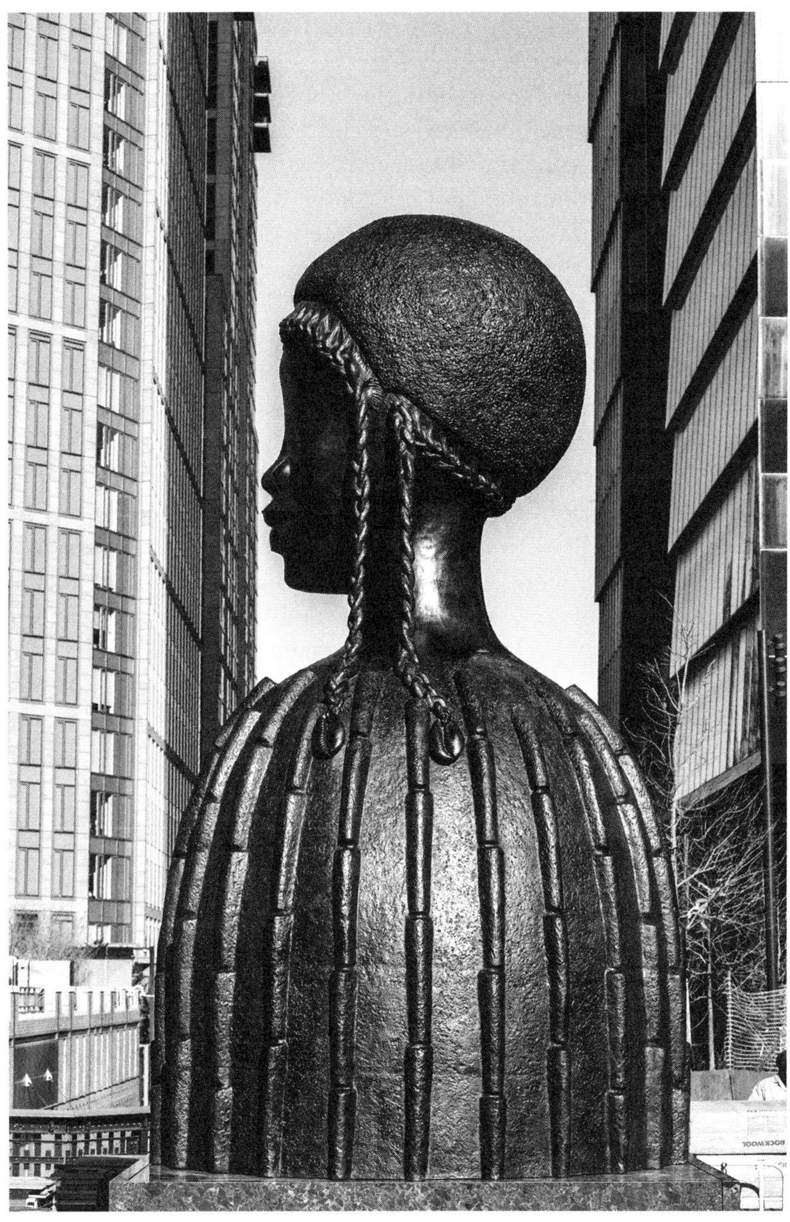

Simone Leigh, *Brick House*, 2019. Bronze. 196 × 114 inches (497.8 × 289.6 cm). A High Line Plinth commission, 2019–2020. © Simone Leigh. Photo by Timothy Schenck. Courtesy the artist and High Line.

"wash'd and rubb'd [them] in salt pickle, lime juice & bird pepper."
To punish the aforementioned Hector for losing a hoe, he whipped
him and then "made New Negroe Joe piss in his eyes & mouth." In
addition to forcing men, women, and children into the back-breaking
work of cutting sugar cane, sometimes he used a byproduct of sugar
for the purposes of torture: "Put him in the Bilboes both feet; gagged
him; locked his hands together; rubbed him with Molasses and exposed
him naked to the flys all day, and to the mosquitoes all night."[6] Lest
it be thought Thistlewood was a lone sociopath, his diary reveals how
he was often allowed to rape the slaves of neighboring overseers and
let them rape his slaves in exchange. And, through it all, Thistlewood
maintained an intimate, thirty-three-year relationship with a slave
called Phibbah, with whom he had his only son, "Mulatto John." They
were apparently warm and affectionate with each other, Phibbah and
Thomas. Once, Thomas brutally flogged his only son for refusing to
work. Once, Thistlewood found himself in competition with his own
visiting nephew—for they were both in the habit of raping the same
slave, "Little Mimber"—and so Thistlewood warned his nephew off
and then viciously beat Little Mimber, as punishment. Once, a fellow
plantation owner sent Thistlewood the head of a runaway slave as a
present and Thistlewood put it on a pole on his estate so that all might
see it. In his will, Thistlewood called Phibbah his "wife," freed her, and
left her property.

What is the correct artistic response to history like that? Which
aspects should be obscured or tidied away or carefully contextualized
to protect the viewer's sensibility? The very word "salacious" withers
before the historical truth. *Salacious; having or conveying undue or inappropriate interest in sexual matters.* What is the appropriate level of interest
in the interrelation of sex and violence in our history?

Caricature and stereotype are not Walker's flaws—they are her sharp-
est tools. She treats them as the very DNA of history, the invisible
building blocks of our social reality, "scripting" for us, informing and
affecting our behavior, and posing the greatest risk not when they are
made explicit but rather when they are allowed to sink into invisibility,
to appear "natural" or "inevitable." It is then that they become most
firmly entrenched as ideology. It's then that we find ourselves abiding by
them unconsciously, without knowing why. "I have always responded,"

Walker has said, "to art which jarred the senses and made one aware physically and emotionally of the shifting terrain on which we rest our beliefs."[7] A striking example of this came in 1998, when Walker traveled to Austria, answering a commission to create a "safety curtain" for the Vienna State Opera. The results were manifestly unsafe. Allowing, once again, for free association without self-edits or self-consciousness, Walker wickedly conjured the Austrian African Imaginary: little black "Turks" in fez holding out cups of coffee, with gold rings in their ears and Aladdin shoes; dancing girls in grass skirts, in banana skirts, stark naked, the whole exotic black *Kabarett*; black bodies inscribed into academic zoological studies, or placed in actual zoos, or made out of porcelain, eternally holding out an ashtray or a serving dish, or sweating underneath paladins carrying Arab kings, or cooling European royalty with those huge feather fans. . . . In *Safety Curtain*, the monograph that accompanied her Austrian experiment, she places, in the same visual frame, a shocking nineteenth-century physiological illustration intended to demonstrate the closeness of the black man to an ape, with an equally poisonous contemporary news photo of Mike Tyson, biting the T-shirt of a blond toddler as said toddler screams in terror. She offers, too, a "before and after" picture—the type of beauty advert still common in the 1990s—in which a childhood picture of Oprah is the "before," and an Austrian-looking blue-eyed blonde is the "after." That is, she makes *explicit* the logic of so many of our contemporary media images: she reveals their DNA. The animalistic black man. Whiteness as purified blackness. Walker shares Warhol's genius for caricature and stereotype, and what she has said she admires in his work—"simplicity and [the] strange mute ability to distil a culture into a single image"—we find also in hers. Like Warhol, she is never subtle, even when making a "subtlety." From her *Notes from a Negress Imprisoned in Austria*:

> I am and shall continue to be the monster in your closet. Prodding at your tightly wound arsenal, your history.
>   Let me out.
>   And. You. shall. seek. to. put. me. back. in.
>   And together we will: in and out and in and out together HAHA![8]

Which is to say, images have intercourse with each other—they fuck each other. They're incestuous. They spawn. And it is when this process is subconscious and invisible that it is most insidious. So much of what was written about Mike Tyson in the 1990s had a long and deadly cultural history, and every time we looked at or thought about him some of that history came along for the ride. Walker sees and makes visible so many of these kinds of historical exchanges, substitutes, echoes, and reoccurrences, but claims no external, objective vantage point upon them. "I don't think that my work is actually effectively dealing with history," she has said. "I think of my work as subsumed by history or consumed by history." The difference between Walker and so many of us is that she knows it.

Walker: "When you have monuments or commemorative things that just simply exist, they sit there and they disappear." Walker's monuments never simply sit, they never stand apart from history as something finished or finalized—and they crave movement. Over the years her cutouts have become animated, and her walls have turned circular, dioramic, and even those notorious "amused" white art patrons have found themselves backlit and cast as shadows, implicated and involved in the art they came merely to view. In 2018, Walker brought her dynamic view of the past to Algiers Point, New Orleans, once a holding area for slaves. A small, inadequate plaque marks the spot. A steam-powered calliope was Walker's typically unsubtle intervention, a catastrophic caravan that took the sentimental organ music of the Mississippi and recast it in a monstrous carved box of black steel, through which steam poured and history seeped. To let off steam, as a calliope must do, is visually cathartic, and the music was black resistance and uplift combined: negro spirituals, "We Shall Overcome," "Down by the Riverside," etc. But the sound each pipe made was somewhere between scream, off-key wail, and—thanks to the huff and puff of the steam itself—a hellish and industrialized machine of torture. The effect was dreadful, in the ancient meaning of that term, and too provoking and active to be called, exactly, a monument. Monuments are complacent; they put a seal upon the past, they release us from dread. For Walker dread is an engine: it prompts us to remember and rightly fear the ruins we shouldn't want to return to, and don't wish to recreate—if we're wise. Dread is surely one of the things we want history to do to us, lest we forget.

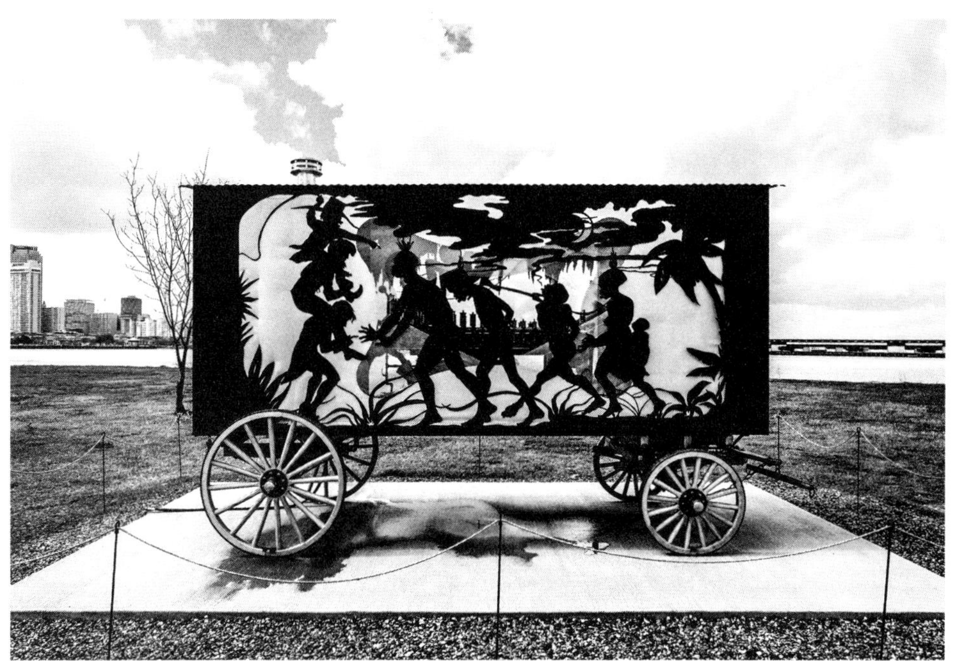

Kara Walker, *The Katastwóf Karavan*, 2017. Steel frame mounted to lumber running gear, aluminum, red oak and muslin wall panels, propane-fired boiler, water tank, gas generator, brass and steel 38-note steam calliope, calliope controller panel with MIDI interface, iPad controller with QRS PNO software. 152 × 215.9 × 100 inches (386.1 × 548.6 × 254 cm). Installation view: *Prospect 4: The Lotus in Spite of the Swamp*, Algiers Point, New Orleans, 2018. Photo: Alex Marks. Artwork © Kara Walker, courtesy of Sikkema Jenkins & Co., New York; Sprüth Magers, Berlin.

But to talk of Walker's art this way, as if history was its only concern, and our "opinions" about that history its only content, is to traduce the art itself. Much has been written about Kara Walker, too much—journalistic debates about her often threaten to subsume any real attempt to *see* this work in all its strangeness and particularity.[9] (Or to allow it the intimate psychology we simply assume with an artist like, say, Tracey Emin, whose engagement with feminist ideas and feminist art history in no way precludes our noticing the personal.) Walker: "The illusion is that it is about past events, simply about a particular point in history and nothing else—and that's really part of the ruse with which I like to approach the complexities of my own life."[10] These complexities have included some masochistic sexual relationships, a long romantic history with white men, a mixed race child, and inconvenient psychic attractions to "heroic" white figures like Scarlett O'Hara in *Gone with the Wind*, that leave her "wanting to be the heroine—and also wanting to kill the heroine at the same time." In art school she was tormented by the sense that she was "going to put my foot in my mouth if I was honest about my own failings as a black woman" and in one early interview recalls a slogan on a popular 1990s T-shirt: *It's a Black thing, You wouldn't understand*: "It inspired a whole way of thinking for me. Because, obviously the 'you' in the saying is Not Black. . . . So what does this mean to the person who is black and still doesn't quite understand?"

These uncollegiate expressions of failure and incomprehension in Walker's retellings reveal—like the border between her black cutout edges and her white backgrounds—something significant in the contrast. For of course you can't fail as a white woman *qua* white women; whiteness is not formulated as a test. A white thing is, by definition, whatever a white person does. Whereas blackness is nothing but test. So many things can threaten a black woman's blackness (in the eyes of white people, black people, herself) that if one allows it to do so the fear of this threat can constitute an entire shadow identity. The wrong kind of art, the wrong kind of husband, the wrong kind of interests, the wrong kind of curiosity, the wrong kind of desires, the wrong kind of confessions. Confessions like this: "If the work is reprehensible, that work is also me, coming from a reprehensible part of me."

One gift an artist might give to other artists is a demonstration of how to make work without shame. Without being cowed or terrified by the opinions of others. As her cousin, the novelist James Hannaham, once said of her: "She has the hermeneutic idea of the role of the artist in society—a person who is strong enough to withstand projection, then can project ideas back to the people in such a way that their minds change. Or not."[11] What kind of shameless black woman imagines a negro boy with a hole in his chest through which a bird has just bust through, stealing his heart? Kara Walker. What kind of shameless black woman imagines a little white boy sucking on the tip of an African girl's banana skirt as the girl also suckles herself? Kara Walker. What kind of shameless black woman imagines rape and chaos while a tiny Abraham Lincoln saunters by? Kara Walker.

The shame is meant to be the shame of being multiple. Of not understanding what the (notably singular) black "thing" is or should be because, in Walker's work, blackness is so many things:

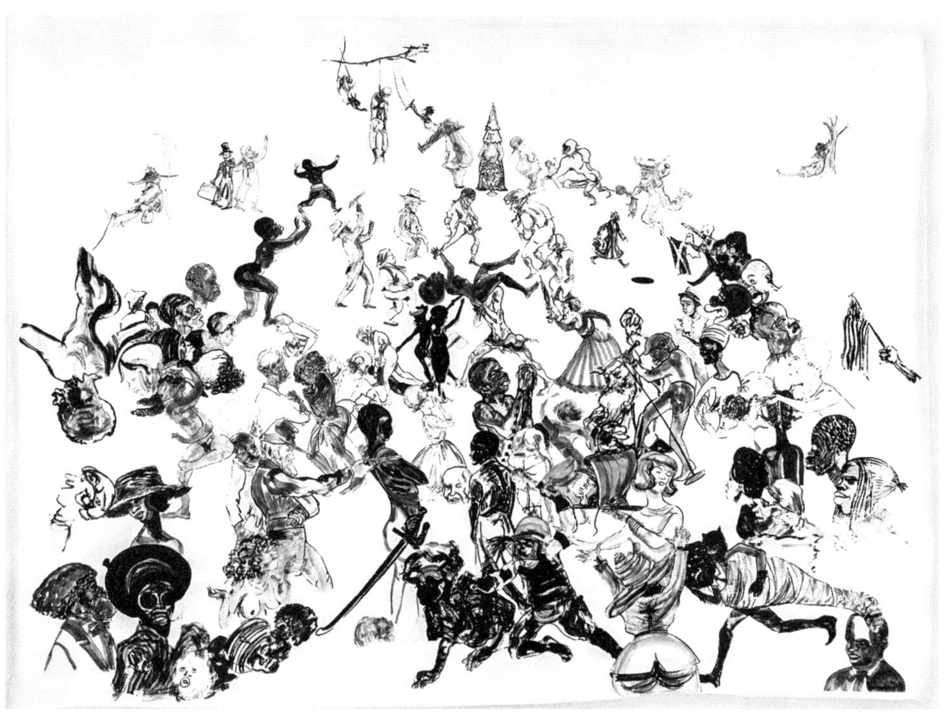

Kara Walker, *Christ's Entry into Journalism*, 2017. Sumi ink and collage on paper. 140 × 196 inches (383.6 × 485.1 cm). Artwork © Kara Walker, courtesy of Sikkema Jenkins & Co., New York; Sprüth Magers, Berlin.

I was looking at the identity politics of the 1970s and 1980s and thinking the idea of a single identity—the militant black woman, or whatever—wasn't enough. At any one moment I felt like 13 different characters piecing themselves together. Some of it was coming out of bizarre lived sexual experiences I'd had with people who will go unnamed, some of it was, like, I don't know, reading *Gone with the Wind*. The feeling I was left with was that it was probably my job to gather all those pieces back into one room. They were all pieces of me and they were unruly.[12]

Into one gigantic space, then, the Turbine Hall, at the Tate Modern, Walker now gathers all her pieces. At the time of writing this work was still in process, and I had access to only drawings and fragments, scraps and ruins and partial models, but I saw a monument rising, a "water feature," not unlike the Victoria Memorial just down the road, featuring waters that seem to flow directly from the Middle Passage—or else from that dreadful stretch of sea between Libya and Lampedusa, currently swallowing up black people at a terrifying rate. I saw a monument in sketch, surrounded by small boats in trouble, that once again suggested to me not only the old trade in humans but the more recent arrival of African bodies to European shores, no longer slaves, but still the desperate subjects of a capitalism red in tooth and claw. That catastrophic caravan of history, circling again.

And atop her fountain, I spotted a typical Walkerian figure of resistance, a spectacular "negress," spurting water from her nipples, and this reminded me of all her soaring birds smashing through slave bodies—as if the urge for freedom could be animated and embodied—and her magnificent swans, lending their wings to the oppressed, and her flying black cherubs and pig-tailed "Topsys" who can often be seen shooting into the sky, propelling themselves above ruin and chaos. Such repeated figures are the not-so-secret glory hiding in plain sight of so many Walker images, obscured by the endless chatter of journalism about her "salaciousness," but not unwitnessed by those who have eyes to see. In England, where so many people still consider it bad taste even to *mention* Britain's long and complex history with the people of the African diaspora, a Walker monument is a thrilling intervention. I imagine awe at the scale. I imagine accolades and protests. I imagine the usual palaver that Walker has already imagined and described herself:

> Students of Color will eye her work suspiciously and exercise their free right to Culturally Annihilate her on social media. Parents will cover the eyes of innocent children. School Teachers will reexamine their art history curricula. Prestigious Academic Societies will withdraw their support, former husbands and former lovers will recoil in abject terror. Critics will shake their heads in bemused silence. Gallery Directors will wring their hands at the sight of throngs of the gallery-curious flooding the pavement outside.[13]

I hope Walker is never ashamed to be the wrong kind of artist/ woman/black person, nor ever tired of our endless projections upon her. Twenty-five years after she exploded into the art world, I hope it continues to be her self-defined job to gather all the ruins of her own, and our, history—everything abject and beautiful, oppressive and free-ing, scatological and sexual, holy and unholy—into one place, without attempting perfect alignment, without needing to be seen to be good, so that she might make art from it. And thus stand up for the subconscious, for the unsaid and unsayable, for the historically and personally undigestible, for the unprettified, for the autonomy of an imagination that cannot escape history, and—more than anything else—for black freedom of expression itself.

Notes

1. Although, in the case of an artist as instantaneously successful and famous as Walker, there is a sense in which all of the art has been "public."

2. Though again, not in the classroom. Diaspora education came informally: from one's parents, from hip-hop, from American movies and books.

3. Interview with Tim Adams, "Kara Walker: 'There is a moment in life when one becomes black,'" *Observer*, September 27, 2015, https://www.theguardian.com /artanddesign/2015/sep/27/kara-walker-interview-victoria-miro-gallery-atlanta.

4. The fundamental peculiarity of this European art practice was long ago pointed about by the late comedian Bill Hicks: "You think when Jesus comes back he's gonna want to see a fucking cross, man?"

5. Betye Saar speaking in an episode of the PBS series *I'll Make Me a World*, 1999. Quoted in Thomas McEvilley, "Primitivism in the Works of an Emancipated Negress," in *Kara Walker: My Complement, My Enemy, My Oppressor, My Love*, by Philippe Vergne, Sander L. Gilman, Thomas McEvilley, Robert Storr, Kevin Young, and Yasmil Raymond (Minneapolis, MN: Walker Art Center, 2007).

6. From entries for July 23, July 30, August 1, 1756, Thomas Thistlewood Papers, James Marshall and Marie-Louise Osborn Collection, Beinecke Rare Book and Manuscript Library, Yale University (ISB MSS 176).

7. In Ariane Grigoteit and Friedhelm Hütte, "Answers and a Little Bit of Wine," in *Kara Walker: Deutsche Bank Collection*, by Kara Walker (Frankfurt am Main: Deutsche Bank, 2002), 7. Quoted in Rebecca Peabody, *Consuming Stories: Kara Walker and the Imagining of American Race* (Oakland, CA: University of California Press, 2016), 118.

8. Kara Walker, "Notes from a Negress Imprisoned in Austria," in *Safety Curtain: Kara Walker*, ed. Johannes Schlebrügge, exhibition catalog (Vienna: Museum in Progress, in cooperation with Vienna State Opera House and P & S Wien, 2000), 23.

9. And the Walkerverse is passing strange. You *think* it's just like nineteenth-century racist caricature until you actually look back at nineteenth-century caricature. Walker's "negro" caricatures have a graphic language of their own—no cartoon red lips, no rolling eyes—and a distinct demonic glee you don't find in their antebellum ancestors. They have designs on your subconscious; they mean to march straight off those walls and into your cerebellum, where they will remain, perniciously lodged, along with the brutal history that created them.

10. Interview by Susan Sollins, Program 5: *Stories, Art:21—Art in the Twenty-First Century*, season 2, New York, VHS and DVD 2003.

11. James Hannaham, quoted in Doreen St. Félix, "Kara Walker's Next Act," *New York Magazine*, April 17, 2017. https://www.vulture.com/2017/04/kara-walker-after-a-subtlety.html.

12. Interview with Tim Adams, 2015.

13. From the press release for Walker's exhibition *Sikkema Jenkins and Co. is Compelled to present/The most Astounding and Important Painting show of the fall Art Show viewing season! . . .* , Sikkema Jenkins & Co., New York 2017.

Page numbers in italics indicate illustrations.